D0341421

SEXUAL TRAUMA IN CHILDREN AND ADOLESCENTS

Dynamics and Treatment

SEXUAL TRAUMA IN CHILDREN AND ADOLESCENTS

Dynamics and Treatment

by

Diana Sullivan Everstine, Ph.D.

&

Louis Everstine, Ph.D., M.P.H.

BRUNNER/MAZEL *Publishers* • New York

Library of Congress Cataloging-in-Publication Data

Everstine, Diana Sullivan, 1944–
   Sexual trauma in children and adolescents : dynamics and treatment
by Diana Sullivan Everstine & Louis Everstine.
   p. cm.
   Includes bibliographies and indexes.
   ISBN 0-87630-529-X
   1. Sexually abused children—Mental health. 2. Sexually abused
teenagers—Mental health. 3. Family psychotherapy.   I. Everstine.
Louis, 1933– . II. Title.
   [DNLM: 1. Child Abuse, Sexual—psychology. 2. Psychotherapy. WA
320 E93s]
RJ507.S49E94   1989
618.92'89—dc19
DNLM/DLC
for Library of Congress   88-26309
                                                                 CIP

Copyright © 1989 by Diana Sullivan Everstine
and Louis Everstine

Published by
BRUNNER/MAZEL, INC.
19 Union Square
New York, New York 10003

MANUFACTURED IN THE UNITED STATES OF AMERICA

10 9 8 7 6 5 4 3

Contents

Preface

The tragic histories of sexually abused children come to light in many ways. The following are poignant examples. Danielle was four when her parents divorced. Her mother thought that she was reacting to the divorce when she became anxious and irritable. Danielle's behavior was particularly difficult to deal with after visits with her father. At approximately age five, Danielle began to masturbate openly, and when her mother told her not to do that in front of other people, Danielle replied, "Why not, Mommy? That's what Daddy and I do."

Doug's father died when he was eight years old. His mother was concerned that Doug would not have an adequate male role model, so she enrolled him in an afterschool athletic league. She thought that the boy was angry and distant because of the loss of his father. But one night a detective who was investigating a child pornography ring came to the house. Doug was one of several boys who had been used for pornography by his coach.

When Donna and Susan were both 14, they experimented with liquor one night. In an intoxicated state, the girls swore to tell each other their deepest, darkest secrets, but Susan was not prepared for what Donna told her. Donna revealed that she had been having sex with her father since the age of four or five—she did not remember exactly when it began.

At the age of six, Alice visited her grandparents regularly. After one such visit, she complained of abdominal pain and refused to sleep in her own bed; she claimed that there were big, brightly colored snakes under the bed that spat poison. When her mother took Alice to the pediatrician to find out about her abdominal pains and strange behavior, it was discovered that the girl had been raped by her grandfather.

Lisa was 16. She had been a model child until age 14, when she started abusing drugs, running away from home, and acting out promiscuously. The parents—in desperation—went to see a therapist. When the therapist took a history, the parents revealed that Lisa's uncle had molested her when she was seven. However, because it "didn't seem to bother her," they just kept her away from him and assumed everything was all right.

During a routine physical exam, Annette, age 16, became extremely tense and anxious when the doctor attempted to reassure her by putting her arm around her. Even though she had known the doctor all her life, Annette pulled away and began to sob. When the doctor questioned her, she learned that Annette had been raped six months before and had kept it from her parents. The doctor explained to Annette that she must report the rape and told her that she would try to help her through the entire process. In an attempt to give Annette some sense of control, the physician asked her if she would rather tell the police or her parents first. Annette's reply was that she would rather start with the police, so the doctor cancelled her appointments for the rest of the day and went with Annette to the police station.

Carol, 30, was a successful professional woman. She entered therapy because she wished to understand why she had such a problem in establishing healthy relationships with men. She had had a long history of abusive relationships and generally described herself as a person who lived at a distance from others: when she tried to get close, she began to feel "numb." Only after months of therapy was Carol able to disclose that her father had molested her, beginning when she was six.

Experiences such as these take their toll on both victim and those who love the victim. Ironically, some victims accept their victimization as what they deserve or, simply, as what life is. Yet they all keep searching until they find someone who will hear them:

> The most important things are the hardest things to say . . . because words diminish them—words shrink things that seemed limitless when they were in your head to no more than living size when they're brought out. But it's more than that, isn't it? The most important things lie too close to wherever your secret heart is buried, like landmarks to a treasure your enemies would love to steal away. And you may make revelations that cost you dearly only to have people look at you in a funny way, not understanding what you've said at all, or why you thought it was so important that you almost cried while you were saying it. That's the worst, I think. When the secret stays locked within not for

want of a teller but for want of an understanding ear. (King, 1983, p. 289)

This book is written for those who are trying to hear.

ORGANIZATION OF THE BOOK

Chapters in the book are organized in the following way. An overview of the problem of the molestation of children is presented in Chapter 1. Chapter 2 offers a systematic approach to the task of assessing whether or not a child has been molested and, if so, the extent of the trauma thus produced. In the next two chapters, treatment issues are discussed in detail, first in respect to the child victim's treatment (Chapter 3) and then the treatment of the adolescent victim (Chapter 4). Chapter 5 analyzes the subject of incest; both treatment and assessment are discussed, including the issue of false accusations. The molestation of boys is considered in Chapter 6.

Chapter 7 takes up the kind of case in which an adult client reveals that he or she was sexually abused as a child. In Chapter 8 the interaction of a psychotherapist who works with victims of sexual trauma and the legal system is described.

GLOSSARY OF TERMS

The many forms of sexual trauma that can be inflicted upon children vary in intensity and by the nature of their psychological impact upon the child. Hence, we believe it wise to give clear definitions of these various forms of trauma.

It is worth noting that much previous research on the subject of childhood sexual trauma was conducted on groups comprised of victims of fondling and exhibitionism, as opposed to those who had suffered such devastating forms of assault as rape and sodomy. The results of these studies are thus of questionable validity, and at the very least one should use great caution in making generalizations from them. There is a considerable difference in the trauma of an eight-year-old who sees an exhibitionist in the park and that of an eight-year-old who is sodomized by a close family friend.

As used here, the term *sexual trauma* encompasses the entire range of the physical categories described below, as well as traumatic events of childhood that are of a sexual nature, such as witnessing the "primal scene" or inappropriate or seductive behavior by an adult. This term is used interchangeably with *sexual abuse*. More specifically, *sexual assault* is used as a descriptor of any form of adult–child sexual contact in which an adult actually touches, fondles, or penetrates the child's body. Within the category of sexual assault, *molestation* refers to an adult's caressing, fondling, kissing, or masturbating a child without making bodily penetration. By contrast, *rape* refers to forced penetration of a child's vagina, either by an adult's penis or finger, or by an object. Forced oral copulation is another form of rape, referred to here as *oral rape. Sodomy* is defined as forced anal penetration by penis or finger, or by an object.

Incest is defined, generally, as sexual activity between two persons who are not permitted by law to marry. In the present context, *incest* refers to sexual contact between a child and (a) a consanguineal parent; (b) a relative, including a stepparent; or (c) someone who fulfills the role of stepparent, such as a common-law husband or wife who is looked upon by the child as a parent surrogate.

Exhibitionism is defined as an adult's exposing his or her genitals to a child.

The term *pedophile*, which originally referred only to those who molest prepubertal children, is here employed as a label for any (nonfamilial) molester of a minor.

REFERENCE

King, S. *Different seasons.* New York: The New American Library, 1983.

Acknowledgments

We came to the subject of this book through our experience in the Emergency Treatment Center (ETC), a nonprofit mental health agency that we described in our 1983 book, *People in Crisis*. The Center, begun in 1975, is still in existence and can be said to have prospered. It recently qualified as a United Way project, and we wish to thank United Way of Santa Clara County, California, for furthering the Center's work.

Since the beginning of this decade, the ETC has received an increasing number of requests for assistance in cases of child sexual abuse. Some of these requests have come from attorneys, some from police sexual assault bureaus, and many from the Victim-Witness Assistance programs of Santa Clara and San Mateo counties.

For the purpose of isolating these cases from the mainstream of referrals to ETC of cases of children and adolescents, and to give them special attention and focus, a Child Trauma Center was established. The Trauma Center's staff is comprised of a combination of senior ETC clinicians and members of the private practice group Affiliated Psychologists of Palo Alto, California. At the weekly meetings of the Center, new cases are discussed and continuing cases are presented for consultation.

A principal sponsor of the Child Trauma Center is Dr. Ben Hammett, a member of the ETC Board of Directors and the Board of Directors of the Mental Research Institute (MRI). Dr. Hammett has been tireless in his efforts to assist and promote the work of both centers, and without his help neither would still be thriving.

We wish to recognize and thank other members of the ETC Board of Directors, who have served the Center long and well. These persons include attorney Liz Shivell, Captain Lucy Carlton and Sergeant Tom Sing, marriage counselor Sarita Ledet, and psychologists Dr. Marguerite McCorkle, Dr. Roger Smith, and Dr. John McNeel. Special mention is due Dr. Arthur M. Bodin, one of the founders of the Center and for many years the Chairman of its Board.

The Child Trauma Center has benefitted from the advice and assistance of attorneys Richard Alexander and Richard Gregg—the latter was our collaborator in writing Chapter 8.

The concepts presented here were described and discussed at international conferences jointly organized by ETC and MRI in Nice (1982), Munich (1984), and Amsterdam (1985). We have been privileged, as well, to be invited to several countries of Europe to speak about this subject at workshops, seminars, and conferences. For this we thank our hosts: Dr. Mony Elkaim of Belgium; Dr. Herman Vergouwen and Bert van Luyn of Holland; Bjørn Reigstad and Knut Sørgaard of Norway; and Dr. Anne Ancelin-Schutzenberger and Catherine Mesnard of France. Their inspiration helped the thoughts expressed in this volume to evolve, and we learned from them that the maltreatment of children is endemic to Western culture.

Ann Alhadeff, our editor, was the victim of a fatal accident shortly before this book was completed. She was a source of help and encouragement at every step along the way. We shall not forget her gentle guidance and her insistence on perfection.

SEXUAL TRAUMA IN CHILDREN AND ADOLESCENTS

Dynamics and Treatment

1

The Problem of Molestation

At last, clinicians are beginning to accept the grim reality of the sexual abuse of children. It is a painful subject, but it is one that we must finally face as a profession and cease relegating to the realm of fantasy created by neurotic children. As long as adults ignore the problem of abuse, it will continue to grow in magnitude, and our children will not receive the protection they deserve. Some people favor the view that there is currently a national hysteria about sexual abuse. Because of this view, it may be that much upheaval will be required to drive the problem out of one of society's darkest corners.

As with other forms of child abuse, many dwell in ignorance of the scope of child molestation in our culture. We can only speculate on the subject, applying whatever multipliers to the currently reported incidence figures as we consider appropriate. Because the rate of *reported* incidents of molestation of both boys and girls has risen from year to year over the past 15 years (Finkelhor, 1984), we may assume a trend toward greater prevalence in the population. That approach is obviously fraught with error, but the compulsion to pursue it is strong. No doubt there was as much or more sexual molestation of children during the Victorian era (to name only one profligate period in history) as there is currently, but the values of the time required that the report be more scorned than the act it reported. What we do know about our era is that more cases of molestation are being brought to light. Reporting of these cases leads to heightened public awareness of the problem. Aware-

1

ness creates a climate that favors reporting, and so on. In sum, it is increasingly likely that we *can* know how much molestation is occurring in our society. That fact raises confidence that we are beginning to draw at least the severest cases into our treatment network.

MISCONCEPTIONS ABOUT THE MOLESTATION OF CHILDREN

Sexual assaults on children are definitely not rare phenomena. According to Finkelhor (1979, 1982, 1987) and Fritz, Stoll, and Wagner (1981), in the general population one may find that between 15% and 45% of women and between 3% and 9% of men have been sexually traumatized as children.* And while reports of *physical* abuse of children increased by 16% nationwide from 1983 to 1984, during the same period reports of *sexual* abuse increased by 59% (Garcia, 1986). Moreover, it is conservatively estimated that only one out of five cases of child molestation is ever reported to the police. Considering this extremely low rate of reporting, it is clearly a mistake to presume that actual occurrences are infrequent. Before the clinical aspects of the sexual traumatization of children are discussed in this book, it may be helpful to review some of the causes of this misconception.

For the most part, adults tend to have a mental "set," in which children are seen as requiring careful supervision and discipline: children are viewed as being "naughty" or unreliable. Many adults believe that they need to be on guard against children's fibs, exaggerations, and "tall tales." In many instances, even if a child has reported being sexually assaulted by an adult, the child is considered to be lying until it is proven that he or she is telling the truth. We consider it to be ironic that in the justice system, one of whose concerns is the protection of children, an adult is innocent until proven guilty, but a child's word against an adult is immediately greeted with skepticism. Also worth noting is that the preponderance of professional literature on the subject of childhood sexual trauma, before 1970, was focused above all on the issue of whether the child was lying or telling the truth, as opposed to the emotional implications of the experience on the child.

In our experience (supported by others, e.g., Finkelhor & Browne, 1985; Geiser, 1979; Green, 1986; Hilberman, 1976; Peters, 1973), the child in a majority of cases is telling the truth. When assessing the veracity of a child's allegations, we prefer to begin with the assumption

---

* The authors believe that the currently accepted percentages for males who have been molested will be revised to 10% or 15% of the population when more accurate data are forthcoming.

that what is said is true until it is proven otherwise in the course of a thorough evaluation (Geiser, 1979). By doing so, one may set in motion a process that will make certain that the child is protected from any possible future abuse.

Another unfortunate source of misconceptions concerning sexual assault against children can be found in the writings of Sigmund Freud. Because he was unable to come to terms with the knowledge that some of his adult patients had been victims of incest, Freud changed certain case studies to portray incest fantasies as opposed to actual incest (Peters, 1973). Why did Freud do that? Peters surmised that Freud already had endured enough professional criticism because of his theories of infantile sexuality, and was unwilling to endure the additional censure that would result in his revealing that a significant number of his patients (for the most part, members of prominent Viennese families) were in fact the victims of incest. In addition, Peters hypothesized that Freud himself, the father of daughters, could not personally cope with revelations of this sort. Unfortunately, few clinicians have thought to question these clinical falsehoods. Hence, this errant point of view may have permitted them to avoid dealing with a particularly painful and shocking aspect of human behavior, by relegating it to the fantasy life of simple children. Despite the current recognition that these Freudian signposts were false, there is still considerable reluctance in the clinical profession to become involved in this issue.*

Another consideration, related to the one discussed above, is that a majority of the adults who sexually abuse children are known by the child's family or are related to the family itself (DeFrancis, 1969; Finkelhor & Browne, 1985). So the child may be reporting assault by a family friend, a member of the community who is known to the family, or a family member. Some parents are simply not prepared to face the family disruption or social pressure that giving credence to such a report may bring. Unfortunately, many parents simply refuse to believe that a family member or the nice man who lives down the street could have done such a thing, because of the popularly held notion that child molesters are either hostile old men, members of another race, or people who are obviously deranged. In point of fact, the person who molests children is very different from those people. A majority of child molesters are of the same race as the child and

---

* We do not intend by these comments to diminish the undeniable value of Freud's work to the field of psychology. We are of the opinion that no one has contributed more to our science than has Freud.

are apparently sane men in their late twenties or early thirties (Groth & Birnbaum, 1978).

The Los Angeles Police Department has compiled a profile of men who molest young boys. The man is usually married, with children of his own, middle class, and a college graduate. In many cases, he has a fairly active sex life with his wife. In general, he does not have good interpersonal relationships, but he is often perceived by those who know him as a respectable citizen. This profile is a far cry from the stereotypical "dirty old man who gives out candy in the playground"; in fact, few children are sexually assaulted by elderly people.

Because most children who are sexually traumatized are victims of people they know and trust, most assaults occur within the child's natural environment. Many pedophiles seek jobs or volunteer positions in places that are frequented by children and that parents think of as safe: e.g., schools, recreation centers, day care centers, nursery schools, the Boy Scouts, Big Brothers, or Big Sisters (Geiser, 1979, p. 93). Because of phenomena such as these, the therapist should consider the child's story to be true until he or she is *absolutely sure* that the story is false. In our experience, when it comes to reporting sexual assaults, children can usually be counted on to tell the truth more often than adults.*

Another facet of this dilemma that may serve to confuse matters and influence adults to disbelieve or blame the child is that in many cases of sexual assault against young children, no extreme physical force is involved. If force is used on a child, it is usually in the form of a verbal threat or coercion (DeFrancis, 1969; Finkelhor & Browne, 1985; Groth & Birnbaum, 1978; Schultz, 1975; Sgroi, 1978). The child is most often lured into the situation in some way. Logically, one can see that adults who intend to molest young children do not have to use much physical force: because the molesters are bigger, they can overpower their victims easily. And, realizing that most child molesters are known and trusted by the child, one can see that *no* force is required in many cases involving children. Because of the notoriety given to child murders and other violent crimes against children, people hold the fixed belief that sexual assaults against children are violent. Hence, when a child tells an adult that he or she has been sexually assaulted, the parent may misconstrue the missing evidence of physical force as evidence of

---

* It is more likely that a false report of sexual assault will be made by an adult, rather than a young child. When a child *does* make a false accusation of sexual abuse, he or she has usually been pressured into doing so by an adult (Green, 1986). For example, a child may falsely accuse a parent of sexually abusing him or her during a child custody dispute as the result of pressure or "brainwashing" by the other, angry parent. The general topic of false reporting is discussed in more detail in Chapter 5.

compliance on the child's part; or, he or she may look upon the child's story as untrue. We have observed that people tend to be relatively more sympathetic toward victims of sexual assault who have been physically injured (whether children or adults) because they can focus their attention upon the victim's physical injuries. In that way, they may avoid dealing with the sometimes shocking sexual aspects of the assault, as well as with the victim's often more profound "invisible psychological wounds" (Everstine & Everstine, 1983, pp. 163, 164).

Finally, there may be aspects of a child's behavior that will cause adults to doubt the reality of the child's story. Some molested children have a considerably flattened affect, which adults tend to misinterpret as being blasé about (or undisturbed by) the event (Burgess & Holmstrom, 1974; Everstine & Everstine, 1983; Green, 1986; Peters, 1973; Sgroi, 1978). The flat affect of these children is actually indicative of childhood depression, shock, or fear, as opposed to indifference or calm. The child's superficial lack of emotion may even lead adults to believe that he or she was unaffected by the assault. It could also lead a clinician to believe that the child is emotionally unaffected by the event, or to doubt that the supposed event occurred because the child is so calm. Instead what may be occurring is that the child is depressed and not capable of expressing himself or herself, or the child may be too afraid or ashamed to express inner feelings to an adult. This phenomenon was described aptly by Sgroi (1978):

> Children can exhibit the entire gamut of behaviors in response to a sexual assault, ranging from the negative to the positive. Unsophisticated observers may note calm and unconcerned behavior or outright denial of the situation or positive response by the child to the suspected perpetrator (all these behaviors have frequently been observed in child victims where sexual assault has been proved) and mistakenly conclude that no sexual assault could have occurred because of the child's reaction. It is essential that helping professionals who come in contact with these children be knowledgeable about the wide range of possible reactions that may be exhibited. (p. 135)

Some children may appear emotionally bland or neutral, while others may exhibit positive feelings or even affection toward those who have sexually traumatized them. By contrast, some children may exhibit intense negative feelings toward the perpetrators; still others react to sexual traumatization by any one of a wide range of somatic reactions— sleep and eating disturbances, bedwetting, or phobic reactions. Because of these complicating factors, there may follow a period of several weeks or months—requiring considerable support—before the child may reveal his or her true feelings about the incident and the assaulter.

Behavior that can lead to the most tragic misunderstanding is that of the (so-called) seductive child. Too often, adults accept the protestations of the child molester that he or she was seduced by a sexually aggressive child. It is our experience, as well as that of others (e.g., Geiser, 1979; Green, 1986; Meiselman, 1978; Porter, Blick, & Sgroi, 1982), that such excuses are rarely, if ever, true. Emotionally needy or neglected children (as many child victims of sexual assault are) may try to please an adult by responding to the adult's overt or covert sexual demands. Children are rarely sexual in front of, or toward, adults—unless they have been previously traumatized sexually by an adult. Many children are sexual with other children in an exploratory fashion, usually out of the sight of adults. However, even if a child were to be sexually aggressive with an adult, most persons would agree that responsibility for self-control and appropriate behavior should rest with the adult.

Children are essentially polymorphous in their sexual orientation. As Schultz (1975) has pointed out, children may be sexually curious but they are curious in a childish manner, i.e., relative to their development stage. When a child's curiosity results in adult, genital sex, the child may become terrified or feel betrayed or confused, because he or she has no way to resolve or release the overstimulation that occurs. What may have begun as curiosity or an attempt to gain an adult's affection and attention often results in a nightmare from which one cannot awaken.

It should be noted that overt sexual behavior on the part of a child is quite frequently a cry for help. In other words, it may be a way of trying to tell the adults around the child what has happened. A traumatized child may act out sexually with other children, may perform autoerotic acts in public, or may behave in a primitively seductive way toward adults. These actions are often an indicator of prior sexual trauma, and one should take care to avoid reacting intemperately to the overt sexuality of the child's behavior, no matter how shocking it may be. The child may be testing an adult, by this means, to see if the adult is going to abuse him or her sexually, just as someone else has done in the past. The child may be portraying, in a pathetic dramatization, what is impossible to say. (The subject of sexual acting out as a cry for help is discussed in detail in Chapter 3.)

Many factors have interacted to cause misperceptions concerning the problem of sexual abuse of children. Clinicians are beginning to realize that the abuse of children is an enormous problem for our society and that there are literally thousands of young victims in need of the care and protection of adults. Moreover, there are other thousands of "silent victims" (Hilberman, 1976; Nelson, 1982), namely those children who were disbelieved or who could not even tell an adult about the abuse that they suffered in childhood, and who have grown into adulthood with the emotional wounds of these assaults.

THE PEOPLE WHO MOLEST CHILDREN

Most sexual assaults against children are committed by men (Finkelhor, 1982, 1987; Geiser, 1979). Finkelhor suggested some factors in the socialization of men that may play a role in the etiology of this phenomenon:

1. Women learn earlier and much more completely to distinguish between sexual and non-sexual forms of affection. In part, because of their preparation for motherhood, they are sensitized to appreciate the satisfactions involved in affection without a sexual component. Men, unfortunately, are not given many legitimate opportunities to practice nurturing and to express dependency needs except through sex. So when men need affection and are feeling dependent they are much more likely to look for fulfillment in a sexual form, even if this is with an inappropriate partner. Women can get such needs met with children without sex entering the picture.
2. Men grow up to see heterosexual success as much more important to their gender identities than do women. When their egos or their competencies suffer any insult, men are much more likely to feel a need for sex as a way of reconfirming their adequacy. If the only easily available sexual partner is a child, it may be a weak confirmation, but it is some.
3. Men are socialized to be able to focus their sexual interest around sexual acts isolated from the context of a relationship. Women, by contrast, fantasize about whole situations and whole relationships. For women, the fact that a partner was a child would make it more difficult to experience sexual interest in that partner. Men, however, could experience arousal because the partner, even though a child, had the right kind of genitals, or could engage in the desired sex act.
4. Finally, men are socialized to see their appropriate sexual partners as persons who are younger and smaller than themselves, while women are socialized to see their appropriate sexual partners as being older and larger. It is less of a contortion for

a man to find a child sexually attractive, because it is merely
an extension of the gradient along which his appetites are
already focused (1982, p. 101).*

We do not intend to imply that women do not sexually abuse children.
In fact, women do, but when women traumatize children, it often takes
the subtler (but nonetheless emotionally damaging) form of inappropriate fondling, caressing while bathing or dressing the child, or sexually
seductive behavior toward the child. The male–female differences in
type and severity of sexual traumatization are complex and multifaceted,
raising questions that warrant continuing research.

GENERAL OBSERVATIONS

We cannot emphasize too strongly how important to the eventual
recovery of a child is the manner in which an adult responds to the
child who has reported being molested. One of the key factors in the
child's successful recovery from a sexual assault is that his or her parents
and relevant adults behave in a way that gives the child a sense of
being protected and supported (Everstine & Everstine, 1983; Finkelhor
& Browne, 1985; Geiser, 1979; Katan, 1973; Peters, 1973; Tufts, 1984).
However, a supportive and/or protective attitude by the child's parents
is not sufficient to resolve the trauma of a childhood sexual assault. It
is our opinion (see also Porter, Blick, & Sgroi, 1982) that child sexual
assault victims need to be in treatment from several months to years
depending upon the severity of the trauma.

In general, treatment of sexually traumatized children requires that
the therapist first conceptualize the child developmentally, then within
the context of his or her family system, and finally in respect to the
greater social system.

Current Level of Development

A clinician needs to assess the child's current level of development
and help the child to *understand* as well as to resolve the trauma. The
structure of the child's individual therapy must provide a safe situation
in which the child can construct a healthy framework for conceptualizing
the traumatic event. A therapist assists the child in creating this conceptual framework by interpreting the child's behavior in a manner

---

* Reprinted with permission from Finkelhor, D. Sexual abuse: A sociological perspective.
Child Abuse and Neglect, 6, 95–102, copyright 1982 by Pergamon Press.

that he or she can grasp at his or her developmental level. The clinician may also assist a child to give vent to feelings through the use of expressive play. The clinician must also be prepared to provide the child with accurate, age-appropriate information about molestation, about the molester, and about the child's relationship with the molester. Unfortunately, molested children are frequently engulfed in misinformation that can lead to a distorted sense of self in relation to the world. This damaged self-perception—if not worked through and changed to a more positive, healthy one—can have disastrous effects in later life. A fuller description of the aftereffects that are caused by unresolved childhood sexual assault appears in Chapter 7 on adults who were abused as children.

The Family System

A therapist will also be wise to work with a child in the context of the family system. This family intervention may take many forms, depending on the nature and degree of the trauma. The family frequently needs considerable support during the initial, discovery phase, and it would be useful for a therapist to spend some time with each family member (individually) during this initial stage, because it is fraught with fear and anxiety. Later, the family therapy may take many forms ranging from monthly parent or family meetings to—in cases of incest—a complete restructuring of the family system (the latter form is elaborated in Chapter 5).

The Social System

Finally, a clinician should help the child or adolescent deal with issues in relation to the social environment. The child and the family may become involved in some aspect of the legal system. We believe that it is important for treating therapists to become familiar with that system in order to guide the family through its complexities and stresses. In addition, those who treat sexually traumatized children and adolescents should be prepared to reach beyond the confines of their offices to assist other professionals such as teachers, the clergy, and pediatricians who may come in contact with sexually abused children, because these children have special needs and may behave—in any sphere of their lives—in a way that can cause misunderstanding.

In summary, the subject of child sexual abuse is a complex one, about which there is considerable misunderstanding and misperception. Therapists who wish to treat these children will be both buffeted by strong emotions and forced to wade through minefields of prejudice.

REFERENCES

Burgess, A. W., & Holmstrom, L. L. *Rape victims of crisis.* Bowie, MD: Robert J. Brady, 1974.
DeFrancis, V. *Protecting the child victim of sex crimes committed by adults: Final report.* Denver: The American Humane Association, 1969.
Everstine, D. S., & Everstine, L. *People in crisis.* New York: Brunner/Mazel, 1983.
Finkelhor, D. *Sexually victimized children.* New York: Free Press, 1979.
Finkelhor, D. Sexual abuse: A sociological perspective. *Child Abuse and Neglect,* 6, 95–102, 1982.
Finkelhor, D. *Child sexual abuse.* New York: Free Press, 1984.
Finkelhor, D. The sexual abuse of children: Current research reviewed. *Psychiatric Annals,* 17(4), 233–237, 241, 1987.
Finkelhor, D., & Browne, A. The traumatic impact of child sexual abuse: A conceptualization. *American Journal of Orthopsychiatry,* 55(4), 530–541, 1985.
Fritz, G., Stoll, K., & Wagner, N. A comparison of males and females who were sexually molested as children. *Journal of Sexual and Marital Therapy,* 1, 54–59, 1981.
Garcia, D. Child abuse increasing, aid money decreasing. *San Francisco Chronicle,* November 11, p. 10, 1986.
Geiser, R. L. *Hidden victims.* Boston: Beacon Press, 1979.
Green, A. H. True and false allegations of sexual abuse in child custody disputes. *Journal of the American Academy of Child Psychiatry,* 25, 449–456, 1986.
Groth, N., & Birnbaum, J. Adult sexual orientation and the attraction to underage persons. *Archives of Sexual Behavior,* 7(3), 175–181, 1978.
Hilberman, E. *The rape victim.* New York: Basic Books, 1976.
Katan, A. Children who were raped: Psychoanalytic study of the child. *University Press,* 28, 208–224, 1973.
Lister, E. D. Forced silence: A neglected dimension of trauma. *American Journal of Psychiatry,* 139(7), 872–875, 1982.
Meiselman, K. *Incest.* San Francisco: Jossey-Bass, 1978.
Nelson, S. *Incest: Fact and myth.* Edinburgh: Stramullion, 1982.
Peters, J. J. Child rape: Defusing a psychological time bomb. *Hospital Physician,* February, 46–49, 1973.
Porter, F. S., Blick, L. C., & Sgroi, S. M. Treatment of the sexually abused child. In S. M. Sgroi (Ed.), *Handbook of clinical intervention in child sexual abuse.* Lexington, MA: Lexington Books, 1982.
Schultz, L. G. The child as a sex victim: Socio-legal perspectives. In L. G. Schultz (Ed.), *Rape victimology.* Springfield, IL: Charles C Thomas, 1975.
Sgroi, S. M. Child sexual assault: Some guidelines for intervention and assessment. In A. W. Burgess, A. N. Groth, L. Holmstrom, & S. M. Sgroi

(Eds.), *Sexual assault of children and adolescents*. Lexington, MA: Lexington Books, 1978.

Tufts New England Medical Center, Division of Child Psychiatry. Sexually exploited children: Service and research project. Final report for the Office of Juvenile Justice and Delinquency Prevention. Washington, DC: U.S. Department of Justice, 1984.

2

Assessment of the Trauma

The role of a therapist in relation to cases of child or adolescent sexual trauma can take many forms. For example, the course of treatment of a troubled child may be interrupted by a revelation of sexual trauma, past or present, in which case the therapy context will be profoundly changed. In another instance, it may be an intuition of the therapist that leads, through exploration of the subject, to a revelation of abuse; in such a case, the role of the therapist will similarly change at once. In another typical sequence of events, a child is brought to the therapist by a worried parent, and the first clinical task is to assess whether or not the child has been abused and, if so, to what extent trauma has occurred. This role is one that the clinician is asked to play more and more frequently in recent years, and for that reason the assessment (or evaluation) function is separated from the treatment function for detailed discussion in this chapter.

In those cases in which an assessment does lead the therapist to suspect abuse, he or she is usually the person who will report the crime (see Chapter 8 for reporting requirements). Once this has been done, it often follows that the person who did the assessment is the one who is asked to treat the abused child. When the clinician accepts this new role, he or she can begin to apply the therapy methods that are discussed in the next chapter.*

---

* When a court has handed down an order that a child be "evaluated" (legal usage) to determine possible abuse of some kind, a different set of contingencies is faced by

Many complex factors go into measuring the degree of immediate and long-term emotional trauma that is being, and will be, suffered by the sexually abused child. Much empirical and clinical research is needed to clarify the methodological issues that remain in respect to this form of assessment. Nevertheless, existing research findings and case studies do suggest some useful criteria for determining the extent of a child's trauma, as well as prognosis in treatment.

Our experience is consistent with that of Schultz & DeSavage (1975), who wrote that the amount of psychological trauma a child experiences can be related to the amount of violence or terror associated with the event, in addition to the severity of physical assault that the child experienced. Landis (1956) found that children who were victims of rape were more severely damaged emotionally than were child victims of other types of sexual abuse. Others have documented that the way in which parents, relatives, teachers, and other adults respond to the child will have a significant effect upon the child's recovery (DeFrancis, 1969; Finkelhor, 1984; Peters, 1973, 1974, 1976). Parents, by their reaction to what has happened to the child as well as to the perpetrator's behavior, can contribute to lasting trauma in the form of guilt and shame on the part of the child. Simply put, children whose parents respond in an understanding and loving manner usually experience less trauma. Further, the child's age is thought to be a significant factor in determining how traumatic an assault has been and how successful will be the child's recovery (Burgess & Holmstrom, 1984; Peters, 1974); in effect, the younger the child, the more vulnerable he or she is to trauma, and the more likely to be overwhelmed by the experience.

Naturally, the number of sexually traumatizing events that were suffered by the child, as well as the length of time during which the child was abused, are predisposing factors to the degree of emotional damage (Yates, 1982). As might be expected, repeated sexual abuse over a long period of time is likely to be more traumatic than one isolated event. Even so, one should avoid dismissing a single event of abuse as less serious until the circumstances and the child's reactions have been thoroughly examined.

---

the clinician. This most often arises in the context of a custody or guardianship dispute, when a judge needs to know what is in the best interests of the child. When a therapist takes on this kind of referral, he or she should reflect that the assessment may result in some kind of formal report being made to a public agency (e.g., police, probation department, or child protective service of the welfare department) or even testimony in an open court. Because of the confidentiality issues that this would raise (among other issues), we recommend that the clinician refer the case to a colleague if therapy is indicated by the evaluation outcome. Conversely, if the child is already in a course of treatment with a therapist when court-ordered evaluation enters the picture, then that therapist should decline to conduct the evaluation, referring to a colleague instead.

The research of Peters (1974), DeFrancis (1969), and Sgroi (1978) has shown that assaults on children by people whom they know and trust may be more traumatic than are assaults by strangers. As Sgroi (1978) stated so well, "In general the greater the emotional distance between child and perpetrator, the less emotional trauma can be expected" (p. 135). These findings emphasize the importance of giving full consideration, when assessing the severity of the trauma suffered by a child, to the nature of the relationship between the child and the perpetrator. The clinician should ask, for example: What needs did this relationship fulfill in the child's life, and what will the loss of this relationship mean to the child? It is important to keep in mind that many traumatized children come from chaotic or emotionally impoverished homes and that the molester may have been perceived as the child's only friend, or as a major source of attention and affection. Hence, the therapist must put his or her own biases aside, and realistically evaluate the secondary gains that a child has associated with the sexual encounter. In that way, it is possible to begin to understand the climate of fear in which a child dreads losing the relationship with the abusive adult. When, later, the child believes that he or she was responsible for the adult's being harmed or imprisoned, the child's unsolvable paradox is complete.

We have found, to our sad surprise, that the degree of support received by a child can be inversely related to the family's fear of what the family may suffer as a result of an assault being made public, such as stigma or scandal. (See also Kaufmann, Peck, & Tagiuri, 1954; Sgroi, 1978.) This is tragically true in cases of incest in which the perpetrator is the father and the main source of economic support for the family. In many of these cases, the mother turns a blind eye toward the sexual abuse of her child(ren), in favor of continuing economic support by the husband.

The early literature reflects considerable controversy concerning how lasting are the effects of sexual assault upon children. The research of Bender (1965), which is frequently cited to prove that children can adjust satisfactorily after a sexual trauma, is less than convincing because the design did not include a control group, i.e., a matched group of children who had, for one reason or another, not received treatment. And in the retrospective study of Gagnon (1956), a majority of the children had been victims of exhibitionism or petting, while fewer than 5% had been victims of rape. In fact, most of the major studies that have suggested that children suffer no lasting trauma from sexual assault have lacked control groups (of nontreated victims) and have incorporated a wide variety of types of abusive incidents—most of which were not physically violent. By contrast, there is growing evidence, consistent with our clinical experience, to suggest that both prolonged trauma and later problems of adjustment result from childhood sexual assault (Bauer & Stein, 1973; DeFrancis, 1969; Finch, 1967, 1973; Finkelhor, 1984; Katan, 1973; MacDonald, 1971; MacFarlane & Waterman, 1986; McCauldron, 1967; Peters, 1974, 1976; Price, 1975).

As an overview, the psychological aftereffects of molestation may depend upon one or more of the following variables (adapted from Katz & Mazur, 1979, p. 247):

1. *The age of the child* is believed to affect the degree to which a child is traumatized. Younger children are considered by many to be more vulnerable to trauma; by contrast, MacFarlane (1978) noted that older children may be hurt more because they are more fully aware of the social stigma that is associated with sexual assault.

2. *The psychological condition of the victim:* Child victims who have had prior emotional problems (or who are emotionally vulnerable because they come from broken or unstable homes) may experience more pronounced problems as a result of being assaulted, and those problems may be longer lasting.

3. *Sexual knowledge or experience:* Children who have had no previous sexual experience may be more vulnerable than others.

4. *The type of assault:* The amount of violence and degree of bodily penetration are positively correlated with trauma. Also, the extent to which the child believes his or her body has been damaged by the event can contribute to the degree of trauma that is experienced by the child.

5. *Repeated assaults:* Repeated assaults may cause more psychological damage than an isolated assault.

6. *Molestation by a stranger versus a known, trusted offender:* Sexual assault by someone whom the child knows and trusts is more likely to cause lasting damage than is assault by a stranger.

7. *Reactions of others:* Negative reactions on the part of police, parents, teachers, peers, and/or family friends or neighbors can contribute to the degree of trauma.

8. *Not being believed or supported:* Children who are not believed or supported by their parents or adult caretakers suffer more emotional trauma than do those who are.

9. *Therapy:* As with adults, child victims of sexual assault who receive psychotherapy are more likely to recover from it than are those who do not receive treatment.

The traumatic sequelae of childhood sexual abuse are best described in two categories: 1) symptoms that usually occur in the first two years after the abuse has ceased; and 2) long-term effects. The initial symptoms exhibited by sexually traumatized children will be discussed in detail later in this chapter and can be summarized as follows: fear and anxiety, sleep disturbances, somatic complaints, regressive behavior, poor self-esteem, inability to trust, depression with its underlying anger and hostility, poor school performance, inappropriate sexual behavior, guilt, shame, and/or self-destructive behavior. The longer-term effects, which will be described more fully in Chapter 7 on adults who were assaulted as children, can be summarized as follows: depression, self-destructive or suicidal behavior, anxiety, feelings of isolation and alienation, negative self-concept, impaired interpersonal relationships, vulnerability to re-victimization, a propensity to choose abusive mates, problems with sexual adjustment, and/or substance or alcohol abuse.

One cannot review the assessment of the degree to which sexual assault traumatizes children without discussing the persistent controversy about whether or not the traumatic impact of assault has been overstated. In our opinion (in accord with Finkelhor, 1984), one must view the impact that such an event has upon a child in terms of a child's perceptions of pain and trauma. It would be foolish to think of the only "true" trauma as that which leads to impairment in the victim's later adult functioning.

Most people are aware that certain traumatic events in the course of adult life such as rape, serious physical injury, or the loss of a loved one may cause excruciating emotional suffering; the seriousness of such events is accepted, even if they do not emotionally impair the adult when he or she becomes elderly. In fact, most persons would be relieved to learn that such traumatic events may not necessarily scar the rest of a person's life. Why, then, are some so willing to dismiss childhood sexual trauma as not being a serious matter unless it is shown to impair the child's life when he or she grows into adulthood? Clearly, the logic does not hold; but what is most disturbing is the reluctance to accept the pain and suffering of childhood as being valid in its own terms.

In conclusion, current research, as well as clinical observation, strongly suggests that children are traumatized and suffer emotionally as a direct result of their being sexually abused. Browne and Finkelhor (1986) put it succinctly:

Because of the general lack of research in this field, clinicians have only recently been able to substantiate their impressions that sexual abuse is traumatic with evidence from strong scientific studies. However, as evidence now accumulates, it conveys a clear suggestion that sexual abuse is a serious mental health problem, consistently associated with very disturbing subsequent problems in some important portion of its victims. (p. 72)

As will be elaborated upon later in this book, the currently available findings of long-term impact are especially persuasive.

KEY SYMPTOMS

The generally accepted array of symptoms that typify the effects of sexual abuse on children are (summarized from Browne & Finkelhor, 1986; Everstine & Everstine, 1983; Green, 1986; Heiman, LoPiccolo, & LoPiccolo, 1981; Meiselman, 1978; Peters, 1976; Reich & Gutierres, 1979; Tufts, 1984):

1. *Fear:* The most common initial reaction. For that reason, the child who expresses extreme fear (and/or anxiety) for no apparent reason should be viewed with concern.

2. *Inability to trust:* Because of the betrayal that the child has suffered at the hands of an adult, and because he or she has been made to feel helpless by the adult, the child is severely limited in ability to trust. This deficit of trust may impair his or her future relationships in many ways.

3. *Anger and hostility:* Children are rarely able to express their anger toward an assailant, and as a result it is often displaced onto others. However, in some cases (usually those that involve extrafamilial abuse) the child does find an opportunity to release his or her anger toward the abuser.

4. *Inappropriate sexual behavior:* Sexually abused children may attempt to show or tell others what happened by doing or acting out what was done to them. A child may also attempt to gain a sense of mastery over the trauma by repetition of the events in a symbolic form; for example, child victims of sexual assault (especially male victims) may attempt to undo their feelings of helplessness by doing to other children what was done to them—a manifestation of "identification with the aggressor."

5. *Depression:* Because of not being able to express their feelings of helpless rage for what was done to them, abused children may become clinically depressed, showing signs of emotional constriction and flat or bland affect, and so forth.

6. *Guilt or shame:* Since young children are by nature egocentric, they may mistakenly accept responsibility for other people's actions toward them; this tendency, when added to the molester's attempts to shift blame onto the victim, often results in the child's experiencing intense feelings of guilt for what has happened.

7. *Problems in school:* A sudden drop in school performance may be a symptom of sexual abuse; even so, in some cases performance does not falter because the child may find security in the structure of the school environment.

8. *Somatic complaints:* Many sexually abused children internalize their trauma and may demonstrate varied somatic disorders such as headaches or stomachaches that have no organic cause.

9. *Sleep disturbances:* Frequently, sexually abused children experience difficulty in sleeping, fear of sleeping alone, nightmares, or even night terrors.

10. *Eating disorders:* Some victims of sexual abuse exhibit eating disorders as evidenced by a sudden marked increase or decrease in appetite, or the hoarding of food. A clinician should be especially observant when treating anorexia or bulimia in adolescents, because those symptoms may mask trauma caused by sexual assault.

11. *Phobic or avoidant behavior:* Child victims may display a wide range of avoidant behaviors, from agoraphobia to school phobia to the fear of someone who even slightly resembles the molester in appearance.

12. *Regressive behavior:* Children may become regressive as a result of sexual trauma. Hence, cases of regression that are not readily explained should be checked carefully for possible evidence of abuse.

13. *Self-destructive behavior or accident-proneness:* These may become outlets for the child's feelings of guilt and shame. Many molested children feel damaged or worthless and their acting out takes this form.

14. *Runaway behavior:* Older children and adolescents may attempt to cope with sexual abuse by running away from home.

INITIAL INTERVIEWS

This section reviews some of the factors that should be taken into consideration when a therapist first meets with a sexually traumatized child and his or her parents. Special attention is given to these first encounters because they are often extremely sensitive moments which, in many instances, can become a pivotal point in the direction and outcome of the treatment course. It is our experience, as well as the experience of authors such as Sgroi (1978) and Green (1986), that if these first contacts with the child and the family are dealt with effectively, the case will more likely have a successful conclusion.

Usually, a sexually traumatized child comes to the attention of a therapist in one of the following ways. The therapist may be called upon to make an evaluation of a child in an emergency or crisis situation, such as might be conducted by a child protective service program or in a hospital emergency room. Or a child is brought in for assessment because a parent is suspicious that "something has happened" to the child. A therapist may also be asked to evaluate a child during a divorce proceeding, in which allegations of child sexual abuse have been made by the child or by one parent against another. Finally, a child may be brought to see a therapist because of some behavioral or emotional problem that could have been caused by a sexual trauma which is unknown to the parents.

Involving the Parents

When the sexual traumatization is unknown (or allegedly unknown) to the parents, the clinician needs to proceed with considerable caution if, during a first or early meeting, he or she learns or has reason to suspect that a trauma did occur. How the parents of a sexually traumatized child respond to the child when trauma is first discovered can have a considerable impact on how well the child will be able to recover from the trauma. Since parental responses to learning that their child has been sexually assaulted can run the entire gamut from sensitive support of the child, to blind rage, to total nonsupport or denial, it is best to exclude the child from a meeting in which parents are informed that he or she has, or may have been, molested. Emotional confrontations or angry scenes can be almost as confusing or even as traumatic to the child as the assault itself, and it is wise to take precautions to avoid them if possible.

A therapist also needs to consider that one or both parents of the child may have suffered his or her own sexual trauma as a child, and consequently the therapist may be forced to discuss complex and sensitive intergenerational issues that may not be appropriate in the presence of an already injured child. It is our experience that many parents of children who suffer sexual abuse have been victims themselves as children, in many cases at or about the same age as their own child's victimization. Hence, revealing to this previously traumatized parent the fact that his or her child has also been assaulted can be an extremely volatile situation, from which a vulnerable child should be shielded.

A further reason for keeping the child apart from this early discussion with the parents, particularly in cases of intrafamily sexual abuse, is that this will possibly prevent the child from being forced to contradict a family member's version of what happened. Often, traumatized children fall silent in such a situation, or they may even change their stories, because they cannot withstand the pressure of confronting a significant adult. Few parents are capable of listening to details of the sexual traumatization of their child and maintaining the accepting, nonjudgmental attitude that is necessary in such situations. The child might misinterpret a parent's distress upon hearing the details of the event as being anger toward him or her. Nevertheless, if the child insists that his or her parent be present, we recommend that the child's wishes be respected, unless there is a strong suspicion that the parent in question may have been the one who abused the child, in which case the child should be interviewed alone.

When the child is reluctant or fearful to be seen without his or her parent, the best strategy is to see both parent and child together initially, engage them in some neutral, nonthreatening discussion for a brief period, and then ask the child again if he or she is willing to talk with the therapist alone. If the child is still reluctant, the parent may remain, but the clinician must be alert for any attempt on the parent's part to influence, silence, or censor the child.

Meeting with the Child Alone

One virtue of interviewing the child alone is that this may serve to protect the child from otherwise well-intended but harmful outbursts from the parents, such as, "I told you not to go there alone," or "Why did you let him . . . ?" Understandable but emotionally charged remarks by distraught parents can often make a child feel that what happened was his or her fault. The therapist must also consider that the person who abused the child may be a trusted family member whose identity the child may be fearful to reveal in the parents' presence. The child may also be hesitant to speak because he or she may, in fact, have been a willing or curious participant at the beginning of the assault. Sadly, sexual abuse sometimes results from a child's innocent curiosity or from feeling flattered by an adult's attention. Also, the child may have been seeking a form of nurturance and concern that was absent in the home.

Most children find considerable relief if they are able to tell an adult what has happened to them and the adult responds appropriately. It shows them that they are accepted and that they did not do anything wrong. In addition, it may serve to negate some of the things that the molester may have said to coerce or seduce the child into cooperating, or as an attempt to prevent the child from telling anyone about the assault. Some common threats that are used by child molesters to silence their child victims are variations of the following:

"If you tell, I'll come back and kill you."

"This is our secret, and if you tell you will be taken away."

"If your parents find out what we have done, they will have you locked up in jail."

"Your parents won't love you anymore if they find out what we have done."

Such threats are frequently very successful in silencing a child and making the child feel immensely guilty. This is especially true in respect to an emotionally deprived child's need for love and attention.

Thus, any hysterical overreaction on the part of a parent or other significant adult that may cause the child to believe that the threats of the molester were true and to retract an accurate report of molestation can be avoided when the child is seen alone. Instances in which children have recanted true reports because of family pressure or the behavior of angry adults who frighten the child are far more frequent than is generally known.

A Frightened Child

The case of three-year-old Adam, who was repeatedly sexually abused by his new stepfather, illustrates this point. His mother and stepfather had been married only five months when the abuse began. The step-father would take Adam into the bathroom (under the pretext of giving him a bath) and sodomize the boy. During the abuse, the stepfather would hold Adam's head under water and say to him that if he ever told anyone, he would be taken away from his mother and locked up in a place for bad children.

As time went on, Adam's behavior began to regress. He started to wet the bed, cling to his mother incessantly, and have unexplainable temper tantrums. Even though Adam's stepfather dismissed the behavior as jealousy and problems in adjusting to a new man in the house, Adam's mother took the child to the pediatrician for a checkup and to ask her advice about the sudden behavioral changes. Adam had known the pediatrician all his life, and so he felt safe with her. During the examination, the pediatrician found evidence of anal trauma. A tearful Adam told the doctor and his mother about what was taking place during the baths with his stepfather.

Unfortunately, the terrified child failed to tell either one about the threats that his stepfather had made. The mother, thinking that she was doing the right thing to protect her child, took Adam to his natural father's house while she went to report what had happened to the police. Even though the mother perceived that taking him to his father's was a caring and protective act, Adam feared that she was abandoning him.

Later on, after the mother spoke with the police, they decided that it would be necessary to talk to the child, and chose to send a police car to the father's home to get the child. When Adam saw the police officer in the patrol car arrive at his father's home, he was convinced that all the threats of the stepfather were coming true. When questioned, Adam said, "No one ever touched my behind." Later, at the police station, he said that "two big blue men from next door did it." Finally, Adam refused to talk at all.

The police called a therapist from the Emergency Treatment Center (ETC) to assist them in this interview with Adam, because they were concerned that even though there was physical evidence that Adam had been sexually assaulted, the child's story was so confused that they did not know who had actually abused him. (In fact, by this time the stepfather was vehemently denying that he had ever touched the child.)

The ETC therapist, after speaking with Adam and his mother for some time, could tell that Adam's being separated from his mother during such a stressful period had been extremely terrifying to such a young child, and that he needed reassurance from her that she was not going to abandon him again. Finally, after the mother had thoroughly reassured him, Adam was able to tell about the threats that had been made to him.

Helping the Child to Feel Comfortable

From the first interview, the therapist must communicate clearly to child victims that they have done nothing wrong and that all responsibility for what took place rests with the adult who molested them. A therapist also needs to be extremely sensitive to the child, reassuring him or her that the discovery of the abuse means that there is the possibility of help and support, rather than the fear of separation or blame that may have been threatened by the molester. Eventually, the child may find an enormous relief in being able to tell an adult what took place, and to find that the adult responds in a kindly and understanding manner. The clinician should be aware that when a child reports one incident of abuse, that may only have been one in a series of sexually traumatic events.

Before talking with a young child, the therapist may find it helpful to learn the family names for male and female genitalia, as well as those for urination and defecation; the child may be more at ease in using these names. Upon first meeting, the therapist should let the child know that he or she is free to talk about what happened, but it is all right if he or she does not want to. If the child does not want to talk about what took place, it will be wise not to force the issue but to begin a play activity such as drawing or playing with dolls or puppets. The child should be allowed to proceed at his or her own pace and should not be pressed for details or information. The main aim is to establish trust and good rapport with the child during these first meetings.

A child's reluctance to discuss the incident in question should not be interpreted as meaning that nothing happened or that the child is unreliable. The child may simply be shy, confused, or frightened. Adults will concede that sex is a difficult topic to discuss for adults, let alone children. Hence, we should not expect a child to be able to discuss freely, with a stranger, what adults have difficulty in discussing with those to whom they feel close. In fact, many parents convey to their children at a very early age that sex and sexual feelings are associated with guilt or wrongdoing; for those children, discussing sexual trauma can seem an impossible task.

A child victim may not be comfortable with an adult in a closed space, especially one the child does not know, because that may have been the type of situation in which the child was molested. The clinician may wish to allow the child not only to select the type of activity that occurs in the first meeting, but a location for the meeting that is outside or away from the office. If the meeting takes place in the therapist's office, the child may be asked to choose whether the door to the office will be left open or closed. We have found that some severely sexually traumatized children may wish to open and close the door to the therapist's office repeatedly, in order to see if he or she can get out. A child may also wish to test the telephone to see if it really works, should he or she need to summon help. We suggest giving the child permission to use the phone or to open and close the door as often as necessary, while gently trying to reassure the child that the therapist will not hurt him or her.

Gathering Information

A child may feel comfortable in describing what happened to him or her by using dolls, or may prefer to make a drawing rather than talking about the event. In general, in a first interview it is not wise to use the anatomically accurate dolls that are used by some police or social agencies, because the sight of these dolls may be too stimulating or frightening for a severely traumatized child to tolerate. This is especially relevant should there be a possibility of legal action being based upon the assessment. A number of recent cases have established that questioning involving the use of these sexually explicit dolls may be discredited as testimony. The rationale is that showing the dolls enhances the likelihood that a child will be asked "leading" questions by the examiner. It is well-known that anxious or confused children are vulnerable to being "led" by questioning because of their dependency needs. Hence, the child could misinterpret what he or she is being shown and misconstrue the purpose of the questioning. The child may feel that the clinician wants him or her to make statements about sexual matters and may reply accordingly, simply in order to please.

As an alternative to the anatomically accurate dolls, traditional boy and girl dolls, or girl/boy animal dolls, are useful and nonthreatening. In some cases of severe sexual traumatization, even these human puppets, dolls, or drawings of human figures may be too frightening, especially if the child is young. In such extreme cases, the clinician is advised to give the child the choice of a neutral play activity or game while the time is used to gain rapport with him or her. However, in most instances, a therapist can ask the child to choose among animal or human dolls or puppets to act out what happened. For example, we have Raggedy Ann and Andy dolls with removable clothes, as well as male and female frog hand puppets, among which the child may choose to reenact the situation. (Specific recommendations for useful toys are presented in Chapter 3.)

While observing the child, a therapist should be alert for those details that signify the child has had a sexual encounter with an adult. For example, if, in a neutral setting, a seven-year-old child describes an erect penis ejaculating semen, the child most likely has been abused. There are only three sources from which a child could have learned about this, namely, (1) by witnessing or participating in some form of adult–child sexual contact, (2) by having it described to him or her by an adult, or (3) by seeing adult sexual activity in a pornographic photograph or videotape.

Although the child may initially refuse to talk about what happened to him or her, evidence of the trauma will eventually surface if the therapist is able to build a positive relationship with the child. Consequently, building such a relationship should be the primary consideration of the first several assessment meetings. One of the principal errors that clinicians make during first meetings is to permit their own anxiety or concern about finding out what happened to result in putting pressure on an already anxious or frightened child. This may cause the child to withdraw or be afraid because now he or she feels attacked or pressured by the therapist. If the child *was* sexually abused or traumatized, it will eventually come to light. A child may reveal this directly in discussion with the therapist or symbolically through play. In addition, projective tests (e.g., drawings, Rorschach, CAT, or TAT) are often useful means to elicit information when the child is too fearful to talk freely.

Understanding the Child

It may require from two to four assessment sessions before the child will begin to communicate about his or her trauma, and even at this point the expression may take a symbolic form through play. During these sessions, the child may be watching or testing the therapist to see if this is a safe and trustworthy adult. The child's testing may take one of the following forms:

1. Flat, rigidly controlled, or disinterested play.

2. Aggressive acting out toward the therapist or toward the toys in the play therapy room.

3. By contrast, the child may give the therapist (consciously or unconsciously) hints about what has transpired and then wait to measure
what the therapist's responses are to these hints. The aim is to see
whether or not it is safe for him or her to proceed with further
disclosures. The clinician should be aware that even if the hints are
unconscious on the part of the child, the child will nonetheless be
sensitive to, and aware of, the therapist's responses to those unconscious attempts to communicate.

4. Possibly there may be sexual acting out toward the therapist or with
a toy. If the child behaves in a sexually aggressive manner, the
clinician should be quite careful about the manner in which he or
she responds to this behavior. In such a case, the child is usually
not attempting to engage the therapist in actual sexual activity, but
rather testing the adult to see if this is a "safe" person. The child
may also be showing the therapist what was done to him or her,
perhaps being too fearful to say it in words because he or she was
threatened not to tell.

   How a therapist responds to such a sexual advance is extremely
critical for the course of the evaluation or treatment. The clinician
must guard against doing anything that a child might misinterpret
as being judgmental or punitive. No matter how aberrant the child's
behavior may be, a therapist should take a calm, neutral stance that
will enable the child to communicate freely what has occurred.

During first meetings with a child victim, the clinician needs to be
extremely sensitive to the relationship issues involving a child victim
and his or her assailant. Because the person who assaults a child may
well be someone who was once trusted or loved by the child, perhaps
in connection with a school or recreation center or in the context of
the child's family, a child may view his or her molester as a sole source
of emotional support or nurturance. In addition, the child may have
been repeatedly assaulted over a period of time. The factor of a long-
standing relationship between victim and assailant can mean that child
sexual trauma is more complex than is experienced by an adult; i.e.,
rape is usually a single occurrence perpetrated by a stranger. A therapist
must consider that the child may be quite confused or ambivalent about
what has happened, and may fear the loss of this relationship with
the molester.

Above all, a therapist should strive to be fully cognizant of how the
child perceives his or her relationship with the molester. Again, the
clinician needs to be careful to keep his or her feelings or biases well
in check, so that the child does not feel judged or additionally stig-

matized for having positive or mixed feelings toward the perpetrator. Adults frequently have considerable difficulty in resolving mixed or conflicting emotions about someone. One must imagine how enormously difficult it is for a child to struggle with such a jumble of emotions. Another reason why a therapist should not permit his or her personal biases to intrude upon therapy is that those biases may contribute to a predetermined definition of what the child's experience must have been like, and thus prevent hearing or understanding of the victim's true feelings.

Finally, the clinician should be aware that many of these children simply do not trust adults in general, and thus will not tell an adult, in any direct manner, what has happened to them. Instead, children may communicate by their behavior and watch to see what the adult does in reply. This kind of case will require much patience and sensitivity on the therapist's part—an atmosphere in which the child can begin to come to terms with what has happened and eventually communicate directly about the event.

Since it may require several meetings to determine whether or not a child has been sexually traumatized, the clinician should conduct these sessions in a relaxed and unhurried manner, bearing in mind that the child may misinterpret pressure on the part of a therapist as evidence of censure or dislike. An important component is to clarify the reason for talking with the child, so that the child does not feel confused or betrayed later on if the therapist reports what was said or done during the sessions. A statement such as, "Your parents [or teacher, etc.] have asked me to meet with you a few times because they [he/she] are concerned that something may have happened to you, and I will be talking to them [her/him] after we meet," will usually suffice. In our experience, it is best to keep such a statement neutral until one learns how the child feels about what happened, and what his or her relationship with the molester was.

Understanding the Family

In addition to making an assessment of the child's current status, a clinician will need to assess the child's family and support system before treatment of the child begins. It may have been the child's search for any kind of adult affection that led to the victimization. One general way of assessing the resources or support that the child has available to him or her is to ascertain how, and to whom, the child reported (if at all) the sexual abuse, and what was done by the family once the child made this report. For example, did the child reveal the sexual assault to a parent (or parents) and did the parent(s) respond in an appropriate, protective, and/or supportive manner toward the child? Or, by contrast, did the child report the event to someone outside the family—a teacher, a counselor, a friend, or a friend's parents? Further, when the outside person to whom the child reported the assault contacted the parent(s), did the parent(s) dismiss the allegation as a "tall tale" or act responsibly?

A significant element in determining the emotional resources available to the child is the length of time that it took the child to report an incident of assault to an adult. For example, in the situation in which a child reports a traumatic incident immediately or quite soon after the occurrence, one generally finds that the child has more sources of emotional support within the family than a child who cannot or will not ask for help right away. The child who is a victim of sexual abuse that continues over time usually comes from the less supportive and more disorganized or pathological family system.

Finally, the child who has never told and who is referred for an evaluation due to unusual behavior may be the most difficult of all to reach. This child may be too terrified by the threats of his or her assailant, or may realize that there is no support for him or her in the family system. In cases of incest, a child may believe that he or she is saving the family from some form of destruction by accepting his or her role as child victim and would ruin the family by disclosing "the secret."

The Child Before the Trauma

When making the initial assessment of a child who has possibly been sexually traumatized, the therapist should attempt to collect information about the child's level of functioning *before* the supposed trauma. The clinician should try to gain consent to obtain such information from the child's school, pediatrician, day care center, or other relevant caretaking agencies. It is advisable to seek additional information from family sources outside the nuclear family as well. One should inquire into how the child attempts to deal with anxiety or stress, and also into the child's cognitive, emotional, and intellectual levels of functioning. With this kind of information, the therapist can begin to measure whether or not a child's current behavior is consistent with his or her more usual patterns of behavior.

AFTER THE INITIAL MEETINGS

If the clinician has reason to believe that a child *was* sexually assaulted, he or she should take appropriate steps to report this belief to the proper authorities and to ensure that the child receives a comprehensive pediatric examination. This pediatric examination can be extremely reassuring for the child, because many sexually abused children feel "changed" or damaged by the experience (Sgroi, 1982). When the examination is done in a sensitive manner, it can serve to reassure the child that he or she is undamaged and that the adults around the child are taking every possible step to ensure that the child is protected and cared for.

Preferably, the examination will be performed by a pediatrician who has experience in the assessment and treatment of sexual assault victims, and who will be capable of testifying as an expert witness should the case eventually go to court. Unfortunately, not all physicians are qualified or knowledgeable in respect to childhood sexual assault, and all too often these examinations are left to inexperienced residents who are on call at a hospital emergency room. Moreover, an inexperienced medical practitioner not only may lack the knowledge to perform such an examination, but also may be more likely to avoid dealing with the shocking or unpleasant aspects of the case, dismissing the child as hysterical or a parent as overreacting.

Unresolved Cases

Probably the most difficult and distressing cases for a therapist to work with are those in which no concrete determination can be made of what actually happened to the child. Cases such as these are, sadly, common. In unresolved cases, the adults, upon learning that nothing legally supportable has been determined, often wish to "forget the whole thing ever happened."

The children in these situations may be those who need treatment the most, for the following reasons. Consider the emotional impact on a child who was, in fact, sexually traumatized, but whose parents do not believe it; or, a known assailant is found not guilty or no charges are pressed because of lack of sufficient evidence (a frequent outcome).* Add to that the fact that a majority of those who abuse children are known to the victim (DeFrancis, 1969; Finkelhor, 1984), which means

---

* Another misfortune can occur if an instance of molestation is not reported before the statute of limitations has passed. The latter varies from state to state (cf. Chapter 8, p. 184).

that the child, in many situations, must continue to see the person who abused him or her. This child may feel totally helpless at the prospect of future assault by that person. What does this do to a child's sense of self in relation to others, or to his or her world view—both of which are still in various stages of formation? The effects on personal and social development of the child could be considerable.

In unresolved cases such as those referred to above, children may feel abandoned and betrayed by the adults whom they trusted to protect them. Those children may themselves grow into people who do not trust others and must always be in control of those around them. Or, they may incorporate the experience in a way which causes them to be masochistic "eternal victims" because they have defined themselves as helpless people to whom "things happen." In another possible life script, they may re-create being victimized again and again in the unconscious expectation that "this time" someone will protect them— which of course never happens. This syndrome of vulnerability to revictimization has been identified in the research of Miller and colleagues (1978), Brandt and Tisza (1977), Fromuth (1986), and Russell (1986). Another pattern being traced by research occurs when these children, as adults, choose abusive mates (see Briere, 1984; Katan, 1973; Russell, 1986).

In summary, initial sessions for assessment purposes should be conducted with utmost care. Children in a situation of this kind may be extremely fearful and their behavior may vary across a wide spectrum. Hence, the clinician must accept that it may take considerably longer than usual to complete an assessment. Further, some children may be too terrified to give a clear description of what took place—ever. It is in those cases that the more symbolic content of such measures as play and testing can be informative.

During the assessment, a clinician should obtain both pretrauma and posttrauma behavioral histories from as many independent sources as possible (i.e., parents, teachers, relatives, pediatricians, and other caretakers), in categories such as the child's emotional state of being, developmental processes, cognitive functioning, coping skills, and typical reactions to stress. Finally, the therapist should weigh these data in the light of sexually abused children in general, as described in this chapter and other sources.

REFERENCES

Bauer, R., & Stein, J. Sex counseling on campus: Short-term treatment techniques. *American Journal of Orthopsychiatry, 43*, 824–893, 1973.

Bender, L. Offended and offender children. In R. Slovenko (Ed.), *Sexual behavior and the law*. Springfield, IL: Charles C Thomas, 1965.

Brandt, R., & Tisza, V. The sexually misused child. *American Journal of Orthopsychiatry, 44,* 80–87, 1977.

Briere, J. The effects of childhood sexual abuse on later psychological functioning: Defining a "post-sexual-abuse syndrome." Paper presented at the Third National Conference on Sexual Victimization of Children, Washington, D.C., 1984.

Browne, A., & Finkelhor, D. Impact of child sexual abuse: A review of the research. *Psychological Bulletin, 99*(1), 66–77, 1986.

Burgess, A. W., & Holmstrom, L. L. Rape trauma syndrome. *American Journal of Psychiatry, 131*(9), 981–986, 1984.

DeFrancis, V. *Protecting the child victim of sex crimes committed by adults: Final report*. Denver: The American Humane Association, 1969.

Everstine, D. S., & Everstine, L. *People in crisis*. New York: Brunner/Mazel, 1983.

Finch, S. M. Sexual activities of children with other children and adults. *Clinical Pediatrics, 6,* 1–2 (Commentaries), 1967.

Finch, S. M. Adult seduction of the child: Effects on the child. *Medical Aspects of Human Sexuality, 7,* 170–187, 1973.

Finkelhor, D. *Child sexual abuse*. New York: The Free Press, 1984.

Finkelhor, D. The sexual abuse of children: Current research reviewed. *Psychiatric Annals, 17*(4), 233–238, 1987.

Finkelhor, D., & Browne, A. The traumatic impact of child sexual abuse: A conceptualization. *American Journal of Orthopsychiatry, 55*(4), 530–541, 1985.

Fromuth, M. E. The relationship of childhood sexual abuse with later psychological and sexual adjustment in a sample of college women. *Child Abuse and Neglect, 10,* 5–15, 1986.

Gagnon, J. H. Female child victims of sex offenses. *Social Problems, 13,* 176–192, 1956.

Geiser, R. L. *Hidden victims: The sexual abuse of children*. Boston: Beacon Press, 1979.

Goodwin, J. *Sexual abuse: Incest victims and their families*. Littleton, MA: John Wright/PSG, 1982.

Green, A. H. True or false allegations of child sexual abuse in child custody disputes. *Journal of the American Academy of Child Psychiatry, 25,* 449–456, 1986.

Heiman, J. R., LoPiccolo, L., & LoPiccolo, J. The treatment of sexual dysfunction. In A. S. Gurman & D. P. Kniskern (Eds.), *Handbook of family therapy*. New York: Brunner/Mazel, 1981.

Katan, A. Children who were raped. *Psychoanalytic Study of the Child, 28,* 208–224, 1973.

Katz, S., & Mazur, M. A. *Understanding the rape victim*. New York: John Wiley & Sons, 1979.

Kaufmann, I., Peck, A. L., & Tagiuri, C. K. The family constellation and overt incestuous relations between father and daughter. *American Journal of Orthopsychiatry, 24,* 266–277, 1954.

Landis, J. T. Experiences of 500 children with adult sexual deviation. *Psychiatric Quarterly Supplement, 30,* 91–109, 1956.

MacDonald, J. M. *Rape offenders and their victims*. Springfield, IL: Charles C Thomas, 1971.

MacFarlane, K. Sexual abuse of children. In J. R. Chapman & M. Gates (Eds.), *The victimization of women*. Beverly Hills, CA: Sage, 1978.

MacFarlane, K., & Waterman, J. *Sexual abuse of young children*. New York: Guilford Press, 1986.

McCauldron, R. J. Rape. *Canadian Journal of Corrections, 9*, 37–57, 1967.

Meiselman, K. C. *Incest*. San Francisco: Jossey-Bass, 1978.

Miller, J., Moeller, D., Kaufman, A., Divasto, P., Fitzsimmons, P., Pather, D., & Christy, J. Recidivism among sexual assault victims. *American Journal of Psychiatry, 135*, 1103, 1104, 1978.

Peters, J. J. Child rape: Defusing a psychological time bomb. *Hospital Physician, 9*, 46–49, 1973.

Peters, J. J. The psychological effects of childhood rape. *World Journal of Psychosynthesis, 6*, 11–14, 1974.

Peters, J. J. Children who are victims of sexual assault and the psychology of offenders. *American Journal of Psychiatry, 30*, 398–421, 1976.

Price, V. Rape victims: The invisible patients. *The Canadian Nurse, 71*, 29–34, 1975.

Reich, J. W., & Gutierres, S. E. Escape/aggression incidence in sexually abused juvenile delinquents. *Criminal Justice and Behavior, 6*, 239–243, 1979.

Russell, D. E. H. *The secret trauma: Incest in the lives of girls and women*. New York: Basic Books, 1986.

Schultz, L. G., & DeSavage, J. Rape and rape attitudes on a college campus. In L. G. Schultz (Ed.), *Rape victimology*. Springfield, IL: Charles C Thomas, 1975.

Sgroi, M. Child sexual assault: Some guidelines for intervention and assessment. In A. Burgess, N. Groth, & L. Holmstrom (Eds.), *Sexual assault of children and adolescents*. Lexington, MA: Lexington Books, 1978.

Sgroi, M. A conceptual framework for child sexual abuse. In M. Sgroi (Ed.), *Handbook of clinical intervention in child sexual abuse*. Lexington, MA: Lexington Books, 1982.

Yates, A. Children eroticized by incest. *American Journal of Psychiatry, 139*(4), 1982.

Tufts New England Medical Center, Division of Child Psychiatry. Sexually exploited children: Service and research project. Final report for the Office of Juvenile Justice and Delinquency Prevention. Washington, DC: U.S. Department of Justice, 1984.

3

Treatment of the Child Victim

In this and the following chapters, treatment issues are separated from those of assessment to fit the type of case in which (1) a therapist has been asked to provide treatment after sexual abuse was discovered (and, of course, reported); or (2) an existing treatment process must be altered because abuse has been revealed. In short, situations in which the existence of sexual trauma *has been established* are referred to here.

This chapter focuses on the treatment of molested children who are, in general, between the ages of five and 11, although some of these concepts of treatment do also pertain to childhood victims of *incest* (a subject to be discussed in depth in Chapter 5). The chapter also includes methods of treatment for other members of the child's family (i.e., parents and siblings), who may not have been directly victimized by the abuse but who nonetheless may be profoundly affected by it.

THE GOALS OF THERAPY

The child's world is a very small one, composed of the building blocks of future personality integration. As children develop, they will utilize these basic elements to construct their world view or concept of "reality," their concept of the self or who they believe themselves to be, and who they are in relation to others. These perceptions of self, reality, and self in relation to the external world can vary in correspondence with the structure of a child's environment and its component parts. The sexual assault of a child by an adult radically alters the basic elements of a child's small world. This assault can introject components such as adult sexuality, betrayal, violence, and helplessness, to cite only a few. Since young children have no adequate frame of reference by which to judge such events, they are dependent upon the interpretations of the trusted adults around them.

We conclude that one of the fundamental tasks of a therapist, as well as the other adults in the child's life, is to help the child understand the trauma in such a way that it is not incorporated into his or her construct of self or view of reality. How these traumas are defined or interpreted by the parent(s) or parent-figures, as well as by the child's therapist, will be a pivotal factor in deciding whether the trauma will be incorporated by the child or relegated to the status of an unpleasant but external kind of event that can be overcome. In the case of a child who is sexually assaulted and whose parents dismiss the event as a "tall tale," do nothing about it, or blame the child, the behavior of the parents can negatively influence the healthy development of their child. It can serve to seal over the trauma and make it one of the fundamental building blocks of the child's future personality.

When a child turns to his or her parents for help, the child is asking for support on many levels: for example, "Protect me." "Explain this event to me." "Do adults do this to children?" "Is this what I deserve?" "Is this what a love relationship is?" "*Is this what I am?*" If the adults dismiss the event or react with inadequate concern (depending upon the child's developmental level), thoughts such as "No one protects me," "I am helpless," "The world can be chaotic and violent," "People can use me sexually," or "To be loved means to be abused" may become incorporated into the child's concepts of self and reality. If significant adults react in an overly aggressive manner, the impact upon the child can be equally confusing, because such behavior can convey a message such as, "If you turn to adults for help, they get angry," or, "If something bad happens, the appropriate response is a violent one."

A clinician must consider not only what the sexual trauma means to the child and the child's family system at this moment, but how the event will affect the child's personality development. A key to accomplishing this task is to assist the child to externalize the trauma from his or her constructs of present and future self. The trauma needs to be defined as something wrong that was *done to* the child, not internalized as "I am the sort of person that these things happen to"—in other words, someone who grows up to see himself or herself as a victim or as a bad or worthless person. Finally, a therapist should carefully facilitate the child's feelings of anxiety and anger concerning the event in such a way that these feelings can be appropriately vented. Eventually, the child will view the abuse as an event that happened to him or her, instead of an event that will define who he or she is.

THE CHILD VICTIM AND THE FAMILY

When a child is brought into treatment shortly after a sexual assault, he or she, and the family as well, are likely to be in a greatly disrupted state. A therapist should endeavor to treat the child within the context of the family. Even though the child may be seen individually in treatment, he or she is usually extremely dependent upon the family for support after such a traumatic event. Because young children are still emotionally and physically dependent upon parents and other family members for care and protection, they often reflect the family's own feelings about the events that take place in their lives. Because of this, it is vital that therapists involve both parents and siblings in the therapy process from the beginning.* This family systems work will take its form from the structure of the family and from the nature of the child's trauma. It could range from traditional, whole family therapy meetings in conjunction with the child's treatment, to meeting with individual family members separately. Even though the session format may differ depending upon the specific needs of the case, what is fundamentally important is to incorporate the family members into the treatment plan in a meaningful way, and not merely to treat the child as an isolated individual.**

The Family's Reaction

Some parents require considerable guidance in grasping what the assault meant in terms of the child's developmental level. They may project their own adult knowledge or sexual experience onto what the child went through, or they may wish to dismiss the event as being nothing because they think that the child could not have known what

---

* This differs from the procedure for evaluation of the child to determine whether or not abuse has occurred—as described in Chapter 2. The latter procedure may involve visits with the child alone in the initial stages.

** In the more complex cases, it is wise to use cotherapists who work together closely, in a team approach, to ensure that each member of the child's family receives proper support and attention so that each can do his or her part to meet the traumatized child's needs. This kind of team approach, if properly coordinated, can also be very helpful to prevent therapist burnout. One should never underestimate how draining severe trauma cases can be for a clinician working alone.

actually took place (in adult terms). Both responses are equally inappropriate. It is significant to note that a child's cognition is so different from that of an adult that it is practically impossible for most adults to think like a child would about an event such as molestation. Hence, one of the therapist's first tasks may be to help the parents conceptualize the assault in terms of their child's own cognitive framework.

An example of an *inappropriate* adult response is the case of a seven-year-old girl who was trapped in the bathroom at school by a man who exposed his erect penis to her and forced her to masturbate him. The child's parents reported the incident to the police and called their family doctor, asking him what they should do. They were told that she would simply forget about it because she really did not know what happened. The doctor further instructed the family not to mention the event again. The parents were, of course, greatly relieved to hear that their little girl would simply forget about the incident, and they followed the doctor's advice.

Over the next few weeks, the child developed several symptoms related to the sexually traumatic event. She began having nightmares, refused to play outside of her house, and began to have temper tantrums at school. When the girl's parents received a telephone call from her teacher, they realized that there had been a considerable change in the behavior of their daughter, who normally was a pleasant, reasonably compliant child. The parents eventually contacted a psychologist after having a conference with the girl's teacher.

What both parents and family doctor failed to realize was that although the little girl was not aware of the full sexual meaning of the assault, she was quite aware that a strange adult had trapped her in a place that she thought was safe and private, had forced her to do something that confused and frightened her, and had caused her to think that he was going to kill her.* This was also a child who had always trusted adults and believed them to be safe. So even though molestation was not the only terrifying aspect of the assault, the girl had suffered serious emotional trauma that needed to be discussed and worked through. Consequently, when the parents abruptly stopped talking about the event, she believed they did not care about what had happened to her.

A family's reaction to trauma, as referred to above, can range from emotionally bland denial of the reality of the event to confusion and

---

* It was also the first time that this little girl had seen a penis, the sight of which caused her considerable confusion about male and female anatomy. And because the man had used his penis in an assaultive manner, she felt even more acute anxiety and fear.

outrage. The latter emotions can be especially magnified if the parents learn that their child was repeatedly victimized over time, while they were unaware of the victimization. Such a situation tends to involve more complex family issues, which usually go beyond the fact of sexual trauma. Few parents are in any way prepared for the victimization of one of their children. Consequently, a therapist should plan, from the beginning of treatment, to assist the whole family in coping with the crisis. In turn, this will help the child to cope and, eventually, to recover from the victimization.

PARENTAL DENIAL

We have found (confirming the work of DeFrancis, 1969; Finkelhor, 1984; Peters, 1975) that many parents tend to underestimate the amount of psychological trauma that results from a sexual assault. This under-estimation is probably caused by the parents' wish that the horrible event had never happened and/or their own feelings of guilt or shame. Such thinking can lead parents to believe that their child does not require treatment because he or she has been unharmed by the event. Finkelhor (1984) also found that many parents believe that they can "handle" the problem themselves. This impulse also serves to keep the problem private, as well as to shield the parents from facing the reality of the trauma. Thus, in some cases a wishful fantasy on the part of the parents can prevent a child from obtaining needed treatment and healing of the traumatic process.

Another problem-causing form that parental denial can take is pretending that, no matter what happened, the child will just forget about it. In this manner, some parents give the child subtle, indirect messages, and some directly tell the child not to mention it or "just try to put it out of your mind." This often well-intended, but misguided, attitude of the parents can lay a foundation for more serious conflicts later on, because the child *cannot* forget about it. Moreover, the parents' "let's-keep-it-quiet" attitude implies that they may be ashamed of what happened to their child. The child may sense, because of such remarks, that he or she is guilty of some misdeed, when quite the contrary is the case. The authors have encountered too many adults who were traumatized as children who, because of such silencing parental comments, internalized the childhood experience in such a way that now they perceive themselves as bad, "dirty," or lacking in worth. This process, at best, leads to a lowered sense of self-esteem and can be a cause of self-destructive or masochistic behavior patterns in adolescence or adult life. (For a fuller account of this process, see Chapter 7.)

Clinicians should let parents know that it is usually important for child victims to talk with the parents about what happened to them. Some children may not wish to tell, but most need to, and some need to tell the story more than once. When a child tells a parent about what happened, he or she is usually looking for acceptance, understanding, and a sense of parental protection. The child seeks reassurance that he or she was not damaged or soiled by the event. And when a parent responds with indifference, it can have far-reaching effects. Many parents will find that hearing about the details of their child's molestation is very painful and stressful, and as a result they will probably need considerable support from a therapist when it happens.

Emotionally Impoverished Families

Another issue which should be taken into consideration when treating child victims, noted briefly above, is that many of them come from emotionally impoverished homes, i.e., family systems that were not (and are not) able to provide for their emotional needs. In such cases, it is as important to treat the family—so it can become more functional and learn to meet the needs of the child—as it is to treat the child. If it is not possible to inspire a family to be more responsive to the child's needs, the therapist may decide upon an alternative treatment plan which incorporates a support network for the child outside the family. This network could be composed of social and clinical agencies, as well as afterschool activities or religious youth activities. Frequently, a child's ability to form one or two healthy relationships outside of an unresponsive family system, along with a supportive course of treatment, can be a crucial factor in the child's recovery. In effect, these cases may require that the role of the clinician extend beyond the treatment of trauma. The therapy process should also provide a socially, culturally, and emotionally enriching experience for the child, with the aim of helping him or her construct a healthier, more affirmative world view. An ego-enhancing process of this kind can, in turn, have beneficial effects upon therapy itself.

The Therapist and the Child's Mother

Establishing a good therapeutic relationship with the child's mother is frequently crucial to successful treatment of the child for a number of reasons. First, many mothers feel that they have somehow failed the child because the molestation occurred. As a result of this feeling of failure, some mothers may perceive the child's therapist as a threat or as a rival. Some of these mothers are emotionally needy, dependent women (especially those who themselves were victims of abuse as children). Because this kind of mother's unmet needs for nurturance can be so overwhelming, she may not be able to permit her child to receive care and concern from the therapist. This kind of mother is usually not consciously aware of what is causing her anxiety and discomfort in respect to her child's therapy. If the clinician is not aware of the underlying anxiety of the mother, it could jeopardize the child's treatment.

A mother's anxiety over unmet dependency needs may reveal itself in one of the following types of behavior. She may intrude into the child's therapy time by talking about her own needs or about parenting issues; or, she may use the time to complain at length about the child's behavior. After the child's session, the mother may quiz the child about what happened during the session or repeatedly ask the therapist to tell her "what's going on" with the child. The mother's interference may also take a resistive form in which she is not responsible about keeping the child's appointments or complains about the imposition that the appointments are for her. If the clinician responds to the mother in the more traditional way by setting limits on her intrusions into the child's therapy or by counseling her to be more responsible, it is quite likely that she will try to undermine the treatment process or remove the child from therapy. Separate meetings with the mother on a weekly basis during the beginning of therapy, or arranging for the mother to see her own therapist concurrently with the child's visits, can usually resolve this problem.

Sexual Acting Out by the Child

When treating a child in the context of his or her family, the clinician should reflect that the child has very likely had a sexual experience far beyond the proper developmental level. The victimization may have been painful or terrifying or confusing or bizarre; but also, it could have been, at least in some ways, pleasurable for the child. And as a sequel to the trauma, a child may act out sexually toward adults and other children in the family. This acting out may also occur with playmates or at school. A therapist may find it advisable to prepare the parents of the child so that, if such acting out does occur, it will be dealt with appropriately. The therapist might also request the parents' consent for consulting with the child's teachers, should any inappropriate behavior occur at school.

When treating this kind of acting out, a therapist will help the parents control the acting-out behavior and at the same time will advise them to be careful not to convey shame to the child. This will occur if the parents can separate the inappropriate behavior from the child's identity, i.e., "You shouldn't do that" versus "You are bad." This approach requires that they communicate, in a calm manner, that the child must stop what he or she is doing. A parent can say, e.g., "An adult [or other child] did something to you that was not right, but what you did just now was not right either." The adult can further reassure the child that he or she is a good person. In most cases, the child will feel relief when an adult places limits on acting-out behavior in a way that helps the child to understand such behavior. If limits are designed in this way, a child can begin to gain mastery over his or her acting-out impulses, rather than feel punished for "being" bad.

This point can be illustrated by a case in which a nine-year-old girl was sexually assaulted by a man who lived in her apartment complex. He had forced her to perform fellatio and engaged her in masturbatory play. Later that night, the little girl told her mother what happened; the mother called the police, who referred both the mother (a single parent) and the child for therapy because they were so shaken by the event.

After the clinician had seen both mother and daughter for two sessions, she received a frantic telephone call from the mother because the latter did not know what to do. Apparently, the man who sexually assaulted her daughter had given the child a battery-operated vibrator, which the girl had hidden in her room and had not told her mother or the police about. That evening, much to her mother's horror, she found the girl in her bedroom, masturbating with the vibrator. The mother was extremely concerned, but she wanted to react appropriately because it was clear that the girl had very mixed feelings about what had happened to her. (One of the reasons why the child was vulnerable to the neighbor's advances was that her father had left her mother for another woman. Neither the child nor her mother had seen the father for the past eight months, and because of her abandonment, the child was searching for a father figure.)

The therapist spoke to the mother for a while in order to calm her down, so that when she began talking with the daughter it would be done in a manner that would protect the child from additional trauma. The therapist instructed the mother to go into the bedroom and ask the little girl to give her the vibrator, ask her where she got it, and then explain to her that it is not a toy for children. When the mother asked her where she got the vibrator, the girl said that the neighbor had given it to her as a "special secret toy." The mother told her that it was not a toy for children, that the man was wrong to have given it to her, and that she was going to take it away.

The mother called back the therapist the next day to let her know how things went: after a minor protest, the daughter had accepted the mother's nonjudgmental stopping of the inappropriate behavior. The mother also said that her daughter even appeared to be somewhat relieved that she had taken the vibrator away from her. The little girl never mentioned the vibrator again.

After this incident, there were two other times when the little girl openly tried to engage other children in sexual play that was similar to her victimization. In both instances, the mother calmly interceded and told her daughter to stop the sexual play because what the man had taught her was wrong. She then explained to the girl that what the man did to her was wrong and that she should not do it with other children. Her mother went on to reaffirm that she was a good girl but the man was a bad man. After these events, the mother continued to reassure her daughter and, as a result of the mother's decisive intervention, the acting out stopped.

In short, this kind of "reactive" sexual acting out must be controlled as soon as it occurs. The intervention should be carefully framed, in such a way that it minimizes feelings of guilt or blame on the part of the child. Further, the child should be helped to understand that, even though some things in life are pleasurable, they are not always good for a person; so people learn not to do those things because not doing them is better for a person.

When considering a traumatized child in the context of the family, the clinician needs to consider another important factor: that the child may have been assaulted during a time when there was an existing serious problem in his or her life. (The same is often true of adult victims of assault.) The case cited above of the little girl who was sexually abused by her neighbor describes a child who was vulnerable because of a crisis in her life, namely, being abandoned by her father. She was accepting of adult attention because she had been deprived of the parental nurturance she needed. Again, one must view these children in relation to the family environment that a child requires in order to mature and grow. If some of the essential components for nurturance are not provided within this milieu, the child will be drawn to other possible sources of support that are not naturally available.

With time, many deprived children become oriented toward pleasing adults to have their normal dependency needs met, so much so that they appear (superficially) to be overly mature children. They are not, in fact, overly mature but are starving for nurturance as a basic element of normal development. In a manifestation of magical thinking, these children feel that the only way they will receive any approximation of parental nurturance is to pay for it sexually. Unfortunately, many professionals who encounter adult-oriented or seductive behavior in children are frequently shocked by it and, too quickly, shift the focus of attention (or blame) onto this behavior. It is our experience that these professionals seldom look beyond the immediate seductive behavior to its source—deprivation.

The unfortunate tendency to transfer responsibility from a molester to the victim serves several purposes. First, it protects others in the child's world from having to cope with the recognition that an adult *like themselves* could do such a thing to a child. Each of us has a tendency to resist looking at the darker side of human nature. Second, shifting the blame to the child will serve to protect the child's parents from having to assume any responsibility for what happened to their child. And blame displaced onto the victim (not unlike what frequently takes place in cases of adult rape, e.g., "I did not rape her; she seduced me") can be particularly "convenient" if the person being accused of the assault is a respected member of the community, a family member, or a family friend.

Siblings

The siblings of a child victim usually require some clinical attention. First, the clinician should assist the parent or parents to prepare an age-appropriate explanation, for the siblings, of what happened to their brother or sister. Siblings will intuitively know that something has happened, and if the parents do not provide them with a reasonable explanation, they will try to figure out what happened themselves. Very likely, the explanation that siblings concoct or fantasize may be wilder and more emotionally damaging (should the victim be confronted with it) than the true story. Also, by not providing the other children with a reasonable explanation of what transpired, the parents may imply that the victim is guilty of some misdeed or is "tainted" in some way. The siblings may need an explanation, if the perpetrator is a known, significant figure in their lives, about why this person can no longer be a part of their lives. This is important lest they blame the victim for some imagined misdeed that caused this cared-for adult to disappear.

The siblings may require special concern because they could be the targets of sexual acting out by the abused child, as a sequel to the abuse. These siblings may also have feelings of remorse that they were not somehow able to protect their brother or sister, or were unable to prevent the trauma from occurring; even worse, they may believe that they were in some way responsible for what happened. (For this reason, a therapist should cautiously explore what the victims themselves think about how and why the assault happened, and what could have been done to prevent it.)

Finally, the sibling of a victim might have been the one who discovered the victimization, and he or she may also have been emotionally traumatized by this encounter. Sometimes the needs of these siblings, who are victims, too, become overshadowed or ignored in the aftermath of an assault.

THE CHILD'S THERAPY

We now consider the treatment of the individual child victim. In this section we include suggestions on how a clinician should introduce herself (himself) and present the therapy situation to the child, as well as the toys and games that a therapist may wish to have available in the therapy room. Suggestions are added concerning the type of structure and limits that a therapist should consider incorporating into the play therapy. The section will also discuss significant aspects of the therapeutic process.

Usually, gaining clinical access to a child who is the victim of extrafamilial sexual assault is not as difficult as it is in cases of intrafamilial assault. Situations in which this may not be so include the following:

1. cases in which the child was repeatedly victimized over a period of time and whose family may be too disorganized to follow through in treatment appropriately;

2. cases in which the parents need to avoid dealing with their being responsible, in some way, for the child's traumatization; or

3. cases that involve a family friend or someone significant to the family, which wants to protect the person accused.

Other extrafamilial assaults can be extremely volatile situations in which outraged parents wish to take justice into their own hands. In such cases, parents need to be told—clearly—by the therapist that their child needs them to stay in control so that he or she will feel safe and protected. As one young child told her raging father, who said he wanted to murder the man who assaulted her, "Daddy, please don't kill him, because the police will take you away and lock you up; then I'll have no Daddy to take care of me."

When beginning a therapy relationship with a child victim (as with the clinical evaluation described in Chapter 2) a therapist should explain his or her role and the nature of the therapy relationship to the child and to the family. Some parents will be rather protective of the child at this stage and wish to question the therapist in detail about his or her type of training and qualifications. A clinician should not be offended by this, because it is usually an expression of the parents' feeling of being "failed protectors" of their child when the victimization occurred. By means of this "examination" of the therapist, they are attempting to regain the feeling of being adequate guardians of the child.

The parents should be told that they will be expected to attend regularly scheduled meetings with the therapist at which the child will not be present. Extremely anxious parents or those whose child was severely traumatized may require weekly conferences of this kind. In less critical situations, biweekly or monthly meetings may suffice. Further, the clinician should express a willingness to assist the parents in coping with any behavioral problems that may arise. Parents may also find it particularly reassuring if the therapist encourages them to call if they have any questions concerning how to respond to a particular situation. The case cited previously of the little girl who was given a vibrator is an example of how such a parent consultation helped to defuse a potential crisis by assisting a frightened parent to stop some acting out on the part of the child victim in an appropriate manner.

Apart from issues concerning duty to warn or to report, the relationship between child and therapist needs to be kept confidential so that the child will be encouraged to express himself or herself. Most parents are able to understand the necessity for the confidential nature of a therapy relationship, but some may require additional reassurance in order not to feel threatened. In general, a discussion with parents concerning the nature of the therapy relationship should contain the following information:

1. Your training and qualifications.

2. General diagnostic impressions concerning the child.

3. Type of therapy to be used to treat the child and what this consists of, i.e., a description of what play and/or other forms of therapy entail.

4. Prognosis and estimated length of treatment.

5. Request for consultation with other significant adults (i.e., teachers, babysitters, etc.) in the child's life, should the case warrant.

6. A suggested schedule for the therapist to meet with the parent(s).

7. Explanation of the confidential nature of a therapy relationship with a child, as well as reassurance to the parents that confidentiality is to help the child feel safer in self-expression, as opposed to a means for keeping things from the parents.

8. A full explanation of any fees that pertain to the child's care.

A clinician should also discuss the nature of the therapy relationship with the child client. In this talk, the structure and limits of treatment should be described, as well as the possible frequency of visits and duration of the relationship. The first step is for the therapist to introduce himself or herself to the child by saying something similar to the following:

Hello, my name is _____ . Your parents have asked me to meet with you because of what happened to you. You can talk about what happened if you want to, or we can play with dolls or puppets about what happened. But if you don't want to talk or play about what happened, that's all right, too.

Next, the therapist should convey to the child that what happened has happened to other children. The message is that he or she is not the only child to experience such an assault. The therapist should also make clear that the child's own feelings concerning the trauma are significant and that the therapist views the child as a unique, important person.

The therapist may continue by telling the child that they will be meeting once or twice a week, depending upon the treatment plan. Next, the clinician should explain that what is said or done (or played) is private, and that he or she will not tell other people unless the child gives permission to do so. (This consideration differentiates the therapy relationship, which needs to be private, from the evaluative relationship that was described in an earlier chapter. Because of this difference, it is wise [but not always possible] to divide the two relationships so that another clinician does the evaluation—which is not confidential and may entail court testimony.)

A therapist should let the child know that he or she will meet with the child's parents periodically; these meetings will be held to help the parents understand what happened to him or her, and before these meetings the therapist will discuss with the child what is to be talked about. At first, the child may not fully grasp the meaning of a statement like this, but as the therapy relationship develops and these concepts are discussed again later in the context of real events, he or she will gain a greater appreciation for its meaning.

Last, the clinician should explain the basic structure and limits of the play therapy situation. The child needs to understand that the therapy hour is basically his or her time to say, or express in play, whatever he or she wishes. There will be a variety of toys and activities from which the child can select. The decision about what to do during therapy is completely up to the child. The only thing that the child cannot do is hurt himself or herself or the therapist.

It is important that the play therapy be structured so that destructive impulses and anger are directed toward symbolic play objects and not people. A clinician also should see to it that any expressions of anger occur only within the playroom. For example, toys that have been the recipient of, or drawings that represent, the child's anger should remain in the room. And even if the child wishes to take these objects home with her or him, they should remain in the playroom. The therapist should assure the child that the play object will be kept in a safe place until he or she returns for the next session, thus ensuring that the play therapy room is seen as a safe environment in which to express such feelings of anger. In this way the child need not fear that such impulses will spill over to his or her family or friends.

We cannot overemphasize the delicate balance that is required in facilitating a child's expression of anger, while providing structure and security, in order that the expression does not cause further misunderstanding of the child. When it surfaces, the anger of some sexually traumatized children can be extremely primitive and intense, and this anger must be clearly directed toward symbolic objects and not people. Apart from these limits, the therapist can assure the child that the play therapy hour is under the latter's control.

Clinicians should also exercise considerable caution in respect to touching a traumatized child. Such a gesture, although well intended, could be misinterpreted by the child as a sexual advance or threat on the part of the therapist. The reader need only reflect that most of these children have already been sexually stimulated by an adult with no adequate means of appropriate emotional release. Consequently, they are extraordinarily sensitive to any form of touching by an adult, and many young victims who have experienced protracted molestation may not be able to discriminate between sexual and nonsexual touching.

Should this be the case, we recommend that a therapist initially explain to the child that he or she knows the child has had a relationship with an adult (or adults) that involved touching, but this relationship (with the therapist) will not include touching. In this new relationship, the therapist and child will communicate by means of talking and playing. The clinician can explain to the child that he or she and the child, in the context of their new relationship, will learn to express the whole range of emotions from affection to anger in this new way. In particular, a therapist must clearly communicate to the child that he or she does not need to exchange touching or sexual behavior for a positive relationship with an adult. Hence, the therapist can frame the treatment relationship in a manner that will permit the child appropriate expression of feelings.

The Play Therapy Room and Suggested Toys

The therapy room should be a place designed to be comfortable for children. It should be warm but neutral, so that a child will be freely drawn to the toys that attract him or her. The room should be modestly appointed so that the child will not become anxious about making a mess or spilling something. There should be a selection of toys that are *below* the child's age level (in case the child needs to become involved in regressive behavior), as well as a selection of age-appropriate toys for various types of play activities. The following is a listing, by categories, of certain toys that may be useful in a play therapy room.

RECOMMENDED THERAPY ROOM EQUIPMENT

Regressive Toys:
  Baby bottle
  Clay
  Finger paint (some very traumatized children may be fearful of
      finger paint)
  Soft, cuddly stuffed animals

Drawing Materials:
  Crayons
  Paint
  A large roll of butcher paper is recommended, so that the child
      can take whatever sized paper is desired

Dolls:
  Boy and girl dolls with removable clothes (we have Raggedy Ann
      and Andy dolls)
  Baby doll

Board Games & Card Games:
   We have: "Uno" cards, a deck of playing cards, "Aggravation,"
      checkers, and chess, among others

Toys to Encourage Discussion and Fantasy:
   Puppets:
      Boy and girl animal puppets (we have boy and girl frogs)
      Obvious villain puppet (we have a snake and a devil puppet)
      Obvious good figures, e.g., parent (mother and father), police,
         doctors and nurses, Prince Charming (we have a unicorn and
         a nurse puppet)
      Assorted neutral animal or human puppets to which the child
         can assign various roles
   Doll house (with furniture and family-member dolls)
   Sand tray
   "The Ungame"
   "Imagine"

A therapist may also have, in the play room, a cuddly teddy bear
or a soft stuffed animal for use with those children who have been so
severely traumatized that they are too terrified to communicate with
another person. Such children may become mute, dissociate, or break
down into primary-process babbling because they are so fragile. In
these cases, a therapist may wish to place a soft, cuddly object beside
the child and talk with him or her in a soothing manner about a neutral
subject. This kind of safe, nonhuman object can help the child to make
the transition back to communicating with people.

An example of the use of a safe, nonhuman object is illustrated in
the case of a five-and-a-half-year-old boy who was referred for treatment. He had been repeatedly sodomized by three men who enticed
him while he was playing unattended at a neighborhood playground.
When his mother and a policeman brought him to the therapist's office,
the mother reported that he was practically mute. She said that the
boy had uttered a few sentences to her about the assault, but had since
become almost nonverbal. When the boy's mother left the room, he
sat on the edge of a chair staring off into space. The therapist made
several attempts to engage him in play and discussion, which were
unsuccessful. He later got out of the chair and huddled on the floor,
looking away from the therapist.

After a few minutes, the clinician's small cocker spaniel dog, who
had been asleep under her desk, woke up. This extremely anxious little
boy had not noticed the dog when he first entered the therapist's office.
The clinician, thinking that possibly the child might feel safer with the
dog, slowly rolled the dog's ball in the direction of the little boy. When

the dog went after the ball, she noticed the boy sitting on the floor; the dog took the ball in her mouth, carried it over to the boy, and tried to engage him in a game. The therapist quietly watched, hoping that the little dog, who is extremely gentle, could make some contact with the child. The dog first sat quietly beside the boy and then nudged him several times with her nose, trying to show him the ball. When the boy remained silent and motionless, the dog dropped the ball and pushed it toward the boy with her nose. As the ball rolled directly in front of the boy, she bumped him once more. Then the boy, with slow, awkward motions began to pet the dog and cautiously rolled the ball back.

The boy spent the rest of the first session quietly sitting next to the dog and petting her. The therapist decided not to intervene in any way in the interaction between boy and dog. At the second visit, the boy hesitantly greeted the therapist and immediately engaged the dog in play. Slowly, over a period of several weeks, he was able to make the transition from playing with the dog to interacting with the therapist. This case indicates how it is possible to bring a child back into contact with people by means of a substitute object.

Some severely traumatized children attempt to cope by means of such primitive defenses that they are not capable of responding to traditional forms of interpretive play therapy. In these situations, the clinician should provide the child with a therapy environment that is safe and nurturing and that will enable the child eventually to arrive at an emotional level that permits the more traditional play therapy techniques. For these severely traumatized children, the initial therapy goals need to be set modestly, in recognition of the child's traumatized psyche.

For example, in the case of the abused boy, the first goal of therapy was for the boy to tolerate being alone in a room with an adult. The next goal was that he attempt to communicate with the therapist in some fashion. From this point, the therapist sought to make therapy a positive and enriching experience for the boy. These goals were achieved only after months of work. Not until these initial steps were taken could the child begin to participate in interpretive play therapy relating to the trauma.

Treatment Dynamics

Children, in general, will respond in one of two ways to a sexual assault or trauma: (1) there will be behavioral or somatic symptoms that become overt immediately after the assault; or (2) there will be a delayed or "silent" reaction, which is usually depressive in nature.

Somatic Symptoms

Some of the *somatic* effects that may rapidly appear following molestation include amorphous aches and pains, gastrointestinal disturbances, sudden changes in normal toilet habits, and enuresis (in younger children). Child victims frequently withdraw from their accustomed activities and relationships by becoming phobic, sometimes refusing to play outside the home, or by becoming school-phobic. Burgess and Holmstrom (1974), DeFrancis (1969), Gibbons and Prince (1963), Tufts New England Medical Center (1984), and Finkelhor (1987) have noted in their studies that a majority of child victims had at least mild to acute posttrauma symptoms.

Night terrors and nightmares are commonly experienced by traumatized children; many are afraid to sleep alone and insist upon sleeping with parents. We do not recommend that a sexually abused child sleep in the same bed with a parent or parents. If the child has been sexually traumatized and cannot tolerate being alone at night, it is a good idea for parents to make up a separate bed in their bedroom, thus maintaining appropriate parent-child boundaries until the child is ready to return to his or her own room for sleep. We also recommend using night lights, as well as keeping a bell or whistle beside the child's bed to summon a parent should he or she become fearful. We have also found it useful to give the child a stuffed animal, saying that the animal has special powers against bad things. The child is encouraged to take the animal to bed and, if he or she becomes afraid, to hold the animal close and make the scary things go away.

We have found, as did Peters (1976), that a fairly lengthy period of play therapy may be required, in many cases, before the child is able to express feelings about the assault. As indicated in Chapter 1, one reason that some find it extremely difficult to express anger toward the adult who traumatized them is that most children are trained not to express such feelings. Children are trained to obey adults and not "talk back" to them. When one further considers that many children were lured into the situation in which they were molested by someone known and trusted, one realizes that the assault has put them in a double-bind situation. The child was assaulted because he or she obeyed an adult. The child may have angry feelings but cannot express them because speaking out against adults is forbidden.

Many children are not able to overcome this double-bind experience. So they resolve the conflict by internalizing the anger and confusion and becoming depressed. If the parents react in a manner that gives the child the message "just forget about it," it confirms the child's notion that anger toward adults is discounted or not allowed, thus deepening the sense of hopelessness. Or, if the parents go to the opposite extreme—becoming overly restricting or supervising the child's behavior excessively—a child may misperceive this overprotective parenting as punishment for angry thoughts. Either extreme parental reaction may serve to cause the child to block his or her true feelings concerning the abuse and prevent the working through of the trauma.

Delayed Reactions

In cases of *delayed* or depressive responses to sexual traumatization, the clinician may need to spend from four to six weeks (or more) playing with the child, conveying the message that his or her feelings are accepted and that the play room is a safe place to express those feelings. We have found that some of Milton Erickson's interspersal techniques, in which the message that a therapist wishes the client to receive is introjected subtly throughout the conversation with the client (Erickson, Rossi, & Rossi, 1976), can be extremely helpful. In addition, a clinician may tell the child something such as this:

I know that you have thoughts and feelings about what happened to you. You may wish to share them with me now, or you may want to tell me about them later. If you don't want to tell me now but, instead, wait until later, that is all right with me.

This is a version of an Ericksonian technique called the "illusion of alternatives." It is a way of giving a person the illusion of having alternatives by "permitting" him or her to choose between doing something now or doing it later; the alternative of not responding at all is not offered.

Another indirect technique that can be used in treating a child who is fearful of disclosing what has happened to him or her is that of storytelling, in which the clinician tells a story about a hypothetical child in a similar situation as a way of interpreting the child's conundrum. For example, in the case of a child who is afraid to talk about the molestation, the therapist might tell a story about a child to whom something happened that was scary and embarrassing; but an adult understood how the child felt, so the child was able to tell this adult what had happened. The storytelling process is especially effective because it fits nicely into the concrete style of children's thinking; the story provides an illustration of how the child might resolve a problem that may be too complex for his or her cognitive ability. In short, a story may serve as a cognitive roadmap to a solution for the child's dilemma. It has been our experience that children respond very well to indirect methods of therapy such as these.

As Treatment Continues

With time, the child will begin to communicate, to the therapist, what he or she thinks or feels about the assault. As indicated above, the therapist can facilitate this by means of Ericksonian or other indirect techniques, but we advise strongly against the use of intrusive or confrontive therapy approaches. As the clinician plays and talks with the child, he or she should be alert to what the trauma meant to the child and to the child's view of the world. As with adult victims, the sexual aspects of the assault may not have been the primary source of the child's traumatic feelings. Just as they do when confronted by the victimization of an adult, persons who know the child may focus on the sexual details, because they are bizarre or shocking, and fail to realize that most victims are primarily preoccupied with the following recollections: either (1) they could have been killed; (2) they felt totally helpless or used; (3) someone whom they trusted has just betrayed them; or (4) the one person who paid attention to them has been lost to them forever.

This is not meant to imply that the sexual issues are not important. They are important but may not be the primary issues that the child victim must face as a result of the trauma. Therefore, each of the issues listed above should be interpreted for the child so that he or she can understand them in the context of his or her developmental level. A therapist seeks to find out *how the child perceived the trauma* and begin there, instead of beginning with his or her own perception of the trauma. As with many other situations in which two people interact, one can never assume that two people share the same "reality."

When thoughts or feelings pertaining to the trauma surface in symbolic form in therapy, they may be expressed in some of the following ways. A child may act out stories that have the theme of "good people" suddenly changing into "bad people," or situations in which one must guess who the good people are and who the bad people are. In such stories, the child is attempting to resolve the anxiety that was caused by believing that someone was nice who later molested him or her, as well as apprehension about how to protect himself or herself in future.

A child may dirty himself or herself in some manner and ask the therapist's help in cleaning it off. When doing this cleaning with the child, the clinician can directly interpret the behavior by interspersing a message such as, "You want to feel clean again after what happened." The therapist could add that the child will, indeed, feel clean again. To reiterate, we have found that it is usually best if such interpretations are made (whether directly or indirectly) in a matter-of-fact tone of voice and simply introduced here and there in the course of conversation with the child.

A child may also become involved in trying symbolically to undo the traumatic experience by repeatedly taking apart toys, spreading out the parts, and putting them back together. He or she may insist upon taking apart each toy that can be disassembled (and some that cannot) and putting it back together, or the child may focus on one toy. During such undoing and reconstructive play, the therapist should convey a message to the child that contains the following elements: broken or hurt things can be fixed and need not stay broken; people may feel broken but they can get better and feel whole again, too.

Some traumatized children may focus upon one specific game and utilize this game for significant periods or throughout the course of therapy. The game becomes a symbolic vehicle by means of which the child works through the trauma. Frequently, the child will change the basic rules of the game to suit his or her needs. By repeating the game over and over, the child may be seeking confirmation that he or she has a constant relationship with the therapist, even though his or her own world is in chaos. One little girl reminded her therapist at the beginning of each session how many card games they had played; by the time therapy ended, they had played 257 games. Some children are compelled to win each game—either by changing the rules or overtly cheating—as a means of erasing their sense of helplessness resulting from the trauma. This creative rule making or cheating usually subsides as the child begins to recover his or her sense of competence. What is essential is that, if a child chooses one game or play activity repetitively, the clinician will continue to engage in the activity until the *child* decides to move on.

Many very young trauma victims go through a regressive period in the course of treatment. This period usually comes early in therapy, but may occur later in the less-frequent cases of delayed response to a crisis. During this regressive period, the child may wish to feed himself or herself (or be fed) with a baby bottle. Or he or she may choose to play with finger paints or clay in a primitive manner. The clinician may interpret this behavior to the child by saying, for example, "Sometimes when we are upset or frightened, it feels safe or helps to do baby things for a while, and to go back to a time when things felt safe."

If the child becomes regressive during play therapy sessions, it may be wise to let the parents know that the child may exhibit equally regressive behavior at home or in school. This may take the form of asking for a baby bottle, or perhaps requesting old toys that the child had played with at an earlier age, or some other kind of infantile behavior. The parents should not become overly alarmed at such behavior, because it will usually pass in a few weeks if they and other adults respond appropriately. While they can set limits on the behavior, they should allow the child the security of this period of regression after a sexual trauma. And since regressive behavior can be very frightening to parents, they may require considerable support and reassurance from the therapist during this time. A clinician can explain regressive behavior to a parent in a reassuring manner by pointing out that the child is attempting, by means of regression, to return to a pretrauma developmental stage; by so doing, the child is trying to reestablish a solid foundation for his or her psychological needs.

Eventually, most child victims will express their anger about what was done to them, but they may require a great deal of help in doing so. Considering the powerful injunctions that *prevent* children from expressing anger toward adults, a therapist may wish to intersperse carefully constructed statements which can assist the child's anger to surface. These messages should convey that, in certain circumstances, children have a right to be angry at adults and to express this anger. What was done to him or her was wrong, and the therapist understands this anger. But the clinician should also explain that it is not all right to hurt people when one is angry. The child's anger, in the context of therapy, will be appropriately directed toward toys or symbolic objects, but never toward people or animals. This period in which a child expresses anger is a critical one; and while a therapist must facilitate the expression, it is important as well to contain it within the play therapy structure.

Even though controlled empirical research on the longitudinal effects of child sexual traumatization on adult personality development is only beginning, we cannot ignore the startling fact that a considerable number of adult sexual offenders were sexually assaulted as children.* For that

---

* Although many research studies of the effects of sexual trauma on the child's

reason, we believe that how a child victim's feelings of helplessness and rage are worked through may have a significant impact on later adult development.

A clinician further needs to consider that, in some cases of child sexual abuse, there may be several victims of the same molester who know each other. Although it is important to consider each case as a separate one, the therapist should be mindful that these children may know each other and talk to each other about "what happened." So despite the fact that a clinician may have taken the appropriate steps to work with the child's parents and significant others in the child's life, the child may be in contact with another child victim who may be giving him or her other, conflicting messages. Therefore, if a therapist learns that there are other victims whom the child knows, he or she may wish to attempt to find out something about them and their own treatment in order to help the child deal with the information that he or she may receive from these children.

TWO CASE STUDIES

These descriptions illustrate therapy with two nine-year-old girls who were victims of protracted sexual abuse and neglect. The two children, although victims of similar types of abuse, had quite different needs in terms of therapy and case management.

The Case of Amy

Amy had fairly good parenting until her mother left her father when she was three-and-a-half. Her father was the "rescuing/caretaking type" of person; therefore, as long as her parents remained together, her life had been stable. Unfortunately, when Amy's mother took her and ran away with another man, her world changed dramatically for the worse. The mother, who had a history of drug addiction before her marriage, quickly returned to using drugs. Amy's father tried to find Amy, fearing what might happen to her if she was left to her mother's care, but his attempts to locate her were unsuccessful.

After about three years, Amy's mother was heavily involved with drugs, had had a series of often abusive relationships with men, and engaged in occasional prostitution to support her drug use. Amy couldn't

---

psychological development have been conducted, none (to the authors' knowledge) contained adequate control groups or a sample appropriately stratified according to the various types of sexual abuse that children have suffered.

remember which of her mother's boyfriends was the first to molest her. Even so, she clearly remembered the first time that her mother gave her to a man to "play with" for money: it was just after her seventh birthday. The man had intercourse with her. Amy said that his name was Ron and that what he did to her hurt a lot. She said that he came back to see her about once a month. Soon, Amy was regularly being forced by her mother to engage in prostitution and pose for pornography. Amy wondered what happened to her father and why he never came to see her. She said she thought that he had forgotten about her.

One night, Amy's mother was arrested in her apartment for selling drugs and for prostitution. Amy was taken to the children's shelter, and it was there that the horrible story of her prolonged sexual abuse came out. When Amy's mother was eventually released on bail, she left town and was never seen or heard from again. Shortly thereafter, Amy's father was found and given custody of Amy.

Soon after Amy came to live with her father, he realized that she had serious emotional problems. While Amy was with her mother, her school attendance had been minimal. At the age of nine, she was functioning at approximately the level of a six-year-old. She frequently wet the bed and soiled her pants when under stress. Her behavior would vary between being seductive and accommodating to having infantile tantrums. For this reason, her father asked the social worker who was assigned to the case for a referral to a child therapist.

When Amy's father first brought her to therapy, she was very reluctant to remain in the office alone with the psychologist. After a lot of reassurance from her father, she agreed to be alone with the therapist but only if the latter promised to leave the door completely open. During this first meeting, Amy postured anxiously and sat as far away from the therapist as possible, totally avoiding eye contact. The therapist thought it would be wise to test Amy before beginning treatment, for several reasons. Above all, some decisions needed to be made about Amy's school placement: she clearly couldn't function in a regular school classroom. Her father was worried that he would be unable to care for her at home and that she might require placement in a special school or, possibly, need to be hospitalized. On several occasions, Amy had come into her father's bedroom at night and had made sexual advances toward him. Such behavior shocked him and made him wonder if he could properly care for her at this time. In addition, the clinician needed to have answers to some specific diagnostic questions concerning elements of Amy's bizarre behavior in her office.

The results of Amy's psychological testing showed her to be a child who was fundamentally intact—in that there was no evidence of a thought disorder or psychosis. The testing also revealed that Amy was suffering from such overwhelming anxiety that she would emotionally "shut down" and withdraw from the world as a defense. This process explained her rigid posturing during the first interview. The tests also indicated that Amy perceived the world as a hostile, dangerous place in which she attempted to survive by alternating between hypervigilance and emotional blocking and withdrawal. Testing further suggested that Amy viewed herself as totally helpless, with no power to influence or change her world. Amy's IQ test results showed her to be a child of above-average intelligence. And, considering all that she had been through, under normal circumstances she would probably have been functioning in the superior range. Even though Amy was fundamentally bright, her level of achievement in basic tasks was two years below grade level.

When testing was completed, the therapist met first with the father and then with the school. It was decided to place Amy in a small class for emotionally handicapped children (in her regular school), and to supplement this with special tutorial work. Because Amy's bizarre, avoidant behavior and sexual acting out clearly appeared to stem from environmental forces rather than underlying pathology, the therapist wanted to try working with the father and with the school to create a structured, nurturing milieu in which Amy could recover from her protracted trauma and catch up developmentally. Although Amy was so emotionally fragile and so badly traumatized that she could have been hospitalized, the clinician wanted to try to avoid institutionalizing her—with the attendant stigma of being labeled pathological. Although some of the professionals who were involved in Amy's care were dubious, the therapist believed that the child could respond to therapy in conjunction with a more healthy home environment.

Initially, the therapist met with Amy twice a week and the father once a week; she routinely spoke with Amy's school and the day care center by telephone. The clinician worked very closely with Amy's father to help him deal appropriately with her sexually inappropriate behavior, as well as to help him accept that even though his daughter was nine chronologically, she was functionally much younger. The therapist also had to help Amy's father come to terms with his rage at his former wife, as well as his own guilt for not taking more initiative toward finding his daughter sooner.

During this initial phase of therapy, Amy could barely tolerate being alone in the room with the therapist. She would repeatedly go to the door of the office and silently open, close, and reopen it. When Amy did this, the clinician would reassure her by telling her that the door would always be unlocked. She was welcome to open it to make sure it was, in fact, unlocked. The therapist would ask Amy if she wanted to talk about doors and what they had meant to her in the past, but Amy would look away and sit stiffly in her chair.

In general, Amy was very accommodating and submissive with the therapist. After the first month of treatment, she invariably carried a soft, stuffed doll with her. For several months, she was incapable of making any form of demand. If the therapist asked her what she would like to do, she would first look away and posture; but if the therapist suggested a play activity, she would obligingly participate in it. When asked about what she was thinking or feeling, she would become unresponsive. It was as though, for her, to think, to request, or to consider her emotions had long ago been forbidden.

Amy's play therapy activities remained regressive for a significant period of time. She would rock in her chair while holding a soft toy or her doll, and drink juice from a baby bottle. If stressed, she would posture or act bizarrely or speak nonsense. It became clear that posturing and odd behavior were how Amy attempted to drive people away who threatened her. Whenever she would do this sort of thing, the clinician would provide her with as much emotional space as possible, while at the same time interpreting Amy's behavior and providing her with alternative ways to get her needs met. The therapist also made sure that Amy's father and others who were working with Amy understood what this kind of behavior meant, so that they could respond to it in similar fashion.

Amy remained in this regressed, infantile state throughout several months of therapy. Although she began to make solid gains educationally and emotionally (outside of the therapy sessions), she continued to function at about the six-year-old level in treatment. The therapist believed this to be a good indication that Amy had stabilized. She was utilizing the therapy time to regress and, in that way, regain an emotional foundation while making progress intellectually—where she felt strongest.

Slowly, Amy's play changed from infantile and regressive activity with soft dolls and stuffed animals to making up stories in a doll's house with themes of feeding, cleaning, and generally caring for children. Then she began to initiate repetitive, projective play in which she was the doctor who examined and treated a little girl who had been hurt. It became clear that she was reenacting the medical examination that she had been given after she was removed from her mother's custody. Amy would very methodically examine the girl doll to make sure all her hurts were taken care of. During this play, the therapist interpreted what was happening for Amy, while interspersing the messages that she is all right now and is a good girl.

Amy continued to improve at school, and in little over a year was achieving at the correct grade level. She was still quite socially withdrawn and fearful. The clinician decided that enlisting someone from the Big Sister program would be a useful adjunct to therapy, to provide Amy with additional female role modeling and to help her develop more social skills. Because Amy's experiences with her teachers and with the therapist had been positive, she responded well to the Big Sister. In time, her behavior at school improved to such a degree that she was placed in a regular classroom.

Eventually, Amy began to take an interest in the board games in the clinician's office; she particularly liked chess. Each time she played chess with the therapist, she was determined to win even if she had to cheat blatantly. When the game progressed as though Amy was likely to lose, she would become extremely angry and begin a tantrum, grabbing pieces from the therapist to ensure that she could win. It was clear that, through the game, she was beginning to express her need for control as well as her anger toward her mother and the adults who abused her. The therapist allowed Amy to win and used the opportunity to let her know what the underlying dynamics of her behavior were.

Naturally, this was a fortuitous development in therapy. The clinician welcomed Amy's displays of anger, even though they were often directed toward her (the therapist). They signified that Amy was changing her view of herself—from accommodating victim to that of a person who had been wronged. The therapist now aimed toward facilitating this expression of anger, but also toward helping her develop socially appropriate coping mechanisms. To accomplish these aims, the therapist explained that Amy could change the rules of the game if she wished; but first they should talk about the proposed new rule and agree to it before resuming the game. Amy responded well to this idea and began to create new games (and new rules for old games) that were reflective of her abusive experiences. She and the therapist went on to create games and rules that represented her current life and issues with which she was currently struggling.

Amy's individual therapy continued until she was 12½. By then, although she was still a fairly shy girl, Amy had developed a healthy self-image, had made some friends, and was an active member of a soccer team. Even though the clinician discontinued regular therapy sessions with her, the process of closure was conducted in a way that would permit Amy to return to therapy as an adolescent if she needed to. This was done so that if she did return to treatment, she would not see it as a failure or as taking a step backward in her life.

The Case of Jean

Jean was the same age as Amy had been when she entered treatment. She was the victim of similar types of sexual abuse, but the treatment process took a markedly different course.

No one is sure who Jean's father was. Her mother, April, had become deeply involved with drugs and motorcycle gangs when she was in her late teens and early twenties. During this time, she was extremely promiscuous both heterosexually and homosexually, and was a heavy polydrug user. In fact, there were large blocks of time for which April had no recall. Jean had first been removed from her mother's care when the mother and a boyfriend were apprehended while trying to sell stolen merchandise. When Jean was taken into placement she was malnourished and showed signs of both physical and, possibly, sexual abuse. Eventually, at the age of three, she was placed with relatives, an aunt and uncle who had two grown children. These relatives had a difficult time with Jean for several years. She would have uncontrollable temper tantrums, during which she would scream, kick, spit at, or bite anyone who attempted to control her. She had severe night terrors and for more than a year could not tolerate sleeping alone. In addition, she was sexually provocative with adults and cruel to other children and animals. After the first two difficult years, Jean seemed to settle down and respond well to the relatives' stable environment.

Even though Jean remained an oppositional child who was sometimes difficult to reach, things were going fairly well until she was six and her mother reappeared, claiming to be a changed woman. From the moment her mother appeared, Jean desperately wanted to live with her. Jean's aunt and uncle agreed that she had almost a different personality when she was with April; in fact, she was both submissive and affectionate toward her mother. The aunt and uncle did not recognize this as the accommodating and pseudomature behavior that is characteristic of abused children, but instead took it as a sign of a potentially healthy relationship with the mother. After much pleading from Jean and many promises from April, the aunt and uncle permitted the girl to return to her mother's care. Soon the mother took Jean and moved away, presumably because she had found a job in a nearby city.

Jean's aunt and uncle did not see the girl again until she was almost nine years old. She had been found when the police raided a house that was notorious for drugs and wild motorcycle gang parties. The mother managed to escape the raid, but the little girl was discovered in a bedroom with two men who were subsequently convicted of child molestation and possession of narcotics. It was learned later that Jean had been the victim of this kind of abuse for several years. The mother had left her in the care of boyfriends who molested her, who had forced her to engage in group sex at parties, and who had given her drugs. A man with whom April lived, a biker, often had intercourse with Jean—including sodomy.

Eventually, Jean was returned to the custody of her aunt and uncle, who were granted full legal custody. The aunt and uncle sought treatment for Jean because, when returned to their custody, she would have uncontrollable temper tantrums much like the ones she had when she first went to live with them. At night, Jean could not sleep alone, and only slept fitfully if her aunt and uncle allowed her to sleep with them. She was occasionally sadistic and/or sexually inappropriate with other children. Her behavior toward her teachers ranged from the placating to the oppositional. She was unable to do grade-level work at school because of poor retention and a lack of concentration. Jean also insisted that she wanted to return to April because her mother needed her.

When Jean first came to therapy, she did not appear anxious about leaving the aunt and uncle or about meeting alone with a stranger. When she entered the therapist's office, she walked around the room carefully inspecting books and toys and various articles of furniture. She then sat down across from the therapist, crossed her legs in a very suggestive manner, and said, "And now what can I do for you?" She was clearly attempting to defend against her fear and anxiety in this new situation with a strange adult by taking an aggressive approach. The clinician responded by stating, in a friendly manner, that she was meeting with her to help her adjust to living with her aunt and uncle, and to help her with what had happened in the past. Jean's reply was that this wasn't necessary because she was going to go back to live with her mother no matter what she would have to do to accomplish it. The therapist told her, in a kindly but firm way, that she could not go back to live with her mother because she had been abused there. After this exchange, the therapist asked her some general questions about her school and her friends and Jean answered appropriately.

When the clinician met with the aunt and uncle, she learned that Jean's acting out—in particular the sadistic and provocative behavior—had become very serious. They were afraid that if things got much worse they would not be able to keep her. In their view, the tantrums were one thing when Jean was a three-year-old, but now that she was bigger they were afraid that she would hurt another child. They added that Jean was especially cruel toward very young children.

The therapist suggested to them that it would be advisable for her to do a complete evaluation of Jean, including psychological testing, before formulating a treatment plan for the girl. In the meantime, she recommended that Jean not be permitted to play with other children without supervision. The therapist asked for their authorization to talk with the school concerning the girl's special needs; to this, the couple consented readily.

During the psychological testing, Jean was hostile but able to perform the more concrete tasks such as those of the WISC-R and the Thematic Apperception Test (TAT). The WISC-R responses showed her to be a bright, extremely angry child who was attempting to defend herself against overwhelming anxiety and aggressive impulses by hypervigilance and compulsive attention to details. Her hostility, intended to ward off feelings of helplessness and inadequacy, was manifested in a steady barrage of criticism of the WISC-R subtests as "stupid, dumb," and so forth, even though in most instances she dealt with them competently.

It became clear that one of the ways in which Jean had survived the abusive experiences of her past was to develop a pseudomature "mantle of competence"; while this enabled her to function surprisingly well, she was extremely fragile beneath the surface. When she felt that this form of protection was under attack, she would quickly counterattack. And because the WISC-R was perceived as a kind of threat to her competency, Jean could only challenge the source of the threat.

Her TAT responses were full of violence. Many of the stories that she told had happy endings in which superpowerful people were able to vanquish enemies; others expressed themes of people ganging up on other people to get even for past misdeeds. The Rorschach test proved to be too much for Jean, and the testing had to be halted short of completion. One inkblot evoked an image that seemed to spill out over the card and onto the desk. She responded to the blot by saying "Broken, burned bones . . . burned bones and blood—no, broken burned leaves." She slammed the card down on the desk and began tearing leaves off a plant that was sitting on the desk, while she chanted, "Burned bones and leaves." The therapist put the card away and guided Jean toward a neutral activity.

The prognosis for Jean did not look good initially. Nevertheless, the clinician thought that by working with the girl's defenses (i.e., her compulsiveness and desire for competence) it would be possible to get some control over her provocative acting out, which would allow her to be more receptive to treatment. The acting out was seen as an attempt at mastery over her earlier abuse by replicating the abuse in some form; at the same time it served to identify and describe aspects of what had been done to her.

The therapist considered, too, that a treatment plan encouraging regression or the ventilation of anger would be a mistake at that time for several reasons. First, Jean did not have the foundation of normal infant and early childhood experiences as, for example, Amy had had, and thus her ego structure was extremely vulnerable. Second, Jean's defenses were *barely* functional and she frequently lost control in very primitive ways. By contrast, Amy's bizarre posturing and avoidant behavior (while superficially more pathological) actually kept her primitive destructive impulses in check. And because Amy's super-ego was fundamentally healthy, once she felt safe she could utilize a regressive process to catch up developmentally. When the latter was achieved, she could go on to express her anger through a constructive therapy process that was truly cathartic. For Jean, a therapy process that encouraged catharsis would not, at that time, have served recovery but, rather, would have unleashed boundless primitive rage.

The initial goal for Jean's therapy was to shore up her ego by ego-building experiences that Jean could accept, in view of her negative self-concept. The clinician also wanted to try to break through the pattern of mastery-by-identification-with-the-aggressor; to accomplish this, she met with one of Jean's teachers and her parents, persuading them to agree to a consistent behavior modification program with daily reports sent home from school.

The therapist also helped Jean's teacher to understand that as a result of the girl's anxiety, her attention span was not that of an ordinary nine-year-old. Thus, her work needed to be broken down into smaller increments than were given to other students in the class. She also recommended that because Jean's impulse control was still very poor, she would have to be supervised constantly. The therapist also explained to the teacher that the girl would probably require a program such as this, with periodic changes, for at least one year.

The clinician began twice-a-week sessions with Jean. She carefully structured these sessions so that they would be both ego-building and super-ego-strengthening. The therapy hour was divided into three 15-minute activity sessions followed by a cleanup period. Activities ranged from putting puzzles together to simple drawings and games. They were meant to be challenging enough not to bore Jean, while simple enough not to provoke her by being stressful. When she would act out, the activity was stopped, and if she made inappropriate remarks the conversation was changed to focus upon (1) the intent of the message that she was trying to send and (2) how the other person might feel when she made that kind of remark. The therapist would then steer the discussion to how Jean must have felt when she was abused.

As therapy progressed—in parallel to the behavior modification program at school and the work of the parents at home—Jean's behavior improved significantly both at home and school. Nevertheless, she continued to act out and to be provocative with the clinician. It became clear that Jean split her world into all bad versus all good. In this context, she was beginning to focus the anger she felt toward her mother onto her therapist—a positive sign; even so, this division of people and things into good or bad meant that she was merely focusing her negative thoughts in one direction in order to function adequately in another. On a brighter note, it also meant that Jean was beginning to develop enough ego strength to tolerate new departures in therapy.

Jean still had an idealized fantasy of her mother, and for Jean to express anger toward her was to risk loss of the fantasy. With a view to breaking through this all-bad/all-good way of judging things, the therapist began telling Jean stories, both during and interspersed between the play activities. The theme of these stories was that sometimes good people make mistakes and do bad things, but one must recognize that doing something bad doesn't make the person totally bad. One can still like the person.

At first, Jean dismissed the stories as "dumb," but began to show more interest when the therapist created serialized stories about one mother and her daughter, and the latter's friends. Soon Jean was asking the therapist questions about the characters of the stories, wanting more details. Then she would ask hypothetical questions about what the characters in the story might do in this or that situation.

One day, Jean asked the clinician to tell about her own childhood and about her school. When the therapist told the girl about the school, she was particularly careful to tell about times when she did not do well and things she did that got her in trouble, as well as the good things that happened. Jean listened intently for a while and then exclaimed, "You got in trouble? . . . You couldn't have gotten in trouble. You are too goodie-goodie, too perfect!" The therapist reassured her that she had done lots of things that were wrong and had made many mistakes. Jean stared at her in true amazement. It was clear that some of the girl's former ways of thinking were dissolving before the therapist's eyes. It was one of those moments that made months of struggle with a very difficult little girl worthwhile.

Jean was full of questions about the clinician's childhood experiences. She would then tell about something she herself had done or felt, and ask the therapist what she would have done or how she would have felt. The structured activities were continued for a short while longer, but it was clear that Jean was ready to move on to expressive, projective play. She began playing in a doll's house, where she would obsessively reenact "night parties" with lots of scary men. She became quite conflicted about this play and periodically would act out. For example, during one session she described a scene in which a man locked her in the bathroom with him; she ran to the dish where the therapist kept some candy, stuffed her mouth with the candy, and then began throwing it around the room.

The therapist crossed over to her and took the candy dish away, telling her that she understood that the dolls had brought back painful memories; it was all right if she stopped. Jean would not have to get angry or say that something scared her in order to stop the game. The clinician went on to tell Jean a story about a little girl who had been hurt so much that she became afraid to be afraid, and how the girl later learned to tell people that she was afraid. By the end of the story, Jean had calmed down and could tell the therapist how frightened she was. Jean's therapy continued to make good progress. At the time of this writing, she is thirteen years old. She comes in once a month for therapy and is participating in a girls' group.

REFERENCES

Burgess, A. W., & Holmstrom, L. L. Rape trauma syndrome. *American Journal of Psychiatry*, 131(9), 981–986, 1974.

DeFrancis, V. Protecting the child victim of sex crimes committed by adults: Final report. Denver: American Humane Society, 1969.

Erickson, M. H., Rossi, E. L., & Rossi, S. I. *Hypnotic realities.* New York: Irvington, 1976.

Finkelhor, D. *Child sexual abuse: New theory and research.* New York: The Free Press, 1984.

Finkelhor, D. The sexual abuse of children: Current research reviewed. *Psychiatric Annals*, 17(4), 233–241, 1987.

Gibbons, T. C. N., & Prince, J. Child victims of sex offenses. Pamphlet published by the Institute for the Study and Treatment of Delinquency, London, 1963.

Peters, J. J. Social, legal and psychological effects of rape on the victim. *Pennsylvania Medicine*, 78, 34–36, 1975.

Peters, J. J. Children who are victims of sexual assault and the psychology of offenders. *American Journal of Psychotherapy*, 30(3), 398–421, 1976.

Tufts New England Medical Center, Division of Child Psychiatry. Sexually exploited children: Service and research project. Final report for the Office of Juvenile Justice and Delinquency Prevention. Washington, DC: U.S. Department of Justice, 1984.

4

Treatment of the
Adolescent Victim

Adolescence is one of the most complex and turbulent stages of life. This difficult period can often try the patience of the wisest of adults to its limits. When a sexual trauma is introjected into this naturally problematic time, it can pose extremely complex questions for the therapist. In cases of adolescent sexual abuse, a therapist is frequently called upon to help the adolescent victim resolve issues relating to his or her still-evolving sense of self, as well as issues relating to the adolescent's developing sexuality. Furthermore, the adolescent's family relationships, as well as peer relationships, may be heavily burdened by the fact of the assault.

This chapter will focus first on some of the major issues that confront a therapist who treats an adolescent victim of sexual assault.* It continues with an explanation of the phenomenon known as the rape trauma syndrome and recovery cycle. There follows a discussion of questions posed by the "silent rape," in which an adolescent victim attempts to hide the assault from her parents. Also considered are the many issues that are raised when an assault was the adolescent victim's first sexual experience. Finally, the chapter presents methods of therapy for the victim, in light of the strained and often anger-filled relationships that

---

* The principal focus of this chapter is the assessment and treatment of adolescent girl victims. While adolescent boys are targets of molestation, by far the majority of victims are girls. See Chapter 6 for a discussion of treatment and assessment issues regarding latency-age boys; these issues pertain largely to adolescent boys as well.

develop between an adolescent and her family, and the impact that the abuse can have upon a family system. Case examples are presented in which the adolescent was abused as a child, including one in which the assault was a gang rape.*

OVERVIEW

It is frequently difficult to treat an adolescent rape victim, who may resist therapy for many reasons. The adolescent may be struggling to prove to herself that she is still "all right" and not emotionally injured by the assault, and thus, like many adult victims, may refuse to admit she needs help. Another issue that can delay treatment is that frequently after an adolescent has been sexually assaulted she may go through a period of self-destructive acting out or a period of intense self-loathing; this may make it impossible for her to participate in a healthy, constructive process such as psychotherapy. Furthermore, the adolescent may have been doing something that was forbidden or wrong which led to the sexual assault, so her guilt may cause her to resist treatment.

An adolescent's family may also resist the therapy process. Many parents' wishful thinking may lead them to believe that the assault did not really harm their child, and thus the parents may avoid seeing symptoms of the trauma. The parents may be overly focused upon their adolescent's acting-out behavior and not realize that she has suffered a terrible emotional wound. Unfortunately, when she hears such anger, it only serves to deepen the adolescent's self-blame and intensify her potential for even more self-destructive acting out.

Even in cases in which the adolescent's acting out has led directly to her victimization, she is nonetheless a victim who is totally unprepared for the horrible reality of the assault. The attack itself is generally totally unexpected, and the adolescent struggles with disbelief and terror as she attempts to deal with the life-and-death reality of the event. Adults who are close to the adolescent must keep a careful check on their anger or frustration at the adolescent's risk-taking or rebellious behavior that may have led to the assault, as well as bear in mind that despite an adolescent's claims that she "knows it all" and has her right to independence, she is still very much a child trying to grow into adulthood. Communicating with a traumatized adolescent can require a delicate attempt to reach the hurt, frightened child inside without offending her appropriate striving for independence. Both aspects of

---

* In respect to adolescents, rape is more prevalent than molestation, and the former term will be used to refer to the kind of assault being discussed in this chapter.

the adolescent's psyche must be worked with in order to conduct successful treatment, and such a feat is not easily accomplished.

AFTEREFFECTS OF RAPE

Some of the psychological perplexities that are engendered by sexual assault are so fundamental that one hardly ever thinks of them. One of the most basic of these dilemmas is the loss of territorial boundaries. A sexual assault is an assault on the ultimate territorial boundary, one's skin. There are only three situations in which our bodies can be penetrated against our will: when we are shot, stabbed, or raped. The involuntary penetration of this very primitive boundary causes the victim to experience a sense of not feeling whole. It is common for a victim to feel a puzzling sense of personal fragmentation and disorientation caused by this kind of temporary disruption of the territorial boundary of the skin.

This sense of loss of personal integrity or wholeness can be particularly devastating to an adolescent who is still in the process of defining who she is and individuating from her parents. Adolescents have a deep need to perceive themselves as whole, separate people, and disruption of this perception may cause serious repercussions in the girl's later development. Consequently, from the beginning of treatment, a clinician should work toward helping the adolescent to rebuild a healthy sense of personal boundaries and of selfhood.

A second fundamental psychological issue that rape calls into question is the victim's perception of her ability to control her environment. This is a process that begins around the age of two, when a child learns the word "no." This process of learning how much control one has over one's environment is in full operation during adolescence. Then, suddenly, the adolescent is confronted with a situation in which she is totally powerless to stop something from happening. Such an experience of total helplessness can be devastating to a young person who is still struggling to discover what degree of command she has in the various aspects of her life.

A third dilemma that arises from the rape trauma concerns the victim's basic trust in others. As most children grow and change, they hold onto the assumption that others will not harm them. This is especially true of adolescents, who are further convinced that their parents' warnings about the perils of the world are stupid and that, no matter what happens, they can "handle it."

A fourth issue is that of the adolescent's developing sexual identity and the role that sex will eventually play in her life; both may be severely affected by being raped. Unlike the sexually mature adult rape victim, who can in most instances clearly distinguish between rape and consensual sex, the rape of an adolescent may have been one of her first sexual experiences. Consequently, an adolescent victim may later confuse sex with rape.

Finally, another perplexity that the adolescent must struggle with is the question, "Why did such a thing happen to me?" Adolescents are narcissistic and egocentric by nature, and they tend to view causality in terms of themselves; hence, they are also vulnerable to self-blame at this developmental stage. A therapist should be alert to the fact that young victims tend to internalize or blame themselves for an assault more often than adults do. Too often an adolescent victim comes to the tragic conclusion that she was raped because she was "bad" or "no good"; or that she was punished for some misdeed; or, now that she has been raped, that she is worthless. A therapist should carefully explore the entire subject of causality and blame with an adolescent victim to make sure that she does not incorporate the assault in such a manner that leads her to believe that she is bad or worthless. In some cases, the clinician may need to devote considerable time to this issue.

A therapist should note that, even in the turbulent lives of most adolescents, there is some sort of order. But after a sexual assault, the adolescent is left to contemplate an inexplicable, random, violent event. The randomness of life is difficult enough for an adult to decipher, but it is even more puzzling for an adolescent, who is less capable of coping with an abstract concept such as randomness. Furthermore, an adolescent's natural grandiosity, which tends to make her see the world largely in terms of herself, hinders her ability to put her own role in the rape incident in proper perspective.

A therapist should also consider the fact that if the adolescent has been previously victimized as a child, this second assault may serve to solidify her self-perception that she *is a victim*, a worthless object of such events. We believe (with Peters, 1976; Browne & Finkelhor, 1986; and Yates, 1987) that adolescents who were victimized as children are at higher risk of being victimized again than are adolescents who were not child victims. In these cases, the clinician should find out whether or not the adolescent victim was reenacting the earlier situation with the unconscious fantasy that the conclusion would not be a sexual trauma this time.

RAPE TRAUMA SYNDROME AND RECOVERY CYCLE

The rape trauma syndrome and recovery cycle are processes that serve to protect the psyche during the trauma itself and help it return to a normal, stable level of functioning after the assault. These processes are fundamentally similar to the grief process as described by Lindemann (1944). During therapy, a clinician needs to facilitate the adolescent victim's progression through the trauma response and recovery cycle, as well as assist her family to understand the process, so that the family can provide her with appropriate emotional support and guidance. If the adolescent victim receives the treatment and support that she needs, she may not be left with the deep emotional scars caused by the untended psychological wounds that are often the most serious injuries caused by sexual assault.

Specific Components of the Syndrome and Stages of the Cycle

Most victims of rape are totally unprepared for the assault. It takes the victim by surprise and, for a few moments, the victim's mind tries to come to grips with the significance of what is happening to her. Thoughts race through her mind such as "This must be a dream," "This must be a bad joke," or "This can't be real." When the cold reality of "Oh my god, it's real" descends upon the victim, she may become momentarily hysterical, but soon her main concern will be survival: "I'll do whatever you want; just don't kill me."

Figure 1 shows the stages of the trauma response and recovery cycle.

Rape Trauma Response
The attack
Disbelief
Realization of the reality of the attack
Cognitive survival state

[RELEASE OR ESCAPE]

Posttrauma Recovery Cycle
Shock
Denial of what happened
Depression
Mood swings
Anger
Philosophical reflection
Laying to rest

Figure 1. Adapted from Everstine, D.S., & Everstine, L. *People in Crisis*. New York: Brunner/Mazel, 1983, p. 168.

When the victim comprehends what is happening to her, she will go into a cognitive survival stage (Everstine & Everstine, 1983, 1986). This is a strangely cold, unemotional state of mind, which persons who are struggling for their lives endure. During this time, the victim's emotions are kept in abeyance so that she can attend to her more pressing survival needs. There also may be time and sensory distortions. Things may seem to go in slow motion during the assault. If the victim struggles or is injured during the assault, she most likely will not feel the full intensity of the pain, because she is by then in a dissociative state.

When the victim is released, she will most likely enter into a shock phase. Some victims present in a hysterical or emotional manner, but it has been our experience that most adolescent rape victims remain in shock from 24 hours up to three or four days. While the victim is in this state of shock, she may have extremely flattened affect. She may appear dazed, confused, or even blasé. Such behavior can easily be misunderstood by the untrained observer as being unaffected by or not caring about the assault. Too often, well-intentioned parents who desire to see their child as being "all right" misread the adolescent's blunted affect; or, parents who may already be angered by their adolescent's acting out may misinterpret their daughter's symptoms of shock as additional evidence of her being irresponsible. In both instances, a therapist should carefully explain to the parents that the adolescent is by no means indifferent, and then clearly describe the clinical components of this state.

When the victim comes out of shock, for a time she will be in a state of denial during which she attempts to show that the rape has not changed or seriously affected her life. During this denial phase, the adolescent may make statements such as, "I won't let him take any more from me" or "I can handle it." It is best if the therapist takes a position that is supportive of the victim, but also helps her to face the fact that something serious did happen, so that she can proceed with the recovery process instead of staying frozen in her denial. The latter state usually lasts from a few days to a few weeks.

Next, most adolescent victims will enter a state of depression, which is anger resulting from the assault turned inward. Often significant people who are close to rape victims have considerable difficulty in grasping why many victims do not express intense anger after a rape. A few victims are capable of instant anger but most are not. Loved ones, who are frequently enraged by the assault, may misread the victim's lack of expressed anger and react with suspicion and dismay. This may be further complicated by the fact that during this depressive stage some adolescent victims go through a phase of promiscuousness or self-destructive acting out, which is a function of the depression and of loss of sense of self-worth. Some adolescent victims perceive themselves as soiled or no longer of value because of having been raped; others may experience an eating disorder or simply gain weight mysteriously as an expression of their conflicts about sexual identity. If an adolescent goes through a self-destructive or self-loathing phase, her parents will need considerable support from the therapist to ensure that the manner in which they handle their daughter's acting out does not intensify her feelings of worthlessness.

It is worth noting that not all adolescent rape victims respond to being raped by promiscuous or self-destructive acting-out behavior. Although it is our experience that most adolescent victims will go through an acting-out phase in some form, there are adolescents who behave in a quiet, withdrawn manner. This type of girl may avoid social contact with boys; and, in some extreme cases, she may develop a school phobia or an agoraphobia. Unfortunately, many adolescents who respond to an assault in a quiet manner are often misperceived as needing no psychological care. This can occur in a family in which the parents' desires for their daughter to recover quickly may cloud their vision so that they do not see her suffering. It is also easier, in such cases, for the parents to avoid dealing with their adolescent's developing sexuality, a subject that some parents find extremely difficult. In fact, the daughter's withdrawal from social (boy–girl) contacts may be a relief to such parents. Or, as Burgess and Holmstrom aptly put it:

> One of the issues that parents must come to terms with is their child's sexuality. With a rape, there is the reality confirmation that their child has been exposed to a sexual situation, and it becomes important to know how the child is treated in terms of this knowledge. For example, do the parents (1) ignore this fact and not mention the rape; (2) become extra protective of the child in normal boy–girl relationships; or (3) deny the impact of the situation? (1978, p. 78)

As the depressive phase of the recovery cycle fades, a victim will go through a period of mood swings. This phase can be quite frightening to the victim because she gets glimpses of her former self before the assault and then some seemingly minor event will propel her back into depression once more. The girl may need considerable reassurance from the therapist that this is yet another stage in the post-trauma recovery cycle that will pass.

After the period of mood swings will come a period of intense anger. If the earlier, depressive stage was properly worked through in therapy, this anger can be directed toward an appropriate object—namely, the victim's assailant. However, when there is the lack of a solid clinical foundation for directing this anger, there may be problems in some of the central male relationships of the girl's life. For example, she may displace her anger onto "safe" males, such as her father, boyfriend, or brother.

This phase of the post-trauma recovery is one in which those who are close to the victim may also need considerable support. Because the adolescent may appear to be angry about everything, the people around her, especially the males, feel they cannot do anything right. The family may need considerable help in not personalizing this anger and in seeing it for what it is—a symbolic expression of the victim's rage at her attacker. Family members may also feel unjustly accused by the victim if the anger is expressed toward them a long time after the rape took place. In many cases, the victim's anger reaches the surface when the family's anger has subsided. Through wishful thinking, they may have underestimated the duration of the traumatic process.

The final philosophical and laying-trauma-to-rest stages, in which the victim sums up how the assault has changed her life and how she will go on from here, are in many cases difficult for a victim to complete during her adolescent years. The reason is that this task requires dealing with abstract philosophical concepts that adolescents are usually not capable of understanding cognitively. The clinician should note that adolescents live in a world that is primarily governed by their emotions. They view things mostly in terms of their still-forming concept of self— i.e., in an experiential manner. Even though many adolescents sound very adult in their abilities to grasp philosophical concepts, this may be mere verbiage if the concepts being discussed have not been fully internalized by the adolescent. The adolescent typically learns by doing, while an adult is more likely to try conceptualizing before acting. Hence it is not a good idea for the therapist to project an adult's cognitive process onto an adolescent victim. Adolescents are more likely to conceptualize the philosophical, laying-to-rest phase of the trauma recovery cycle in a superficial manner; if so, it represents a temporary but not a real closure to the recovery process. For example, few 16-year-old girls can fully grasp why they went through a period of promiscuous acting out after being raped, but later, at age 20, they may be more capable of understanding their behavior and of coming to terms with it more adequately.

The significance of these delayed reactions is that an adolescent victim may need to return to therapy for a brief period of time during her late teens or early twenties. If the therapist feels that may be necessary, he or she can assist the victim in going through the trauma recovery cycle at her current level of understanding. In addition, the door should be left open for the adolescent to return to therapy again later on, if needed.

THE SILENT RAPE

Even though it is said that approximately half of all rapes are committed against adolescents, we have observed that the adolescent may be the least likely person to report what has happened to the authorities. Sadly, many adolescent victims do not tell their parents or family members. When one takes into consideration what an ordeal a rape victim goes through during the trauma response and posttrauma recovery cycles, it is particularly tragic if *no one* around her knows what has happened to her. Some rapes are undetected for long periods of time and, as a consequence, parents may misread an adolescent's apparently strange behavior. For a therapist, it is worth considering that some of his or her adolescent cases—referred for a myriad of reasons—may be those in which the girl is a "silent" victim of rape.

Some of the symptoms that adolescent rape victims present are the following, according to Hilberman (1976) and Everstine and Everstine (1983).

1. sudden personality change
2. rapid drop in school performance
3. withdrawal from school or social activities
4. flagrant promiscuous behavior
5. sudden phobic behavior
6. withdrawal from social activities
7. obvious self-destructive, risk-taking behavior
8. drug abuse
9. eating disorders such as bulimia or anorexia
10. sudden unexplained alienation from peers or family

Any of these behaviors should be viewed as an adolescent's cry for help. When a therapist inquires whether an adolescent client has been sexually assaulted, he or she should be aware that many adolescents may not feel safe telling strange adults about what has happened to them. Hence, if the girl's initial reply is evasive or negative, the clinician should not assume that the reply is accurate or complete until he or she has had time to establish a relationship with her. In these instances, the therapist may wish to make a neutral-sounding statement to the adolescent such as, "You are just getting to know me and I am sure there are some things that you may not feel comfortable telling me just now. Later on, when we know each other better, you will probably want to tell me about them."

In general, it is important for psychotherapists to reflect that literally thousands of "silent" adolescent victims of sexual assault are not recognized as victims. Instead, they are shamefully mislabeled as delinquent, promiscuous, bad, or "sick" kids.

TREATMENT OF THE ADOLESCENT RAPE VICTIM

The Family

As in the case of an adult rape victim, the response of those who are involved with the victim's emotional needs can be one of the critical factors in determining how well an adolescent will recover from a sexual assault. The need for her parents to behave in an appropriate manner cannot be overly emphasized. It is true that, in many cases, an adolescent's acting-out or risk-taking behavior may indirectly or directly have led to her being assaulted. Even so, the adolescent probably did not have the faintest notion that her behavior would lead to rape, despite the fact that her parents may have perceived the risk beforehand and may have tried to warn her of the dangers of her behavior.

Unfortunately, parents who are already angry at their daughter for some reason may rashly take the position that the daughter deserved being raped because of recent acting-out behavior. This insensitivity is doubly unfortunate; first, because it assumes that the adolescent was capable of realizing that her behavior could lead to rape; and, second, an acting-out adolescent may have been doubly traumatized by the rape because her risk-taking behavior was the result of preexisting problems in her family. The victim has already been taught a ghastly lesson and does not need to have it reiterated by those whom she needs for love and support.

It is advisable for a clinician to meet with the adolescent victim's parents as early as possible in the treatment process. One should bear in mind that they are victims of the assault as well, and they may need considerable help in coming to terms with what has happened to their family. Some of these meetings should be without the daughter's presence because the parents may need a private setting to express their feelings about what has happened; also, some of these feelings may best be not expressed in front of the victim.

During these parent sessions the therapist can go over issues such as: (1) the parents' feelings and prejudices concerning rape; (2) the parents' feelings of helplessness or failure for not being able to protect the child; (3) how their daughter's behavior may have led to the rape; (4) how they should discuss the relevant issues with the daughter; (5) their daughter's sexuality; and (6) how to discuss the subject of the rape with (when appropriate) siblings. These are all difficult subjects, and many parents of victims will require guidance from a therapist.

Rape, despite our culture's many steps forward toward understanding it, remains a profoundly misunderstood subject about which many people still hold unfortunate stereotypical ideas. The clinician should help the victim's parents understand that their daughter may need to learn to be more cautious and responsible for her actions; nevertheless, teaching her this will not be accomplished by angry outbursts. And no matter how much they may wish to shelter their child, they cannot always protect her from some of the cruel facts of life.

Sex is a difficult subject for most people to discuss; many parents dread the day that they will have to have "that discussion" with their adolescent child. Above all, the rape of a daughter forces the parents to deal with her sexuality; and because the rape may have been her first, or one of her first, sexual experiences, it is imperative that she is helped to separate the meaning of the assault from that of consensual sex. This is not always a simple task, but it can be made much easier if the parents are receptive to hearing about her feelings concerning the subject. The "Let's-pretend-it-never-happened" approach simply will not do.

Next the parents should be given an explanation of the rape trauma syndrome and recovery cycle, in order that they may more fully understand their daughter's behavior after the assault. Finally, they should be given an estimation of the length of time that will be required for the victim's recovery from the assault, lest they make the unfortunate assumption that their daughter should return to normal as soon as the bruises heal. In our experience, a minimum of six months in treatment can be expected. In some cases, several years of therapy is necessary.

Sources of Complication

There are factors that can make the treatment of adolescent rape victims possibly more complex. First, the adolescent may have known her assailant or assailants; e.g., they may attend the same school. If she reports the assault, she may be the brunt of cruel gossip or threats by an assailant or his friends. One must bear in mind that during the entire criminal proceedings, an accused assailant may well be free and attending school. Second, if the victim does not report the rape or the case cannot be prosecuted, the victim may have to face her attacker or attackers daily. Either situation can be excruciatingly painful for the victim. A therapist will need to help prepare the victim to decide what she should do in these situations.

An adolescent may have been the victim of a gang rape, and may or may not know who the assailants were. To complicate matters, she may be one of several victims whom she may know or not know. It is our opinion, along with Burgess and Holmstrom (1978, p. 67), that each assault requires separate clinical attention. The clinician should not treat a gang rape as one event in order to avoid listening to the gruesome details of each assault. Instead, a therapist should strive to be aware of his or her own inner feelings about such events and be careful not to unknowingly silence a victim from working through her feelings concerning each rape and each assailant. In case there were more than one victim of the gang rape, the interactional and relationship issues are multiplied. In such cases, each victim will have to work through her feelings concerning her relationship to each other victim during, as well as after, the assault, if the others had been friends before the assault.

Listening Without Judging

The therapist should not aggressively press for details of a rape, so that he or she is not misunderstood as being morbidly curious or as having no regard for the girl's personal boundaries. Instead, the therapist should convey concern and a willingness to hear the details, bearing in mind that there is a subtle but vast difference between encouraging and pushing. Because of the profound damage that rape inflicts upon a rape victim's sense of personal integrity, it is vital that the clinician communicate to her a sense of respect for these already compromised boundaries.

A therapist's best strategy is to assume a nonjudgmental role that is supportive of adaptive coping, while nonsupportive of pathological coping mechanisms. If the adolescent victim is not capable of admitting to the clinician or to herself how traumatized she was by the rape, it is recommended that this "I'm-fine-and-the-rape-didn't-hurt-me" attitude not be challenged. If the therapist questions this facade, the girl is likely to perceive such a challenge as a second assault. If not carefully thought out, any statement that is intended to make the victim face the seriousness of her situation may, in fact, drive an already terrified adolescent away from the therapy relationship. Or, as one young client put it, "Thank you for not telling me how messed up I was. You know, if you had said it then [just after she had been raped], I would have never come back to see you. I would have hated you." Even at 15, this victim knew how vital it was for the therapist to respect her boundaries.

That the adolescent should take precautions so that she does not become a victim again, is another sensitive issue that must be dealt with during the course of therapy. Even so, a therapist should not bring up the subject in such a manner that it ascribes blame for the past assault onto the adolescent. Instead, one can reframe the subject of responsibility and blame by suggesting that the adolescent should value herself, and because she values herself, she should take good care of herself. A shift as radical as that in her frame of reference may take considerable time if the adolescent has already internalized the idea that she *is* a victim or a worthless person. If this is the case, the clinician should intersperse information that contradicts such an unfortunate self-image whenever possible during the (entire) course of therapy.

Acting Out

Some adolescent rape victims tend to sexualize relationships with boys or men, often in a very inappropriate manner. This usually occurs because the young girl has cast herself in the victim's role, and because her self-esteem has reached such a low ebb that she perceives her only value to the opposite sex as being sexual. Unfortunately, this inappropriate seductiveness becomes self-confirming when boys or men who do not know what has happened to her misinterpret what she is doing.

When treating a young person who does this kind of acting-out behavior, a therapist should be cautious lest the girl mistake his or her reaction for being critical. Instead, the clinician should focus on how the girl views herself. During this process, the therapist can try to provide her with information from which she can begin to build a new, more healthy self-image, thus facilitating more appropriate future behavior.

When Unresolved Trauma Is Revived

When entering adolescence, a young person undergoes dramatic cognitive growth; as a result, concepts that were once beyond the person's understanding suddenly come into focus. When that happens, any previous sexual trauma that was not revealed or resolved by the child can suddenly revive for the adolescent. In other words, a child of six may not understand the full sexual or social meaning of having been molested, but a 14-year-old will. The effects of a previously unrevealed sexual assault may suddenly return to the surface, often in the form of inexplicable behavioral or personality changes. In fact, it is more likely that an adolescent will reveal past sexual trauma by her behavior than by directly telling an adult. To make matters worse, many adolescents who have experienced unresolved childhood trauma may not know why their behavior has changed, nor even that it has. They may project their internal turmoil onto the adults in their lives and perceive the ensuing conflicts as due to the adults' unfairness or lack of sympathy. When a family system reaches this sad state, the conflicted parent-child interaction can perpetuate itself, even though both parents and adolescent believe that they are merely reacting to the misguided actions of the other.

Because of these potential dynamics, clinicians should pay close attention to cases in which adolescent clients display sudden behavioral changes, particularly during early adolescence. The symptoms of an unresolved childhood sexual assault are quite similar to those noted earlier in the discussion of "silent rape," namely changes such as an inexplicable drop in school performance, withdrawal from school or other social activities, promiscuous behavior, self-destructive behavior, substance abuse, sudden alienation from the family, runaway behavior, or the onset of an eating disorder—particularly bulimic binging and purging. We have encountered a significant number of cases in which an eating disorder that emerged in adolescence could be traced to childhood sexual assault.

Unresolved trauma may surface slowly, but in our experience the overt symptoms often emerge quite rapidly—usually in conjunction with an adolescent's awakening to the opposite sex, as well as to her own burgeoning sexual development. As one 16-year-old put it, "I don't know what happened when I turned 14. Something snapped and I just didn't care anymore. I was mad at everyone and I hated myself."

When this girl began therapy at age 16 because of her beyond-parental-control behavior, substance abuse, and two suicide attempts, she did not mention that a group of teenage boys had gang-raped her when she was nine years old. When this event was revealed in the course of taking the girl's history (and after considerable exploration), the girl mentioned it matter-of-factly and quickly added that she had not told her parents at the time (or later) because she was afraid of the boys. She went on to claim that the event was not such a "big deal" anyway, because at the age of nine she did not know what was really happening to her. This girl's blasé attitude was clearly a defensive maneuver to help her avoid dealing with a painful, terrifying event.

It took considerable reassurance before the girl could begin to disclose her true feelings about the assault, namely the belief that there was something about her that caused the boys to choose her to be raped. She had gone to a garage with them, willingly, because she was flattered that older boys wanted to play with her. Then, later on, when her mother had discussed the subject of sex with her for the first time, the mother told her that only "bad" girls have sex with men to whom they are not married. This unfortunate but well-intentioned talk occurred only a few months after the assault; it prevented the girl from telling her mother what happened to her because she believed that her mother would think she was bad. When this information was revealed, the girl's adolescent acting-out behavior was cast in a new light, and the therapist was able to work with her and her family to resolve the trauma.

CASE STUDY

The following is a case study of an adolescent girl whose childhood sexual assault was not revealed for many years. Jackie was 16½ when she was referred for therapy. She said that she did not know when the sexual abuse first occurred, but thought that she was probably two or three years old. In any event, she did remember that being sexually abused had always been part of her life. She did not realize that there was something "wrong" or different about her experience until she was about 11 or 12. Then she "just began hating everyone," especially herself. By the time Jackie first entered treatment, at 16, she was at least 30 pounds overweight.

Although Jackie was a bright girl, her grades were poor in grammar school. She barely passed in junior high; and now, in high school, she was virtually failing in a majority of her classes. Her attendance was poor, and when she was in class she was argumentative and disruptive.

According to Jackie, she first began experimenting with drugs in grammar school. By the time she was in junior high, Jackie drank and used cocaine, marijuana, and amphetamines regularly. Socially, she had a few girlfriends, but she was not particularly close to any of them. She had a reputation for possessing an explosive temper, and she had been thrown out of school several times for fighting. Jackie's relationships with boys were paradoxical. She rarely dated, and when she did it was usually with boys who were younger or less mature than she was. Nevertheless, she claimed that she preferred boys to girls as friends. Jackie said she felt that boys were more reliable and interesting than girls and she enjoyed their company more.

Jackie's relationship with her family was strained at best. Her mother, Corinne, shook her head in dismay when describing Jackie in contrast with her other two children, both of whom were good students and attending college. Corinne added that neither of the other children had been a behavior problem apart from average "kid stuff." She said that Jackie had basically been a happy little girl until she was about three years old, when she suddenly became difficult to deal with. At first, Corinne thought Jackie was going through a "difficult" stage. But, when the tantrums and oppositional behavior did not stop, she simply resigned herself to the idea that the first two were easy children to raise, while this one was just a more difficult child by nature.

Jackie's father, Larry, said that he had a better relationship with his daughter than did her mother. He said he understood her somewhat because he had a bad temper as a young man and had to learn to control it. But even Larry admitted that he was not close with his daughter, and when she was in one of her "moods" even he kept his distance.

Jackie spoke with considerable detachment when she referred to her mother and older sister, describing them as "simps" and "goodie-goodie bitches" who spent all their time shopping and looking at themselves in mirrors. Jackie's relationship with her brother was better. Although they were not close, she enjoyed doing things with him when he came home from college.

Jackie's childhood molestation did not come to light until she was 16. One evening when she was visiting a girlfriend, the two girls got very drunk and decided to tell each other their "heaviest secrets." With an indifferent tone, Jackie told her friend that for years she had been having sex with one of her father's best buddies. Over the next few days, Jackie's friend became more and more worried about what she had learned from Jackie. Eventually, she told her own mother who, in turn, became concerned and called Jackie's mother. When she heard this, Corinne knew that, horrible as it was, the story was true. This was confirmed when Jackie's older sister, who was at home when the call came with the news, said that the same man had tried to molest her when she was about eight. The sister had told him to go away or she would tell someone. The two women decided to wait until Jackie's father came home from work. When he had heard the story, the parents decided to talk with Jackie and then to report everything to the police.

When Jackie's parents let her know what they had learned, they were surprised and offended that Jackie was cool-tempered and somewhat hostile toward them. Jackie told them that it probably would not have happened if they had been around more when she was little, instead of spending all their time working in their business while leaving her with the molester and his wife.

When the father's friend was first accused of the molestation, he vehemently denied it, calling Jackie a "slightly retarded delinquent." Later, when other girls in the neighborhood whom he had molested came forward, he pleaded *nolo contendere* to the criminal charges.

Jackie was referred to our clinic by the district attorney who was prosecuting the criminal case. When Jackie began therapy, she was angry and suspicious. She would start her therapy sessions by announcing that she had absolutely *nothing* to say to another stupid adult, and then talk nonstop for the whole session. Because Jackie was so angry and defensive, the therapist decided to see her individually and meet with her parents separately in regard to parenting issues.

Jackie's parents naively expected her to "snap out of it," now that everyone knew about the molestation and people were doing something about it. They felt personally attacked when Jackie's behavior did not suddenly improve. In fact, her behavior got worse because she felt so exposed, vulnerable, and confused when the molestation became public knowledge.

The first step that the clinician took in working with Jackie's parents was to help them formulate reasonable expectations of a girl who had been through so much. Even though they wanted to, they simply could not place the same expectations on Jackie that they had on their other two children when they were Jackie's age. The therapist let the parents know that Jackie would need several years to catch up, developmentally, and to recover. Further, they would most likely be the targets of future anger as Jackie progressed. The therapist supported the parents by letting them know that they had tried their best, and that she (the therapist) would be there to help them, as parents, get through the process. The parents seemed relieved by this offer of support and guidance, and even though they were not told what they wished, they left the session with a sense of direction and some clearer expectations.

Jackie's therapy sessions continued to be turbulent, as she struggled with questions of why her parents had not known that she was being abused, and why her siblings (who were frequently at the father's friend's house with her) were not molested; and why they couldn't do anything about what was happening. It took considerable clinical work before Jackie could understand and accept how young and vulnerable she and her siblings were at the time when the molestation began. It took time for her to realize that she had been too small even to know what was being done to her. Only when she had thoroughly worked through the guilt and accountability issues, and had described some of the molestation in graphic detail, was she able to face the fact that she did have a form of relationship with this man. In retrospect, she acknowledged that in her mind the molestation had been a funny game that they played together; and, that she had not been aware of what these games were or that there was anything wrong with them.

The therapist saw Jackie as a teenager who was intensely vulnerable and depressed. She was utilizing her anger to protect herself from experiencing other emotions. Jackie's drug use could be seen as an attempt at self-medication to cope with her depression. The therapist approached the issue of Jackie's drug use directly, telling Jackie that she was using drugs to try to stop emotional pain; and that if she was to get her life back under control and "not let that man take any more" from her, as she claimed she wanted, she was going to have to stop using drugs and learn to develop coping strategies that worked. The clinician told Jackie that if she wasn't prepared to make a voluntary commitment to stop, she would insist on regular urine tests as a required part of treatment. The therapist was careful to make sure that the message conveyed to Jackie was not a punitive one, but instead clearly communicated that she cared about her and would not passively sit by and let her do destructive things to herself.

During this critical phase of treatment, the therapist worked closely with Jackie's parents to help them learn to set appropriate limits with their daughter in a manner that conveyed concern and consistency. The parents' previous way of interacting with their daughter, in terms of setting limits, was to first underreact to her behavior because they did not want to deal with her temper, then to overreact in an extrapunitive manner out of frustration, and then to feel guilty because they had overreacted. The therapist believed that it was essential to Jackie's treatment that her parents express their responses to Jackie's acting out more evenhandedly. A key factor in helping them to do this was to help them deal with their feelings of guilt for being so involved in starting a (now very successful) business that they allowed their daughter to be exposed to the molester. The clinician guided them toward redirecting their emotional energy into Jackie's healing process, rather than toward past wrongs that could not be undone. The clinician was eventually able to help the parents to see that there were going to be periods of acting out that would be unpleasant, but that these were necessary aspects of Jackie's eventual recovery.

At first, Jackie responded to the new rules and limits with strident defiance, but soon she settled down—still occasionally testing limits. She began to make slow but visible progress once the family began to respond to her in a more consistent manner. She learned to identify emotions within herself and then, in turn, try to think about how she should behave, rather than simply act out defensively. Learning to express herself emotionally was a difficult process for Jackie: for example, phrases such as "I need . . ." and "That hurts" virtually stuck in her throat. Consequently, she would assume a belligerent posture that caused her to be completely misunderstood. To Jackie, showing another person her emotional needs meant that this person had power over her and could hurt her with the knowledge.

Another significant issue in Jackie's treatment was that she felt marked by the abuse. She believed that people could tell she had been molested just by looking at her. This feeling kept her from dating or trying to make herself attractive; since she already felt "soiled," she was sure that no boy would want her. The therapist thought that some work in a girls' group would be a useful process to help Jackie work through some of her fear of being stigmatized. (Jackie often said that because of what happened to her, she felt like "a real freak.") When the therapist discussed the idea with the person who was conducting the group, it appeared that Jackie might fit in well. The group had four members at the time, and two were also victims of the man who had molested Jackie. When the clinician suggested this group to Jackie, she was quite taken with the idea and was particularly fascinated by the notion of talking with the other girls who had been abused by the same man as she.

Later, Jackie admitted that the thought of meeting with a group of strangers had been a bit frightening. Even so, the experience turned out to be extremely helpful to her. She was able to realize that she was not the only young girl who struggled with certain issues. Something else transpired in the group that, ultimately, helped her relationship with her parents immeasurably. Jackie learned that when two of the girls in the group—one of them a victim of the same man as she—

had tried to tell their parents about being molested, the parents had not believed them. When Jackie heard that, she acted out against her parents in a way that typified her conflicts about attachment, dependency, and intimacy.

On the following weekend was her mother's birthday. An expensive dinner was planned for this occasion at an elegant restaurant. Jackie had never revealed to either parent the details of what the molester had actually done to her. She decided that this dinner was the ideal time to do so and started to tell her mother the horrible details. Her mother responded by saying, "For God's sake, I don't want to hear about that now." Naturally, a big scene ensued. Jackie stormed out of the restaurant, leaving her mother in tears. The therapist received two phone calls, one from a wounded Jackie who argued that she had finally tried to share what had happened with her mother and her mother had cruelly rejected her; the second call came from Corinne, who said that Jackie had intentionally tried to ruin her birthday party. The therapist, knowing that neither of these accounts accurately reflected what transpired, suggested some joint mother-daughter sessions. During these sessions, she helped Jackie and her mother gain an understanding of what had happened at the dinner. Jackie had wanted to tell her parents about what had been done to her for a long time but was afraid of exposing herself emotionally and causing her mother to reject her. So, unconsciously, she chose a totally inappropriate time and a public place with friends and relatives present, thus ensuring that her mother would respond negatively. Then Jackie could assume her angry, self-protective posture and storm out of the restaurant.

Once Corinne realized that what had transpired in the restaurant was not an attack but the defensive maneuvers of a frightened adolescent, she responded in a very appropriate and nurturing manner. Even then, Jackie went through considerable struggle before she could permit herself to be emotionally vulnerable to her mother without lashing out at her.

After this incident, Jackie's therapy proceeded quite well. By the time she was in the second semester of her senior year in high school, the clinician had been meeting with her only once a month and was preparing to end therapy when Jackie began to act out once more. She began to have temper tantrums at home; one day she hit her sister when the sister made a negative comment about her. Jackie also started cutting school again and, despite the fact that her grades were now Bs and she had been accepted for admission to a local junior college, she began to refuse to do her homework, claiming that school was just for stupid jerks. Besides, everything her parents said was "stupid," "dumb," or "wrong." The parents became panicked, seeing all the girl's progress begin to unravel.

The therapist realized that Jackie's sudden burst of acting out was being caused by her fear of graduating from high school, where she had just learned to feel secure and confident. Unconsciously, rather than face the risk of a new social environment—namely, college— Jackie was setting herself up to fail in her senior year so that she could remain in a familiar, comfortable environment. To resolve this transitional crisis, the clinician began to see Jackie weekly again and to meet more regularly with her anxious parents. During these sessions she confronted the girl with how she perceived her current behavior. The therapist also tried to help Jackie feel more confident about the social and emotional gains she had already made. In addition, she assured Jackie that the end of regular therapy sessions did not mean that she could not come back to see her if she had a problem in the future. The therapist continued to see Jackie until she had successfully completed high school and had been enrolled in college for half a semester.

Adolescence is a turbulent time of life when a young person is learning to "push limits" in an effort to begin the process of separating from his or her parents and set forth on the path to selfhood. Those who become the victims of sexual assault at this critical stage of development may become thwarted in fulfilling this quest. As a consequence, the treatment of an adolescent victim consists in helping her to resume the healthy developmental tasks of identity-formation and individuation. The therapist tries to sustain the delicate balance in an adolescent's struggle to replace the thoughts and feelings of a child with those of an adult. Another balance is fostered between the adolescent's need to depend upon her family versus her need to become an independent person. These tasks, when performed to the best of the therapist's ability, can be rich in intrinsic challenges and rewards.

REFERENCES

Browne, A., & Finkelhor, D. Impact of child sexual abuse: A review of the research. *Psychological Bulletin, 99*(1), 66–77, 1986.

Burgess, A. W., & Holmstrom, L. L. Complicating factors in rape: Adolescent case illustrations. In A. W. Burgess, A. N. Groth, L. L. Holmstrom, & S. M. Sgroi (Eds.), *Sexual assault of children and adolescents.* Lexington, MA: Lexington Books, 1978.

Everstine, D. S., & Everstine, L. *People in crisis.* New York: Brunner/Mazel, 1983.

Everstine, L., & Everstine, D. S. *Psychotherapy and the law.* Orlando: Grune & Stratton, 1986.

Hilberman, E. *The rape victim*. New York: Basic Books, 1976.

Lindemann, E. Symptomatology and management of acute grief. *American Journal of Psychiatry, 101,* 141–148, 1944.

Peters, J. J. Children who are victims of sexual assault and the psychology of offenders. *American Journal of Psychiatry, 30,* 398–421, 1976.

Yates, A. Psychological damage associated with extreme eroticism in young children. *Psychiatric Annals, 17*(4), 257–261, 1987.

5

Incest

The work of Mara Selvini Palazzoli's group in Milan has taught us that a paradox occurs when the logic of relationships is cancelled, i.e., when someone is asked to play two or three incompatible roles at once (1984). A child or adolescent who is caught in an incestuous family system is immersed in such a paradox because he or she must be a child, a "lover" to his or her parent, and a "parent" to the sexually uninvolved parent. In the incestuous paradox, time is also suspended for a child because it is at once halted and accelerated. The child is thrust into a complex sexual relationship beyond his or her years, which accelerates time; but this, in turn, has the effect of stopping time for the child, because the relationship is so overpowering that it arrests some of the significant aspects of personality development.

Incest was once thought to be a rare and bizarre form of human behavior. Weinberg, writing in 1955, expressed the common view in this way:

> Incest, the universal crime, violates a taboo that is as forceful among primitives as among sophisticated moderns. . . . It is the recourse of very disturbed and very perverse persons. . . . Despite the social force of the . . . taboo, incest occurs, however rarely, in all Western societies. (pp. 3, 34)

Currently, behavioral scientists regard this view as being far from the truth. There are tens of thousands of incest victims each year; they come from every socioeconomic group and culture. Although incestuous thoughts, fantasies, and impulses are part of the normal developmental process of every person, society bans even discussion of the subject. That reluctance to discuss the subject only serves to isolate or silence children who are at risk, and prevents the actual victims of incest from being able to ask for the protection they so desperately need. The authors prefer to be guided by the approach of Anna Freud, who wrote:

> Far from existing only as a phantasy, incest is [thus] also a fact, more widespread among the population in certain periods than in others. Where the chances of harming a child's normal developmental growth are concerned, it ranks higher than abandonment, neglect, physical maltreatment or any other form of abuse. It would be a fatal mistake to underrate either the importance or the frequency of its actual occurrence. (1981, p. 34)

This chapter reviews research and theoretical work pertaining to incest, describes the evolution of the most common types of incestuous family systems, and discusses some factors that may be helpful in assessing these families, including the issue of false accusations. The chapter concludes with a discussion of the treatment of the incestuous family.

Our subject here is principally the phenomenon of father-daughter incest. As defined in our Preface (p. vii), we include in this category incest by any person who takes the role of father in the child's life (e.g., stepfather, mother's live-in boyfriend, foster father, custodial grandfather). We believe it vital that one consider the nature of the relationship that the person who commits incest has with the child victim. For instance, one should not assume that incest committed by a stepparent or parent figure is any less traumatic than incest committed by the child's biological parent; and one should measure carefully the significance of the parenting role that the person played in the victim's life.

We are well aware that incest is often committed by brothers or uncles or male cousins of a young girl, but we are concentrating our attention on fathers and father-figures in order to provide a clear focus for the discussion.

THE INCEST TABOO

Even though incestuous thoughts and impulses dwell in the fantasy realm of all adults and children, when they depart from this realm and enter the real life of a child, the result can be tragic. The incest taboo, being virtually universal, draws its strength from sound biological, sociological, and psychological reasons. The taboo, so powerful that it is unspoken, serves to protect family structure and promote the healthy development of the human species. Although there are some exceptions to this taboo, they are very rare, and when permitted are rigidly restricted to royalty or specific religious rituals (Meiselman, 1978, p. 3). The very few cultures that do permit incest in specific situations strictly condemn and punish incestuous behavior that occurs beyond the context of the prescribed instances, and the majority of these cultures only permit incestuous relationships between brother and sister. In general, even the most primitive societies forbid incestuous unions within the nuclear family (Murdock, 1949).

Many theories exist concerning the origins and reasons for the incest taboo. Freud's attempt (1913) to invoke a theory of the "primal herd" never gained wide approval, and Freud himself was not pleased with this rationale for the incest taboo. Freud described a "primal herd" ruled by a harsh and tyrannical father who forbade his sons access to the women of the herd. Because of the father's tyranny, the sons united to destroy him; in a cannibalistic ritual, they devoured him. Yet because the sons also loved their father, they were afterward overcome with grief. Then they realized they would be in competition with each other for the women. In order to resolve this conflict, the sons created the incest taboo and promised to practice exogamy. Today, few believe that this allegory successfully serves to explain the purposes or functions of the incest taboo.

The anthropologist Malinowski (1927) put forth a theory which attempted to explain the taboo in terms of the structure of the family system. Malinowski maintained that incestuous relations would confuse roles within the family. Because of the intense feelings that are caused by sexual relations, the necessary balance of power within the family would disintegrate in such a way that the family would no longer be able to function as a socioeconomic system.

To the sociological, anthropological, and psychological evidence supporting the significance of an incest taboo can be added strong biological evidence. Meiselman (1978) summarized some of the biological research that has been done on nuclear family incest. For example, a study that revealed sound biological reasons for the incest taboo was that of Seemanova (1971) in Czechoslovakia. In this study, 161 children resulting from nuclear family incest were studied for an eight-year period. The children of incest were contrasted with a control group of their half siblings who were not the offspring of an incestuous union. Twenty-five percent of the children born of incest were found to be moderately or severely retarded, by contrast with no retardation in the control group. Twenty percent of the children of incest were found to have congenital malformations or serious physical abnormalities. Only 43% of the children of incest were considered to be normal, as opposed to 89% in the control group.

In short, the incest taboo has sound sociological, biological, and psychological justification. It protects the structure and function of the family system, it promotes the psychosexual development of children, and it safeguards the healthy evolution of the species.

THE INCESTUOUS FAMILY SYSTEM

The incestuous family system evolves in essentially three ways. First, one may find incest occurring in undersocialized aggressive family systems, such as those found in some remote rural areas like Appalachia. In these families, the pattern of incest is likely to have been going on for several generations and may be established as a "normal" part of life. Often the incestuous behavior occurs not only between father and daughter, but also between siblings.* In fact, the father may introduce a son to incestuous sexual relations with a sister or with his mother (Cooper & Cormier, 1982; Raphling, Carpenter, & Davis, 1967). Such a family could be described as a "polymorphous" incestuous family.

In a second type of incestuous family system, the parent or parents in the system may themselves have been victims of incest (Cooper & Cormier, 1982; Everstine & Everstine, 1983) and may be repeating what happened to them by acting out against their own child. Once the incest taboo has been broken, it is easier for subsequent generations to breach it (Meiselman, 1978; Raphling, Carpenter, & Davis, 1967) because it is no longer an unthinkable act. Parents of this kind attempt to resolve their own conflicts from childhood incestuous experiences through the experience of the child. In some cases, a parent has figuratively recreated the incest experience by reexposing a child to the *same person* who had an incestuous relationship with him or her (the parent). In other cases, the parent may select a mate who had similar

---

* Consensual incest between siblings, even though usually not as traumatic as parent-child incest, can have profound effects upon the participants' future lives. Sibling incest occurs most often in families which can best be described as emotionally impoverished. The parents are often not nurturing or affectionate toward their children, and so the children turn to each other for satisfaction of these needs. An incestuous relationship can have the effect of blocking these children's abilities to establish love relationships other than this forbidden relationship. And when a love object is found within the family, especially when the object is age-appropriate and nurturing, a child often finds it very difficult to move beyond this arrested stage.

characteristics to the family member who committed the earlier incest, so that this person would recreate the incest with a child of the subsequent union.

A third form of incestuous system has its origins in the relationship that the mother in this incestuous family system had with her own parents—the incest victim's maternal grandparents. Her relationship with her own mother (the child's grandmother) could best be described as a "Cinderella" type of relationship, in which she desperately attempted to please a mother who was impossible to please. She was emotionally starved, and as a result she constantly strove to please her mother to gain her love. But, sadly, the love she was constantly reaching for was always just beyond her reach, because one of the ways in which the mother controlled her daughter was by withholding love and approval. Some of these mothers of "Cinderellas" are schizoid persons or chronic schizophrenics.

In many cases of this type, the woman's father (victim's grandfather) was emotionally unavailable to her as well; i.e., he may not have been involved or concerned with the emotional needs of his daughter. Perhaps he was preoccupied with his professional career, was only interested in male children, or may simply have been an uncaring, unreliable father. On the other hand, there could have been the total absence of a father in this woman's family of origin. If so, her early experiences with male–female relationships may have come from her interactions with the various men in her mother's life.

It is from the frustrations and longings of such a childhood that the initial seeds of a future incestuous family system are planted. Because of the nature of her relationship with her own mother, the "Cinderella" woman has an internal definition of the mother–daughter relationship as one in which *the daughter serves the needs of the mother*. What it means is that she has managed to get the relationship between mother and daughter fundamentally reversed, a concept that will become a "ruling fiction" when she becomes a mother herself.

Because of her emotionally impoverished childhood, this woman's desires and expectations for marriage envisage a relationship in which she will receive the unconditional love and nurturance that she was denied as a child. The tragic sequel is that she chooses a mate who may superficially appear to meet her needs, but who is fundamentally similar to her father or father substitute. The man she marries, chosen by misunderstood urges, proves incapable of satisfying her striving for dependency. Hence, when a daughter is born, these unmet dependency needs emerge.

By marrying, the woman had unconsciously hoped that her desire for unquestioning love and nurturance would be met by her husband. When she sees the daughter cast in the dependent, nurtured-child role, by a tragic paradox she begins to envy her own child's place in the family system. With time, she will move toward changing places with the daughter within the family structure. She may leave the girl un-attended with her husband for long periods of time; she may insist that the husband perform child-care activities requiring that he touch the girl (e.g., bathing her or showering together). In the more extreme cases, mothers have actively encouraged incestuous relationships be-tween father and daughter.

The evolution of an incestuous family system can be seen as one in which the traditional generational boundary lines change in relation to one or more of the children (see Figure 2). A predisposing factor, as mentioned above, may be that one or both parents were victims of incest in their families of origin. Or, the rotation of the generational boundary line may have its prologue in the mother's relationship with her own mother, which leads to her changing places with her daughter.

The Mother in an Incestuous Family System

The scenario of the mother in an incestuous family system may read as follows. Very likely she has romanticized ideas concerning what "being married" is like. She may have thought that she married someone who was "safe," according to the model of her fantasized "father–husband." This image of a man who is both idolized father and romanticized husband is, in many cases, projected upon a man who is far from either.

Denial is often the primary defense mechanism (Everstine & Everstine, 1983; Kaufmann, Peck & Tagiuri, 1954; Meiselman, 1978; Machotka, Pittman, & Flomenhaft, 1967; Weiner, 1962). It protects the mother initially from seeing the less-than-ideal aspects of the man she marries, and later serves to help her miss seeing the abuse that her child is suffering. She may be extremely inhibited sexually or nonorgasmic. This sexual dysfunction may be a result of her infantile personality or sexual traumatization by her own father. In either case, sexual relations between the parents have probably ceased for a considerable period of time prior to the beginning of the actual incestuous relationship between father and daughter (Everstine & Everstine, 1983; Lustig et al., 1966; Maisch, 1972; Weiner, 1962).

NORMAL FAMILY

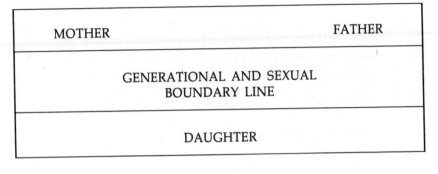

MOTHER	FATHER
GENERATIONAL AND SEXUAL BOUNDARY LINE	
DAUGHTER	

TRANSITIONAL PHASE

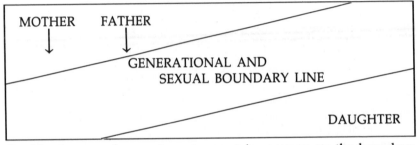

MOTHER   FATHER
↓   ↓

GENERATIONAL AND
SEXUAL BOUNDARY LINE

DAUGHTER

(In this phase, each parent exerts a certain pressure on the boundary, in an attempt to change its position.)

FAMILY IN WHICH INCESTUOUS THREATS OR ACTS ARE OCCURRING

MOTHER	GENERATIONAL AND SEXUAL BOUNDARY LINE	FATHER
		DAUGHTER

Figure 2. Adapted from Everstine, D. S., & Everstine, L. *People in crisis.* New York: Brunner/Mazel, 1983, p. 150.

Because the mother's original expectation of finding a "husband-father" were sadly unrealized, the marriage has become a disappointment to her or, at best, it has become a "truce" relationship. The sexual demands, dirty dishes, and responsibilities of motherhood have dashed the dreams born of her emotionally impoverished childhood. The denial that she relies upon as a defense is very important to the internal functioning of this kind of family system (as in other abusive family systems), because it serves to blind parents to what they are doing to their children. In fact, such a mother is frequently nonsupportive of her victim–daughter (Everstine & Everstine, 1983; Kaufmann, Peck, & Tagiuri, 1954; Meiselman, 1978), and her denial of this nonsupport is particularly difficult to break through, because its origins are so primitive.

The Father in an Incestuous Family System

The father in an incestuous family system may, as noted earlier, have been a victim of incest himself. He may have witnessed incestuous acts by his father; or he could have come from a family in which other types of incestuous behavior took place. The probability is high that he is alcoholic. He may be the sort of person who is capable of presenting a fairly "normal" exterior when sober, but who becomes quite primitive when he consumes some form of intoxicant. This father may well be a self-involved man who is not able to fulfill the emotional needs of his family. Outwardly, he may appear to be quite competent professionally and socially. Even though many of these fathers function adequately in their professional lives, their emotional and social abilities are quite limited and superficial. Many are controlling, dominant figures; but beneath this dominant facade dwells a personality fraught with paranoiac fears and sexual obsessions. Some of these fathers are openly obsessed with sexual concerns (Cooper & Cormier, 1982; Gebhard et al., 1965; Raphling, Carpenter, & Davis, 1967); but even though they are overtly sexual, many are neither sexually knowledgeable nor sexually adept. The incestuous father's reaction to the wife's rejection of her adult sexual role with him is usually self-centered, hostile, and confused. He may not be able to recognize his anger toward his wife. The incestuous father (and for that matter the entire family) may outwardly profess great mutual respect and love.

An example of a father's thinly veiled rage and sadistic manipulation of his family was a case in which the father spoke of great love for his three daughters and concern for their normal sexual development. According to this father, he was determined that his daughters would grow up to be healthy sexually. So to ensure their "healthy sexual development," he decided that he should be the one to introduce them to the pleasures of sex. He began having sexual relationships with each daughter when she was between the ages of 10 and 11. He told each girl that he was introducing her to sex because he loved her and that he would continue to have sex with her until she proved that she was sexually healthy by having regular orgasms. Each daughter, in turn, was totally trapped in her terror and her guilt by this father.

Clinicians need to be wary about the concern for the family that often is professed by the father in an incestuous family system. Protecting home and family against "destruction" is a frequent theme with these fathers. And beneath this veneer of concern for the integrity and security of the family may lie tremendous anger, mistrust, and shame. Consider that, when a father chooses one of his children for an extramarital partner, he is selecting the very partner who will be the most catastrophic for the maintenance of the family system.

Another product of this emphasis upon loyalty and love of family is that it places a tremendous burden of responsibility—and frequently the guilt for the incest—onto the sexually involved child. If she allows the secret to escape the family, it will be her fault if the family is "destroyed." Moreover, even if the secret is never allowed to escape the family, this kind of family myth nonetheless shifts the focus of blame from the incestuous parent to his daughter.

THE CHILD AS VICTIM

The child in an incestuous family system is a truly tragic figure and a victim in every sense of the word. As Yates (1982) so aptly put it, "They are the victims because they have neither the responsibility nor the capacity to participate in the decision-making process. Even in the unusual cases of the experienced seductive child who approaches an inexperienced reluctant adult, it is the adult's responsibility to decline the invitation" (p. 482).

It is particularly shameful, in our view, that some children and adolescents are doubly victimized by those in the helping professions who are supposed to protect them. Portions of the literature concerning the victims of incest are unfortunately reminiscent of the misguided writings of 20 or 25 years ago on the subject of rape, which shifted the responsibility for rape from the rapist to the rape victim. By alluding to the rape victim's behavior as passive or seductive, certain authors totally avoided dealing with the pain and horror that the victim was suffering. Figuratively, these victims were subjected to further assault, namely, what Symonds (1980) referred to as "secondary assault," by members of the helping professions.

Authors on the subject of incest such as Rosenfeld, Nadelson, and Krieger (1979) and Henderson (1972) made similar errors when they placed too much clinical attention on the child's seductive or complicit behavior, possibly leading their readers to suspect that children bring on their own victimization and conspire with the incestuous parent to continue the relationship. A foundation for erroneous conclusions of this sort was laid by the research of Bender and Blau (1937) on children's "sexual relations with adults." The sample that was studied consisted of only 16 children, certainly not enough cases to make sweeping generalizations to the population of child victims. The sample selection of mixed ages and various types of sexual assault included no victims of incest and lacked any control group. Sadly, Bender and Blau's research probably best serves the cause of defense attorneys who wish to absolve their client of guilt by blaming the client's behavior on the child. We believe that this research should be laid to rest among other antiques, such as Wilhelm Fliess's notion that nasal disorders were the cause of neurosis.

It is true that some incest victims are seductive, but if a therapist allows himself or herself to be deluded by this behavior, he or she will never grasp what lies behind it. Behavior of this kind is properly seen as a symptom. Moreover, directing attention to seductive behavior and a child's enjoyment of the sexual relationship can also serve to protect the clinician, because a clinician can focus on the child's "secondary gains" and not face the pathological nature of the child's family system. Certainly, many incest victims derive considerable secondary gains from participating in an incestuous relationship, such as affection, attention, and special privileges. But one must ask: Are these children freely participating in the relationship, or are they bargaining with sexual favors for the affection, attention, and sense of being important that children should have by birthright?

It is true that children are sexual, but they are not sexual in an adult, genital way. A child's sexuality is primitive, autoerotic, and exploratory. Yet precisely because a child's sexuality is primitive and in the process of developing, the child can be taught to enjoy many forms of sexual contact (as noted in Chapters 2 and 3), even those that are beyond his or her normal developmental level. This is particularly true when a child is already affection-starved, as is the case in many incestuous family systems (deYoung, 1982; Everstine & Everstine, 1983; Peters, 1976; Sgroi, 1979; Yates, 1982). Children have an enormous need for adult closeness and nurturance, and frequently they pay a tragic price for it.

One should not forget that it is adults who initiate children into, and define for them, the fantasy we refer to as "reality." From an early age, the adults in a family system ascribe a role or roles to each child; they also provide children with mental maps or blueprints of their world. These maps clearly delineate what a child must see or not see, believe or not believe, in order to function within the family system. One cannot ignore how small a child's world is and how much power adults have over this ever-evolving world. The parents of an incest victim exercise this power to mold the reality and self-definition of the child in such a way that he or she has no choice but to become oriented to adult sex. DeYoung (1982) described quite clearly the quandary in which a child is placed by the parents in an incestuous system, and how it is resolved by assuming a seductive identity, when she wrote:

> Since young children are dependent on their parents for definitions of both reality and morality, many enter incestuous relationships willingly, and, when they later realize that this behavior is both illegal and morally repugnant to others, they already may have been inextricably bound to that relationship for years.

> The child may then give herself or himself a new identity of harlot or whore—an identity that may be reinforced by the deviance disavowal techniques of the incestuous parent. A self-fulfilling prophecy then may ensue, in which the child engages actively in a behavior, in this case incest, which is commensurate with her or his new identity. By doing so, the child reduces any cognitive dissonance which could produce overwhelming anxiety during the incestuous relationship and essentially frees her and himself from the burdensome responsibility of terminating the incestuous relationship or of disclosing it to someone else. (p. 58)

Hence, these children are *taught* to be what they are. It is the family dynamics—in particular, the role-reversal of daughter and mother—that create pathological behavior on the part of a child (deYoung, 1982; Everstine & Everstine, 1983; Furniss, 1984; Maisch, 1972; Meiselman, 1978).

When a child passively accepts or actively participates in a parent's incestuous behavior, one need only investigate the dynamics of the family system to explain this behavior on the child's part. As a starting point, one will note that the system gives a child no real alternative to acceptance of the incest relationship. A lack of role models will be conspicuous, as well as the absence of someone to protect her. In this context, it is not surprising that many incestuous relationships continue for years. Another reason why a child may participate passively in an incest relationship is his or her fear of separation and loss. Many of these children have already experienced separation or loss (deYoung, 1982; Finkelhor, 1979) and are particularly vulnerable to the threat of additional family disruption; hence, they may comply with the incest if they believe that by doing so they are keeping the family together.

The victims of incest confuse some fundamental issues with regard to relationships. Above all, many are unable to discriminate between erotic forms of contact and those which are simply affectionate or friendly (Yates, 1982, 1987a). They tend to sexualize most close relationships, either as a form of testing in order to determine whether the person is safe, or because they know no other way to establish a relationship or be close to someone. Some, unfortunately, have learned that they must pay for the affection to be found in relationships with sexual favors.

This problem of not being able properly to discriminate what is and is not appropriate and to sexualize relationships is further complicated when a child possesses inadequate social skills. Superficially, the child may appear to be socially mature far beyond her years, but this maturity is more shadow than substance. As noted earlier, the child's parental role modeling is likely to be inadequate.

And the incestuous relationship tends to consume so much of a child's or adolescent's emotional energy that it interferes with social development. Yates (1982) put it this way: "The highly cathected focus on sexual learning seems to detract from social learning and a more even distribution of libido" (p. 483). Frequently, many such children are believed capable of grasping the full social significance of what they say or do, when in point of fact they cannot. Examples of this range from that of the five-year-old incest victim who explained to one of the authors with great animation, "I suck my daddy's cock and it tastes so good," to an adolescent prostitute, the victim of incest until she ran away from home at the age of 14, who described her sexual exploits coldly and in explicit detail.

Therapists who work with child victims of incest should be prepared for such behavior, and shocking as it may be, should not allow it to sidetrack them from the more fundamental issues that the children are struggling with. Of course, the clinician will attempt to teach them to control such behavior, because it will only lead to other forms of abuse and social rejection, with cruel accompanying labels such as "tramp" or "seductive child." Our experience with incest victims is consistent with that of Yates (1982), who found that "the degree of eroticization seems closely related to the intensity and duration of the incestuous union" (p. 842).

Whenever a clinician learns of this type of promiscuous or sexually aggressive behavior on the part of a young person (especially on the part of a preadolescent child), it would be wise to look into its origins. One should be equally concerned about a child who demonstrates a difficulty in attaching to others, or in allowing people to get close without being seductive toward them.

Another issue that complicates the case of many incest victims is the difference between anger and sexual feelings, as when being hurt and having sex have become confused. By contrast, the following thoughts are more typical of healthy development: "Sex and affection and being close feel good; but when I am hurt or feel angry or fearful I may not want to be close to you." But, in many cases of incest, the reasoning becomes, "I was close to my father and he used me sexually; I feel impossibly confused, anxious, and angry." We have found that as a result of this contradiction of normal ways of thinking, many child and adolescent victims of incest act out in a promiscuous manner, particularly when they are anxious or depressed.

It is well known that much of the foundation for future relationships has its source in the form and structure of the relationship between parent and child. From this original bond of trust—"my parents will protect me"—comes the ability to create friendship and love. Hence, a fundamental psychological building block is damaged or destroyed by incest, and from this some of the most serious emotional problems may arise. The cause is not exclusively the incestuous sexual union, but what that union does to the basic and very precious trust relationships between parent and child and within the family system. And because one's self-image is first created and given definition in a family context, in turn this betrayal of trust leads the child or adolescent to a deficit of self-worth.

LONG-TERM EFFECTS

In our experience, most incest victims have considerable difficulty in establishing healthy trust relationships later in life. Many cannot or will not keep close friends as a result of the experience. As soon as someone begins to become intimate with them, they will either avoid or end the friendship. On the other hand, they sexualize, often quite inappropriately, the relationship and drive away a potential source of help. If something happens to the woman that is anxiety-producing (e.g., being hurt by someone), some resolve the conflict by promiscuous acting out or by self-destructive behavior, much in the same way that, as a girl, she may have resolved the original conflict by assuming the role of "whore." In this way, a pathetic life script can be written that will be enacted long after the original abuse.

Another way in which a damaged parent–child relationship may affect the future direction of a child's life is when she compulsively chooses a mate who will abuse her or her children, as the morbid cycle repeats itself. Or, the victim may form a dependent bond with either or both parents and simply never leave home. Another victim might utilize obsessive–compulsive defense mechanisms that allow her to encapsulate the incestuous trauma. She might adopt an asexual or homosexual lifestyle, as a method of coping with the original incestuous conflict, designed to protect her from the source of trauma in possible future sexual contacts. It is sad that these quiet victims who do not act out are rarely recognized for the victims that they are.

A question is often raised concerning why many victims of incest develop character disorders. We believe that at least part of the answer lies with the incest taboo itself. In a sense, this is the most powerful of societal proscriptions, more powerful than the taboo against murder. One can discuss an urge to murder in most social situations but, should someone bring up the subject of incest in even the most liberal of social environments, the atmosphere will immediately become chill—because incest is an unthinkable, unspeakable deed. When a child or adolescent realizes that she has been involved in the most reprehensible of deeds, other prohibited acts pale in its shadow.

Other reasons why these children develop character disorders can be found in the structure of the incestuous family system. These systems are similar to schizophrenic family systems in that they define a child's identity by function. In a schizophrenic system, the function of the child in question is to be crazy; by contrast, in an incestuous family system, the child's function is that of a person who is *used* as a sexual object. Hence, the child learns, on a very fundamental level within the system, that people can use other people even to do unthinkable things. The "framing" (construction) of this child's world view usually begins to occur at such an early stage of moral development that he or she does not possess an alternative model for defining the meaning of relationships. So, the dominant theme taught by the family system is, "You can use people for your needs even if the needs are forbidden." Considering the type of role models that are available to these children within such a system, as well as the retardation of appropriate social learning that is caused by their prolonged sexual overstimulation, one can plainly see why many of them develop as they do.

THE ISSUE OF FALSE ACCUSATIONS

The treatment of an incestuous family must take into consideration the validity of the child's accusation. Yet clinicians should bear in mind that, except in situations in which they are appointed by a court, it is not their function to determine the validity of children's claims. The claim should be reported to the proper authorities in a manner which is consistent with the child abuse reporting laws where the clinician practices (see Chapter 8). Then the therapist should permit the person who is appointed to determine the truth or falsity of the accusation. In our view, the dual role of therapist and evaluator is one that the wise clinician will decline.

All too often an unsubstantiated claim of incest has been simply dismissed as an "incest fantasy," the tale of a disturbed child, or the accusation of a child who is caught up in an angry divorce. There is considerable clinical evidence that most accusations of incest, particularly by young children, are true (Bresee, et al., 1986; Cowie, Cowie, & Slater, 1968; Everstine & Everstine, 1983; Faller, 1984; Finkelhor, 1984; Green, 1986; Peters, 1976; Yates, 1987a). Whether a child makes a veiled suggestion of incest or a direct accusation, it should be taken very seriously. It has been our experience (see also Yates, 1987b) that when children are asked about significant events in their lives they are usually accurate reporters of information. If the story turns out to be untrue, the child may be suffering from serious psychological problems.* Or, a child may merely be trying to extricate himself or herself from a family situation in which he or she feels trapped and desperate.

An example would be that of the child who is trying to rid himself or herself of a new stepparent who is viewed as an emotional threat. Another situation in which a false accusation of incest may occur is in the course of divorce proceedings. A clinician needs to proceed with *extreme caution* in such volatile situations and not jump to conclusions despite how things may appear superficially. For example, if the child is no longer living with the accused parent, he or she may make a false report of incest in order to please the other parent. In fact, a particularly dependent child could be "brainwashed" into making such

---

* In the case of a severely disturbed child or adolescent who reports incest, a thorough psychological assessment, including psychological testing, will usually reveal whether or not the young person is capable of adequate reality testing.

a report (Green, 1986). These and other "secondary gains" could motivate false reporting.*

A general rule, mentioned above, that the younger the child the more likely his or her report of incest is to be true may not strictly apply in this context. In divorce cases, a therapist should consider that the younger a child is, the more emotionally dependent he or she is on a parent, and thus may be more vulnerable to the manipulations of a vengeful marital combatant. One should not underestimate how torn and terrified some children are by divorce. Many do desperate things to placate one of the parents whose presence and love they are fearful of losing.

A Case Example

The following case illustrates how a child can get caught up in an angry divorce and subsequent custody battle. The marriage of Valerie and Mike was troubled from the beginning. In retrospect, Mike realized that he married Valerie because he felt sorry for her. Valerie left home at 16 because her father, an alcoholic, had abused her physically and sexually. When Mike met her, she had a job and was struggling to finish college. They had been dating only a short time when Valerie announced that she was pregnant. Although Mike had some misgivings about marrying her because of her chaotic lifestyle, he thought that marriage and a child would give her the stability she needed; if he was patient, she would settle down. The marriage was embattled from its inception: it seemed that living together tended to amplify differences rather than ameliorate them. Mike and Valerie had totally different views on child raising. She, because of her abusive background, was extremely permissive, while Mike had stricter standards. He believed that rules, limits, and structure were good for children.

After they had been married two-and-a-half years, Mike had a brief affair with a woman he knew at his job. The affair troubled Mike because, fundamentally, he didn't believe in extramarital relationships; he knew that the marriage would be endangered. He went to see a psychotherapist because he felt that he needed help in sorting things out and deciding what he should do. After about six months of therapy, he realized that he was only staying in the marriage for their daughter Christina's sake, and that his relationship with Valerie had gone from

---

* The clinician may wish to consider that a child could be describing something that was seen in a pornographic videotape or magazine. We have found (as has Yates, 1987a) that while children's fantasies may be powerfully stimulated by such an experience, few children act out sexually as a result of it.

bad to worse. Mike decided to ask Valerie for a divorce, and to tell her about the affair because the secret still bothered him. The therapist suggested that it might not be wise to tell Valerie about the affair, because it had long since ended, and because telling her might serve only to hurt and enrage an already vulnerable woman. Despite this advice, Mike felt that he had to tell Valerie everything in order to make an honest, "clean" ending.

A very angry divorce ensued. Valerie believed that she had been wronged and set forth to avenge herself in every way possible. At first, she would not admit Mike to the house to get any of his belongings, spent money lavishly, and even refused to allow Mike to see Christina (now three). Valerie claimed that she had a right to keep him out of the house and to spend money as she wished; she said that Mike was morally unfit to see his daughter. A long and bitter legal battle began. Eventually, Valerie was awarded a reasonable property settlement and Mike was awarded joint custody of Christina, who was to spend alternate weeks with each parent.

Valerie fought this coparenting arrangement from the start, claiming that she and Christina could not bear to be apart from each other. She would find every possible excuse not to allow Mike to see the girl. Frequently, when he came to pick up his daughter, he was confronted by Valerie crying and holding a sobbing Christina. Valerie would say things such as "Mommy knows you don't want to go." This joint custody arrangement, although fraught with difficulties, continued for more than a year. Valerie repeatedly alleged that Christina did not want to see her father and that Mike was an unfit parent.

During this period, Mike began to date again and eventually began to see a woman named Nicole who had two young children, ages four and six. Mike was enthusiastic about the relationship because he and Nicole had a lot in common. He believed her to be a good parent, and thought Christina (now four) would enjoy having Nicole's son and daughter as playmates. Thinking he was doing the right thing, Mike made a point of bringing Nicole and her two children with him when he would pick up Christina. He wanted Valerie to know who Nicole was, in case Christina should mention her name.

Suddenly one day, Mike learned that Valerie and a therapist had reported Mike and Nicole to the police for sexually abusing Christina and exposing her to cocaine use. According to Valerie and the therapist, Christina had demonstrated—with anatomically accurate dolls and anatomically explicit drawings—how her daddy and Nicole touched her "wee-wee," which hurt as a result; also, that Mike and Nicole had gotten mad at her when she played with their special white powder.

Finally, Christina allegedly had said that Nicole's children were mean and had beaten her up. Mike's visitation rights were immediately suspended and a police investigation of the sexual abuse and drug charges began.

A woman detective interviewed Christina on two occasions, but Christina did not make any clear accusation of sexual abuse during these interviews. Then Mike voluntarily took a polygraph test and passed it. As a result of these events, the criminal charges were dropped. Nevertheless, Valerie pressed forward in her attempt to obtain sole custody of the girl and to cancel Mike's visitation rights.

One of the authors was appointed by the court to do an evaluation and make recommendations for the court's decision in the custody case. Although Valerie resisted working with the psychologist as much as she could and continued to see her private therapist with Christina, an evaluation was conducted that included detailed taped interviews with both parents, Christina, and Nicole. A full battery of psychological tests, consisting of the MMPI, the Rorschach, the Thematic Apperception Test, a Sentence Completion Test, and the Draw-a-Person Test, was given to each adult involved, because of the seriousness of the charges. Also, the evaluator thought that testing could yield data about whether or not one of them posed a threat to Christina.

Christina was given the Rorschach, the Thematic Apperception Test (which we prefer to the Children's Apperception Test in evaluations of this kind because it can elicit more relevant information), and the Draw-a-Person Test. Christina was also engaged in play sessions that utilized dolls, puppets, and a doll house. During the doll-play sessions, the evaluator was extremely cautious not to lead Christina in any way. She asked open questions such as, "Tell me about when you stay at Daddy's house," and "Tell me about living at Mommy's house." Christina was allowed time to respond and then was asked for details and clarification. An effort was made by the evaluator to refrain from reinforcing Christina for responding in one way or another. It was felt that accurate information was vital and could only be obtained by remaining neutral and patient, working within the cognitive capabilities and attention span of this four-year-old.

The evaluator also chose not to utilize the anatomically accurate dolls or explicit drawings in this evaluation because the dolls and drawings, in and of themselves, can lead a child to thinking along sexual lines. Because children are accustomed to playing with dolls and seeing drawings of people that are genitally neutral, being brought to a professional's office and shown dolls or drawings with genitals sends a message to the child that this adult is interested in issues related to gender or sexuality. And, if a child is vulnerable already, or has been coached or pressured in some way, he or she may respond with sexual references purely to please an adult who is perceived as being powerful. Hence, in these evaluations we recommend that clinicians avoid using such devices, even though alternative methods may be time-consuming.

The evaluator spoke with Christina's pediatrician and her babysitter, and made a visit to each of the girl's residences; at Nicole's house, she met Nicole's children. In addition, she spoke on the telephone with the therapist who had made the initial report, and reviewed records of the treatment given. From this information, the following story began to unfold. Christina was caught in the middle of an unresolved divorce. Although mother was legally divorced from father, she was not divorced from him emotionally. The psychological tests and interviews revealed that Valerie was an hysterical personality who was projecting her own childhood abuse onto the current divorce experience. She was emotionally enmeshed with Christina, and whenever she let the girl go to Mike's house, she felt emotionally wounded. When Mike began a serious relationship with another woman, it became more than Valerie could bear; she grew to be convinced that all sorts of things were going on at Mike's place.

By contrast, the evaluation showed Mike to be a logical but idealistic person who used obsessive–compulsive defenses to protect himself from emotional pain. He was basically a well-intended man who could become overly self-involved and could be insensitive to the emotional needs of others. The evaluation did not show him to be an impulsive or naturally aggressive person; instead, when Mike acted out his anger he was more likely to do it in a passive-aggressive manner.

At first, Christina had made progress toward adapting to two single-parent homes, one strict and one permissive, where she was at least the center of attention. But when Nicole and her two children came into Christina's already troubled lifespace, it was too much for her because now not only did she have to share her father with Nicole, but she had to contend with two rival children. The fact that her father did not perceive the crisis that she was experiencing simply pushed the child further into fear and anger. She began to have tantrums and resist going to her father's home.

From Christina's pediatrician, the evaluator learned that the girl had had a very severe case of poison oak that summer. The rash was all over her arms and legs and the genital area. As a treatment for the poison oak, a lotion had to be applied several times a day to the parts of her body affected by the rash, including her genitals. The application of this medication turned out to be quite a problem because it was painful and Christina vigorously resisted it. For this reason, Nicole frequently helped Mike to apply the medication because it was such a chore. This explained what happened when Valerie took Christina to a therapist: apparently, when she heard Christina say that her daddy and Nicole had touched her "wee-wee," the therapist brought out the anatomically accurate dolls and asked Christina to show what they had done; then, of course, Christina demonstrated being touched on her "wee-wee."

This procedure had been conducted with Valerie present in the room (as, in fact, had all sessions with this therapist), and afterward Christina was praised by her mother and the therapist for being a brave girl and telling what Daddy had done. In effect, Christina was given a clear understanding of what she was supposed to do at this lady's office, namely say bad things about Daddy. The therapist did not inquire into the reason for Nicole and Daddy touching her genitals. Moreover, none of these sessions was audiotaped or videotaped, and no documentation of the sessions was made other than the therapist's notes. Later, the evaluator learned that the white powder Christina had played with at her father's house was the substance TSP, which Mike was using to clean the outer walls of his house prior to painting. When he found her playing with it, he had taken it away and scolded her for getting into it.

As the evaluation proceeded, it became clear that Christina had not been molested. In fact, her behavior during one evaluation session was quite revealing. Christina played pleasantly in the doll house for the better part of an hour; the theme of her play was things that she did at Daddy's house. When she met her mother in the waiting room later, she spontaneously said: "See, Mommy, I don't have to go to Daddy's house anymore." In sum, Christina gave the impression of being an oedipal-age girl who was in conflict about the new rivals in her life, and was suffering from the cumulative effects of her parents' protracted divorce struggle. Apparently, she had been led or encouraged by her mother and the therapist to make critical statements about her father. In general, the evaluation showed Christina to be a psychologically intact child who was responding emotionally to the trauma of divorce rather than the trauma of molestation.

The evaluator's final recommendations were that the father's joint custody be restored immediately and that there should be a court-appointed therapist for Christina, whom neither parent could dismiss. In addition, Mike should work with this therapist toward being more sensitive to Christina's needs. For her part, Valerie should begin in-

dividual therapy, in order to work through her unresolved issues from
the divorce, as well as from the abuse she experienced in childhood.

This case shows how a divorcing parent who projects his or her
malignant fantasies onto the other parent may actually draw an already
anxious or confused child into a delusional system. These manipulations
are made possible by the parent's withholding approval, thus increasing
the child's dependency needs. Frequently, a child is bombarded with
misinformation about the other parent and then subsequently interro-
gated by the accusing parent until forced to give in. A therapist needs
to be extremely cautious about how he or she proceeds in such cases,
because they can be extremely volatile; in fact, both parents can be
equally capable of destructive behavior in these situations.

There are cases in which actual incest may not have occurred, but
instead seductive or inappropriate sexual behavior has taken place. If
so, this will require clinical attention for its own sake. In the vast
majority of such cases, a careful clinical examination of the child and
the relevant adults will reveal what are the real issues. In our opinion,
a confrontation scene between an accused parent and an extremely
anxious, traumatized child, of the kind advocated by some clinicians,
rarely accomplishes anything except adding to the trauma already experienced. The same can be said for the suggestion by Green (1986)
that the child be interviewed with the accused parent present in order
to observe and evaluate their interaction. The latter would amount to
a confrontation in veiled form, and it is not likely that a seriously
traumatized child would have the emotional strength to endure it.

Most children are sensitive enough to know when something unusual
is happening or something has gone wrong—even when adults try to
hide the event—but they may not know the right words to describe
what is taking place. What the child describes may sound like a direct
incestuous attempt has been made when, in fact, it has not been made.
What he or she may be trying to express could be the force of some
sort of misdirected threat or some sort of tension in the family system.
For example, the child may have been overstimulated or exposed to
inappropriate sexual behavior on the part of the parents. What he or
she describes (something half real, half fearful fantasy) may be a
premonition of trouble yet to come. Children are frequently aware of
the basic dynamics of the family on an intuitive level that the parents
may not want to acknowledge. A child may feel that there is something
wrong or about to happen, but what it really is may be unknown to
the child or beyond his or her ability appropriately to express. One of
the possible reasons behind this kind of vague accusation may be that

the child is asking for protection from a parent because he or she senses either inappropriate sexual behavior on the part of the parent, an impending sexual threat, or a shifting of sexual roles within the family (such as the shifting of family roles that takes place during the "courtship period" prior to actual incest; this "courtship period" will be discussed later in the chapter).

Finally, a clinician should be keenly aware of the personal feelings or biases that he or she brings into such a situation. Would the therapist prefer "the whole nasty mess" to be a figment of the child's imagination so that he or she will not have to deal with it? One cannot ignore the fact that many children who were victims of incest were being seen by clinicians who did not detect what was happening to the child, or did not provide a setting that was emotionally safe enough for the child to disclose what had happened.

To summarize, the process of determining whether a child's allegation of incest is true or untrue should be undertaken with great care. When a therapist is part of this process, he or she should approach the evaluation in an objective, clinical manner—not allowing herself or himself to be drawn into the emotional storm such accusations can stir.

The following are suggested guidelines that may assist the clinician in such situations:

1. Evaluate the psychological condition of the child or adolescent to determine whether or not the child is capable of perceiving the world accurately, to a degree consistent with the child's developmental level. Does the child suffer from a psychological condition that could impair his or her judgment?

2. Evaluate the child's or adolescent's behavior according to the criteria that are diagnostic of sexually abused children (in Chapter 2) or diagnostic of sexually abused adolescents (in Chapter 4).

3. Carefully assess *both* parents individually, as well as in terms of their current interaction. In other words, does one parent have something to gain as a result of an accusation of this type, and may that parent be overtly or covertly influencing the child? Does either parent have a history of psychological problems or substance abuse that may disinhibit his or her behavior and cause him or her to be more at risk to act irrationally?

4. In the more complex or serious cases, it is advisable to have the evaluation of both the parents and the child done by a separate, court-appointed therapist in order to ensure an unbiased evaluation—as well as to protect oneself from undue pressure.

5. A therapist should take into account the parents' sexual views in order to determine what they consider to be "normal," what each parent believes is appropriate for a child to be exposed to, and how each parent feels that affection should be expressed toward a child. The clinician need not be surprised to learn that, particularly in divorcing parents, there may be widely differing points of view.

6. A clinician should be prepared to meet with significant adults, as well as caretakers such as babysitters, teachers, pediatricians, and relatives, to obtain relevant data pertaining to the child's emotional state and behavior and to gain any information that may confirm or disconfirm the allegation of incest.

7. Issues of secondary gain ought to be cautiously explored. In most cases when the accusation of child sexual abuse is true, the child gains nothing. Instead, a child fears the loss of or the disruption of the family, guilt, and shame. Consequently, most children who are sexually abused are fearful or reluctant to tell. Hence the possibility of secondary gain by the child for making a false accusation is worth investigation.

8. Steps should be taken to ensure that the child is adequately protected and shielded from pressure as much as possible. The less pressure there is on a child, the more likely the information obtained from the child will be accurate. Too often the evaluation of an allegation is inadequate, owing to the time requirements that are placed upon a clinician.

9. Each evaluation session should be audiotaped or videotaped in order to demonstrate that the child or adolescent was not led or coerced, as well as to provide documentation that the evaluation employed correct, unbiased methods.

10. The child should have an independent therapist who is *outside* the evaluation process and with whom the child has a confidential relationship. Many children in this kind of situation (particularly divorce) feel that they have been tossed into a war zone in which there is no safe place. This protected therapy relationship can provide the child with a haven in which he or she can work through his or her beleaguered feelings.

ASSESSMENT OF INCESTUOUS FAMILIES*

How do incest cases come to the attention of therapists? As we have discussed previously (Everstine & Everstine, 1983, Chapter 9), many

---

* This and the following section solely describe assessment and treatment of cases in which father-daughter incest has occurred.

surface through the child's actions, such as running away from home, sexually aggressive or sexually inappropriate behavior, self-destructive or suicidal behavior, and/or a sudden change in school behavior or performance. In another context, an incestuous family may enter treatment by the following route: a daughter reaches adolescence and wishes to participate in age-appropriate behavior such as dating boys and becoming more involved in peer activities away from the family, but her father reacts like a jealous lover and places inappropriate restrictions on her; she, in turn, reacts to the father's excessive rules. When the daughter acts out or runs away, the family may seek counseling, not because of incest but to regain control of their wayward daughter. The main issue to be concerned about is that despite recently increased awareness of this subject, incest families tend to be closed or isolated systems, and they rarely seek treatment voluntarily for the incest problem itself.

Incestuous intercourse may cease when the daughter becomes old enough to conceive a child. In some cases the form of sexual contact shifts to oral or anal copulation, or the father may select a younger daughter for his sexual partner. This changing of sexual partners may also cause a crisis within the family that brings it into treatment. Even so, most incestuous families come to the attention of therapists because of what they define as some kind of problem behavior on the part of a child; or, the incest has been discovered and they are ordered to seek treatment by the authorities. The following is a list of risk factors which, in our experience, may suggest that father-daughter incest has occurred or might occur in a family (excerpted from Everstine & Everstine, 1983; see also Browning & Boatman, 1977; Finkelhor, 1984, 1979; Meiselman, 1978):

1. Alcoholic father;

2. Father who is unusually suspicious and/or puritanical;

3. Violent or authoritarian father;

4. Mother who is "absent" or very passive or incapable of being a protective force in the family;

5. Daughter who plays the role of mother, assuming many of the mother's household functions;

6. Parents whose sexual relationship is troubled or nonexistent;

7. A situation in which the father must often be alone with the daughter;

8. Factors that may limit the self-control of the father, such as drug dependency, psychopathology, or limited intelligence;

9. The sudden onset of promiscuity on the part of a young girl;

10. A child who does not allow people to be close friends with her;

11. Parents who are reluctant (or refuse) to allow a clinician to talk with their child alone;

12. A hostile or paranoid attitude toward outsiders on the part of one or both parents, especially the father;

13. Previous incidents of incest in the nuclear family (families) of one or both parents;

14. Parents who had deprived childhoods in which there were inadequate role models;

15. Extreme jealousy displayed by a father whose daughter has recently reached puberty.

These events or characteristics can serve the clinician as possible indicators that incest is occurring. Another frequent sequel of incest is sudden wild or bizarre behavior on the part of a child, particularly if it includes delusions of a sexual nature. Geiser (1979, p. 58) found that, in a clinical population of disturbed children, at least 20% may have been incest victims. We believe that because clinicians are becoming more aware of the problem of incest, numerous victims will be identified among severely disturbed or institutionalized children and adolescents.

Approaching the Subject of Incest

How does one bring up the subject of incest with a young girl, or ask if it has occurred? If the child is 10 or 11 or older, when the parents are not present one might say something like this (adapted from Everstine and Everstine, 1983): "As you know, relationships between fathers and daughters can become very close. But some of the things that you told me gave me the feeling—and you may stop me if I'm wrong because I am not always right—that something might have happened between you and your dad that hurt you or frightened or confused you."

If the child has actually alluded to incest, the therapist may say: "What you told me is understandable. A lot of people think it is terrible, but even though it can be very frightening it happens in a lot of families, and it is not the end of the world. Just because it happened in the past doesn't mean it has to happen again, and I shall do everything I can to keep it from happening in the future. But I think that it's important that I know the truth. Is there more you can tell me about this?"

When incest is suspected, a therapist should try to establish a situation in which the child will feel as comfortable as possible about telling her story. Then the clinician can proceed in this way: "Now it might not have been actual intercourse or sex, but . . . ." At each step the therapist gives the child a chance to move toward the subject and a chance for her to test the therapist's reactions. "Maybe there was some touching" is another approach. In this way, the child is permitted to describe a portion, but not the entire event, and is given the option to change the conversation if necessary.

Make sure that the child is permitted sufficient emotional "distance" to retreat if she feels threatened, without having to withdraw from this line of questioning entirely. Using the "illusion of alternatives" technique of Erickson can be helpful in obtaining a more complete story from a frightened child. The therapist can say, "You can tell me as much about what happened with your father as you are comfortable in telling me now, and we can wait a while before you tell me the rest." Hence, the option of not continuing is omitted, but the child is given a measure of control over how much will be revealed and when.

When Incest Is Discovered

When incest is found to be occurring in a family, it is not always necessary or wise to recommend removal of the child from the home or to advocate breaking up the family system. Of paramount importance is that the therapist be keenly aware of his or her own feelings concerning this subject, so as not to overreact or underreact. Either kind of response on the part of a therapist may only serve to substantiate the family myth that "doom and destruction" would follow if the secret were discovered, and may also have the effect of causing a victim to recant his or her story because worst fears have been confirmed.

As noted above, the merest mention of the subject of incest can introduce tension into a conversation—far more than does the subject of physical child abuse. This is probably one reason why for years people found it more comfortable to ascribe an accusation of incest to the fantasy world of a naughty child. On the other hand, the subject of physical abuse evokes a certain mutual understanding, probably because almost everyone can admit to having had, at one time or another, the urge to strike an unruly child. And while most people have had incestuous thoughts and impulses, it is not socially acceptable to admit them to another person. It is even a difficult subject for clinicians to discuss among themselves. But therapists do know what an impact one's own feelings and prejudices can have upon a family that one is treating. Therefore, it is a good idea for those who work with incestuous families to do so as part of a therapy team. Teamwork is helpful because a therapist will have other resources for double-checking his or her clinical impressions. A team or group that meets regularly for case consultation can also help because it provides the clinician with emotional support. One should not underestimate how emotionally draining the work with these families can be.

The discovery of incest in a family may mean that enormous pressure will be brought to bear upon a clinician to refrain from reporting the incest to the authorities (Everstine & Everstine, 1983, p. 147). As mentioned above, it is not uncommon for a victim to recant her story and try to convince the therapist to drop the entire thing. The underlying threat is that, should the family be broken apart by revelation, it will be the therapist's fault. This is another effort to shift responsibility for what was done from the sexually involved parent to someone else. Most incestuous parents are adept at evading responsibility for loss of self-control, and their shifting of responsibility is often reinforced by other family members who share the same myths.

This conspiracy of fear is one of the principal devices by which incest families sustain and protect themselves. The clinician who permits himself or herself to be drawn into the conspiracy will be taking a dangerous step into the family's pathological *modus vivendi*, with its complex network of alliances. Instead, by being frank with the family about a therapist's duty to report suspected cases of incest, he or she will be showing the family a healthy, straightforward way to confront problems; in addition, the therapist will, in effect, be saying to the family, "I am not going to enter your system; I shall establish clear, strict rules and abide by them."

Both incestuous and abusive families are notorious for trying to avoid treatment. They tend to fear change, and they especially fear facing the insidious problems that they have kept so well hidden. Because of this tendency, it may be necessary to take advantage of the court's jurisdiction over the case as a means to induce these families to stay in treatment beyond the initial, frightening stages. It is our experience that incest will not stop, even after it is reported, unless the family receives treatment; very likely, stringent court supervision will be required as well.

Questions to be Answered Before Treatment Begins

It is worth emphasizing that some incestuous families are able to reconstruct themselves in a healthy manner if they are provided with treatment and adequate support services. What is essential is that incestuous families are carefully evaluated before treatment, in order that a treatment plan for the family can be devised which ensures adequate protection for the child. Thorough evaluation of the family may also help the court to decide what degree of supervision or separation is appropriate for the family to have during the treatment process. Therapists can expect that, in some cases, a child will need to be removed from the custody of his or her parents. This may become an extremely difficult situation, and one that can be very traumatic to the child. There are cases in which it may be as traumatic as the incest itself; nevertheless, when there are insufficient resources within the family to protect the child from future abuse, the child should be removed from the family for his or her safety.

The mother is a key figure in an evaluation of the family, as one tries to determine whether there are adequate resources within it to protect a child from future abuse. The clinician will be called upon to answer important questions with regard to whether or not the mother is capable of assuming an appropriately protective maternal role in the family. Of course, one should first assess both the mother's and the father's basic mental stability to see if they are psychologically capable of being adequate parents. Next, the therapist should consider how the mother learned of the accusation of incest against her husband and how she responded to it. Did the mother behave in a rational way? Did she take immediate steps to protect her child and seek help? Was there a fundamental logic to her actions, even though she felt initial shock and dismay? Were her actions focused upon caring for the child, or was her response to the disclosure one of nonsupport or denial? Did she dismiss the accusation as a lie or fantasy, refusing to consider its reality? Did the child confide the secret to someone else because she was afraid to tell her mother? If the child attempted to tell her mother, did the mother give her the message that she wouldn't listen? In our experience, when there is such massive denial and lack of support for the child by the mother, court supervision as well as removal of the child from the home is usually necessary.

A therapist should also consider the frequency and duration of the incest experience. If, after the first incident, the child went right away to the mother for help (and got it), one may assume that there is less serious pathology in the family system than if the incest had continued for a considerable period of time. Could incest have been occurring for years without the mother being aware that such an event was taking place? It is not likely. In most cases in which incest should have been detected and reported years earlier, considerable emotional energy has been spent by more than one member of the family to maintain the status quo of the incestuous system. And because more than one family member has been involved in either actively or passively protecting the incest, a clinician should be particularly cautious in evaluating such families.

The therapist would do well to consider the question of why this problem is coming to light now. Why didn't the child turn to the mother for help earlier? Usually the answer is that the child knew that no help was available from her. That could be because the mother was being terrorized by a brutal husband. Or it could be the sort of family system in which the mother passively colluded with incest and only now is willing to acknowledge her complicity. In such event, the clinician will want to find out whether or not this mother is genuinely trying to stop the incest once and for all. Or, is some other factor causing the mother to come forward at this time, while she is, in reality, attempting to preserve the incestuous family system?

An example of this kind of situation occurred when a mother came to our clinic to report finding out that an incestuous relationship had been going on between her husband and nine-year-old daughter for three years. According to the mother, the girl had just the day before confided the horrible truth to her. Outwardly, this mother appeared to be a truly tragic figure who was deeply distressed by discovering the incest and was determined to protect her daughter from future abuse. Only later, when other suspicious circumstances caused the therapist to look more deeply into the situation and consult with the physician who had previously seen the girl, did the therapist learn what had really happened. This physician, when giving the girl an examination, had found evidence that she had been sexually abused; he informed the mother that she had 24 hours to report the abuse to the authorities or he would. In addition, the therapist later learned, from the daughter, that the mother had been in the room on several occasions when incest was taking place—a fact later substantiated by the father's confession. Thus, in cases of long-standing incest, a clinician needs to be very sure that he or she has the full story. One should not assume that the family members will tell a therapist all that has transpired.

Finally, an issue that needs to be taken into consideration by a therapist when evaluating an incestuous family is the age difference between the sexually involved parent and the child (Everstine & Everstine, 1983, p. 157). If the clinician suspects that incest is occurring between a two- or three-year-old child and an adult, the intervention needs to be more thorough and aggressive than if the child were older because one can expect to find more pathology on the part of both parents. Because there may be more risk that the sexually involved parent may lose control again, a child of two or three will be in need of immediate protection. By contrast, if the victim is a teenager, the therapist may wish to intervene more cautiously—with the aim of developing a trust relationship with the victim. Adolescent victims sometimes have more options available to them, but younger children have fewer means to find aid and protection.

BASIC TREATMENT ISSUES

When incest comes to light in a family, the clinician should consider the *entire* family to be in a state of crisis. Those who work with the family should act in concert to protect the child, provide the family with support and structure, and give the family as much clear information about what is transpiring in the legal process as possible.

The System and Its Individual Members

A therapist should be alert to the fact that, during this initial crisis-of-discovery phase, *each* family member is at considerable suicide risk. The parents, the victim, and her siblings should be carefully monitored in terms of suicide potential. The siblings of the victim are not to be ignored because later it may be discovered that they, too, were victims. Or, they may believe themselves to bear some guilt for the incest. Hence, the therapists involved should be prepared to take an active, directive role until they are *sure* that the crisis has passed.

A child victim must be permitted to be a child, develop age-appropriate behavior, ventilate and work through her feelings concerning the incest, and eventually try to catch up on the social learning that was missed during the incestuous episode. Only rarely can this pivotal early clinical work be done within the context of whole-family sessions. Even so, before conducting *any* therapy that includes the perpetrator, a clinician should receive assurance that the father has accepted complete responsibility for the crime and is prepared to make a genuine apology to his child. We hold the opinion that until an abusive parent takes responsibility and fully apologizes, it is not appropriate for a therapist to foster contact between him and the child.

In the initial stage, the parents should be seen individually as well as together if they have remained together. If they separate, they should be seen as individuals, with occasional joint sessions for subjects pertaining to the children (when possible). This is not to say that family therapy is being neglected during the initial stage of treatment. Family therapy is taking place, but with the individual members of the system, so that they can eventually come together and work as an *intact* entity in the usual sort of family therapy session. And even in those cases when the family does not reunite, it can be said that systems work is being done through the medium of individual therapy for the relevant family members. Furniss (1984) wrote:

> In child sexual abuse, family oriented therapeutic work does not necessarily mean that all or even most therapeutic meetings have to be conjoint. It often is unavoidable or seems indicated to see different family members or subgroups separately. . . . But even individual work needs to maintain the family perspective and it should become integrated through close cooperation between the different agencies involved. (p. 309)

In summary, whole-family therapy sessions can be viewed as a possible goal to work toward during the initial phases of treatment, but are not the modality of choice when beginning to work with most incest families.

At the outset of treatment for these families, it is wise to structure therapy to reflect the way in which one would like to see the family system change. For example, the parents must learn to function as adults who are capable of attending to their own emotional needs, without using their children to gratify those needs. In addition, the parents may have to work through unresolved psychological issues with their own parents and families of origin.

When each parent has a different therapist and the child has her own, the basic structure of a system in which the parents are two individual adults, with a clear generational boundary line between their identity and the child's, is modeled. At this stage it is vital that the therapists work together as a team that helps the family members develop as independent elements of a healthy system. If the individual work goes well, the therapy team can move toward establishing healthy subsystems in the family. For example, the couple can begin meeting with a therapist to work on issues pertaining to the marital and parental subsystems. A clinician who works with the couple during this period should direct them toward understanding that the marital subsystem is best kept separate from the parental subsystem, and that certain issues such as the parents' sexuality should remain within the former sub-system. Most of these parents are dysfunctional as a couple and will need considerable work on sexual compatibility in order to achieve a functional status.

When an incest family contains more than one child, a therapist should try to strengthen the generational boundary further by helping the children to develop a separate sibling subsystem. This can be accomplished either by means of sessions with the siblings or by means of a children's group. This decision should be based upon the complexity and severity of the case, as well as the ages of the children. Only when the functioning of the component subsystems is secure can the clinician begin to consider inaugurating whole-family therapy.

A critical issue that a therapist must address with the parents in incest families is that neither parent can re-create through children a lost or fantasied childhood. Although it is necessary for the clinician to know what happened in the histories of such parents, endless analysis of it will lead to a blind alley. As Selvini Palazzoli (1984) observed, "The present contains the past," and it is the past contained in the present that must be dealt with in order to help these parents begin to function as adults in the here and now.

The clinician who works with incest parents needs to be structured and directive, keeping a clear treatment plan in mind and focusing clearly on changing current modes of behavior. The therapist in many ways will be modeling a healthy parental role for these people by setting clear behavioral expectations and prohibiting rationalization or manipulative attempts to shift the responsibility for controlling them-selves to others.

Working with the Child*

The victim of incest needs her own therapist for the following reasons. She requires the reassurance of an independent person with whom she may eventually feel safe enough to share her feelings concerning what happened, as well as clear separation of her process from that of her parents. It is often not simple to establish a trust relationship with the victim of incest, and everything possible should be done to help her feel that the relationship with the therapist is private and safe. Nor should the clinician be suspicious if the child's initial reflections on the incest are emotionally bland or even (superficially) positive. Again, one

---

* A more detailed description of the individual psychotherapy process with preschool and school-aged children is presented in Chapter 3, pp. 43–55. A description of individual therapy methods for adolescents is presented in Chapter 4, pp. 75–80.

should not be surprised if the child makes overt sexual advances to the therapist, is generally seductive, or behaves in some other sexually inappropriate manner. This behavior will end when she begins to feel safe with her therapist. As mentioned in Chapter 3, if a child engages in this kind of inappropriate behavior the clinician should clearly convey the message that the child is accepted but the behavior is not. And as with a case of molestation, a therapist should work toward the goal of the child's being able to externalize the abuse as an event that happened to her, instead of as part of her concept of the "reality" of who and what she is. This process of externalization will be vital to the child's future personality development, contributing to a healthy self-concept and a sense of self-worth.

In general, it is not a good idea to push an incest victim (nor any victim of childhood sexual assault) to confide her entire story immediately, unless it is vitally necessary to do so, because issues of trust and personal boundaries are essential in doing therapy with these children. Most need to talk in full about what happened to them, but they should not be pressured to do so. First, the child may misunderstand it as sexual curiosity or some form of sexual advance on the part of a therapist. Second, if the child is involved in the court process, she will undoubtedly have to tell her story to adult strangers numerous times; and telling and retelling the details of the abuse can itself become a kind of verbal sexual performance for the child, as well as a form of inappropriate adult–child stimulation. Finally, because more has happened to the child than a pathological sexual relationship, the clinician should focus on treatment that is relevant to the context in which the child lives. If a therapist places too much emphasis on getting the child to tell him or her the sexual details, this process will further the myth of the child as a sexual object in respect to child–adult relationships, and not as a whole child. In turn, it can weaken the essential structure of the therapy relationship with the child, which needs to be a safe, neutral model of child–adult relationships, in which the child does not need to reciprocate with sexual favors. It is within this milieu that a child may be encouraged to tell her story, but on her own terms.

At the beginning of therapy, it is wise to consider carefully how much the young person can or cannot accept (Everstine & Everstine, 1983, pp. 158, 159). Often, the first thing a therapist may wish to do is to reach out and reassure the child. Even though the clinician's intentions in reaching out to comfort the child may be genuinely caring, he or she should take into account, as noted above, that because of their histories these children tend to sexualize relationships and may not be able to discriminate between nonerotic and erotic forms of touch

(Yates, 1982, 1987a). Since many cannot properly interpret social cues and types of touching, it is wise that the clinician not touch (or use great caution in touching) these children during the course of therapy.

Because the trust of the victim of incest has already been betrayed by an adult whom she thought to be trustworthy, the therapist should be prepared for considerable probing, provoking behavior on the child's part. Even if a child's initial response is clinging dependence, on another level he or she will be checking to see if the therapist is safe. This issue of trust is one of paramount importance. In the process of establishing a relationship, the child may "test the limits" of a therapist for a long time to see if his or her concerns are genuine (Everstine & Everstine, 1983, pp. 158, 159; Yates, 1982, 1987a).

Primary issues that will emerge in the process of therapy with incest victims are varied and complex. First, the victim must resolve the confusion that occurred as a result of her mother's exchanging roles with her, preventing her from being a child in the fullest sense and from attending to the necessary developmental tasks that are essential to childhood. Second, there is the damage caused by the breach in the fundamental trust relationship between parent and child, with its subsequent effect on other relationships, that needs repair. Third, an attempt should be made to help the victim resolve the acute anxiety caused by being stimulated sexually before she had developed an adequate identity and understanding of sexual release. This process of the definition of self and development of the person's perspective on life cannot be underestimated, because it is the fundamental stuff of which either positive life scripts or self-fulfilling prophesies are made.

Working with the Father

In the course of his individual therapy, the incestuous father must give the therapist a full accounting of what he did to the child and assume full responsibility for it (Everstine & Everstine, 1983; Furniss, 1984). Extracting a full admission is not always an easy task. Some fathers rationalize by trying to diminish the severity of the event or by claiming that the child enjoyed the relationship; others believe that by confessing what was done they can now magically wash away all their responsibility. Confessions and claims of having become a changed person, dramatic as they may be, should be viewed with considerable suspicion by the clinician. Rarely do people undo lifelong patterns in an instant.

When the perpetrator of incest tries to evade responsibility, the prognosis for treatment of either parent is not good. Even so, admission of guilt by the father should realistically be viewed as only a beginning, because there is considerable clinical work to be done on issues such as impulse control, the appropriate expression of anger, assuming a healthy parental role in the family, and the ability to nurture his children adequately. In effect, the father must learn to express affection and relate to his daughter(s) in a way that is not sexual. He must cease to equate sex with power. In the process, he may be guided to develop a more healthy, "reciprocal" (Jackson, 1968) sexual relationship with his wife. In addition, if the father is believed to be involved in some form of substance abuse, one cannot consider the home to be safe for a child victim until the abuse is resolved. If the incestuous parent has a drug or alcohol dependency problem and is living away from the home, we believe that he should not be permitted to return home until the problem is under control.

As stated above, a critical step in the father's efforts toward resuming his role as a parent will be to apologize to his daughter for what he did. This is not always a simple matter, and often must be carefully planned and supervised. A balance must be struck according to when a parent is capable of apologizing and when the child is prepared to hear the apology without feeling guilty for it or, instead, seizing the opportunity to express greater anger toward the parent. Many children of incest go through a period of intense rage or uncontrolled fluctuations of love and hate toward the incestuous parent; hence, the planning of how and when such an apology should occur may require considerable thought. The fundamental purpose of the apology is not to humiliate the parent but to begin the process of helping him learn to fulfill an appropriate adult role and to be responsible for his behavior.

Working with the Mother to Rebuild a Mother–Daughter Dyad

It is our experience that a good working clinical relationship with the mother in these families is vital to successful treatment, whether or not the spouses remain together. In many cases, the mother has such strong unmet dependency needs and such profound internal conflicts concerning her own mother that until she is successfully engaged in treatment herself, she will undermine the therapy of her child. As with the mother of the molested child (Chapter 3, pp. 38–39), this kind of mother may attempt to sabotage therapy by bringing the child late to sessions, intruding into the child's therapy time, forgetting appointments, or divisively complaining about one clinician or agency to another clinician or agency. The best preventive is extensive individual work with the mother until she feels safe enough, emotionally, to tolerate her child's treatment. One of the fundamental issues that needs to be worked through, early in treatment, concerns the emotional "wound" that may have led to incest in the first place—namely, the mother's anger at her daughter's demands for care and nurturance while hers were generally unmet. Added to this could be the love/hate relationship with her own mother that, as a consequence, renders her incapable of fully accepting the role of mother herself.

A therapist should take care, during this initial phase of treating the mother, not to get sidetracked—by her manipulations—into focusing solely on her acting-out behavior against therapy and/or her child's therapy. To do that would be to permit the mother to "seal over" the key issues that she must face in the process of doing battle with the therapist.

From another perspective, the clinician should be sensitive to the fact that many mothers in incestuous families come from backgrounds that may have included severe abuse and/or neglect; some were incest victims themselves as children. In such cases, emotional scars from this original maltreatment must be addressed in order for the mother to be able to function according to her proper role in the family. Once she begins to come to terms with the issues that prevented her from functioning as an effective and protecting parent, and she becomes more capable of resuming her maternal role, the therapist can actively work toward shaping a healthy mother–daughter dyad.

Restoring the mother-daughter dyad should be considered a fundamental aspect of treatment, whether the family remains intact or separate. This therapeutic work can be done in the context of joint mother–daughter sessions or in a group for mothers and daughters. The treatment modality of choice can be selected according to such factors as the age of the child and the severity or complexity of the clinical issues to be addressed. The goals of this component of treatment (group or conjoint) are to establish an emotional bond between mother and daughter and to help them gain a sense of empathy for one another. It is by means of the fortification of this empathic bond that further abuse will be prevented. In order for mother and daughter to achieve this kind of relationship, a therapist should be prepared to cut through much in the way of fantasy, anger, and projection on the part of both mother and daughter. One might begin by engaging them in some mutually pleasant and nonthreatening experience such as listening to music, drawing, storytelling, or looking at pictures together. The clinician can ask each one to tell the other what she is thinking and how she is feeling. Then, he or she can ask how each thinks the other is feeling. A therapist should not be surprised to find that even in the context of a simple, neutral activity, both daughter and (particularly) mother have considerable difficulty in understanding and interpreting each other's thoughts and feelings. In the early phase of treatment, the therapist will likely need to take a fairly active role in teaching both mother and daughter to recognize and respond appropriately to each other's feelings. As they become more capable of understanding one another, the clinician can shift his or her role from being directive and instructional to being more facilitative and interpretive.

When mother and daughter are able to "read" the other's emotional cues fairly well, a therapist can move on to create a deeper emotional bond between the two by utilizing some of the nurturance or bonding techniques described by Long (1986). If the daughter is quite young, one might ask the mother to hold the child on her lap and cuddle or rock her while the therapist engages them in talking about how the other person is feeling. In the case of an older daughter, the mother may be asked to hold her daughter's hand or hold her in her arms; each could gently caress the other's face while learning how the other is feeling. As in the earlier stages of this approach, the clinician may wish to take a directive role at the outset; if it proceeds well, one can transfer the more active role to the mother, as her ability to understand and nurture her daughter develops.

When a therapist believes that the mother has developed a reasonable measure of empathy and nurturance, he or she can begin to explore a deeper level of clinical work. The therapist can ask each to describe an event from the present or recent past according to the other's perspective. In other words, the mother is asked to describe how her daughter felt about the abuse in question, and vice-versa. Then, when this process is going fairly well, the therapist can lead them toward working through the incest experience.

Working with Grandparents

In the case of an incest family in which the mother had a "Cinderella" type of relationship with her mother (the victim's maternal grandmother), a clinician should never underestimate the power that these grandparents have in the family system. If the therapist does not account for them in the therapy process, he or she may be in for a difficult time. Sometimes the role and influence of the grandparents are obvious, but more often they are subtly expressed; nonetheless, they are a major force within the family and must be reckoned with. It is often the case that when these mothers first separate from their husbands, they are particularly vulnerable to the negative influence of their own mothers, sometimes returning to live with them in the wake of the separation. We have observed that until the victim's mother is able to individuate and, in the process, work through the symbiotic relationship with her own mother, she will not succeed in providing adequate protection and nurturance for the victim. The reason is that her own conflicts about what a mother is and does are so profound.

Group Therapy

Many incest victims respond well to group therapy as part of a treatment program. These groups should be well structured and conducted by experienced clinicians. The children and adolescents who participate in the group should be clinically screened to find out if they are ready, emotionally, for group work. Each participant should be working on issues that are consistent with those of the other children or adolescents in the group. We recommend that these groups be limited in size: for example, between three and 10 group members was proposed by Furniss (1984) and Furniss, Bingley-Miller, and Bentovim (1984). This group work can be a useful way to help the victim break away from her feelings of isolation and being different from other children.

In addition to children's groups, parents' groups can be a very useful treatment adjunct, once the parents have done the initial individual therapy work. Mothers' groups and/or groups of mothers and daughters are potentially useful media for conducting some of the mother–daughter work that was described earlier. Also, fathers' groups for perpetrators of incest can be a very powerful treatment mode, when led by a wise and forceful male therapist. Such groups require a well-trained group leader who is both solid enough to cut through these fathers' strong defenses and complicated self-protective manipulations, yet also capable of providing them with a caring and encouraging role model or alternative father-figure.

When a therapist considers that a family member is ready for group therapy, it should begin as an added component of individual therapy. Transfer to a group as the primary treatment modality should not take place until agreement on this move is reached by the treatment team. Because of the clinical complexities posed by these families, we must emphasize the team concept and stress the wisdom of consulting with team members before making major alterations in the treatment plan.

A therapist will be wise to consider that not all incestuous families can reconstruct themselves in a healthy way; many put unrealistic demands on themselves, thus ensuring failure. It is important that the clinician should proceed cautiously in this respect, mainly because little research has been done on treatment techniques for sexual offenders (see also Finkelhor, 1987). In fact, there is a lack of valid assessment methods for discriminating those offenders who are amenable to treatment from those who are not. As a consequence, the therapist will need to evaluate each family member thoroughly to find out the likelihood of reconstructing the system; this may be a lengthy process, accomplished only by extensive individual therapy with each member. And because some families will never achieve reconstruction, a therapist should note that his or her role in helping those who cannot reunite is as important as with those who can.

When a family cannot be made whole, the clinician's task will be to see to it that the parental separation takes place in a manner that is least damaging or traumatic to the child victim. Moreover, it will be the therapist's responsibility to help a child understand the reasons for separation, so that she can come to terms with it appropriately without feeling that she bears some fault. Of course, in the vast majority of cases, the daughter will remain with her mother after the separation, and a crucial role of the therapist will be to ensure that the child is protected from any future abuse.

REFERENCES

Adams, M. S., & Neil, J. V. Children of incest. *Pediatrics*, 40(1), 55–63, 1967.
Bender, L., & Blau, A. The reaction of children to sexual relations with adults. *American Journal of Orthopsychiatry*, 7, 500–518, 1937.
Bresee, P., Stearns, G. B., Bess, B. H., & Packer, L. S. Allegations of child sexual abuse in child custody disputes: A therapeutic assessment model. *American Journal of Orthopsychiatry*, 56(4), 560–569, 1986.
Browne, A., & Finkelhor, D. The impact of child sexual abuse: A review of the research. *Psychological Bulletin*, 99(1), 66–77, 1986.
Browning, D. H., & Boatman, B. Incest: Children at risk. *American Journal of Psychiatry*, 134, 69–72, 1977.
Cooper, I., & Cormier, B. M. Inter-generational transmission of incest. *Canadian Journal of Psychiatry*, 27, 231–235, 1982.
Cowie, J., Cowie, V., & Slater, E. *Delinquency in girls*. Atlantic Highlands, NJ: Humanities Press, 1968.
deYoung, M. Innocent seducer or innocently seduced? The role of the child incest victim. *Journal of Clinical Child Psychology*, 11(1), 56–60, 1982.
Everstine, D. S., & Everstine, L. *People in crisis*. New York: Brunner/Mazel, 1983.
Faller, K. C. Is the child victim of sexual abuse telling the truth? *Child Abuse and Neglect*, 8, 473–481, 1984.
Finkelhor, D. *Sexually victimized children*. New York: The Free Press, 1979.
Finkelhor, D. *Child sexual abuse: New theory and research*. New York: The Free Press, 1984.

Finkelhor, D. The sexual abuse of children: Current research reviewed. *Psychiatric Annals, 17*(4), 233–241, 1987.

Freud, A. A psychoanalyst's view of sexual abuse by parents. In P. B. Mrazek & C. H. Kempe (Eds.), *Sexually abused children and their families.* New York: Pergamon Press, 1981.

Freud, S. (1913). *Totem and taboo.* (A. A. Brill, Trans.) New York: Vintage, 1946.

Furniss, T. Organizing a therapeutic approach to intra-familial child sexual abuse. *Journal of Adolescence, 7,* 309–317, 1984.

Furniss, T., Bingley-Miller, S., & Bentovim, A. Therapeutic approach to sexual abuse. *Archives of Disease in Childhood, 59,* 865–876, 1984.

Gebhard, P., Gagnon, J., Pomeroy, W., & Christensen, C. *Sex offenders.* New York: Harper & Row, 1965.

Geiser, R. L. *Hidden victims: The sexual abuse of children.* Boston: Beacon Press, 1979.

Green, A. H. True and false allegations of sexual abuse in child custody disputes. *Journal of the American Academy of Child Psychiatry, 25,* 449–456, 1986.

Henderson, J. D. Incest: A synthesis of data. *Canadian Psychiatric Association Journal, 17,* 299–313, 1972.

Jackson, D. D. *The mirages of marriage.* New York: W. W. Norton, 1968.

Kaufmann, I., Peck, A. L., & Tagiuri, C. K. The family constellation and overt incestuous relations between father and daughter. *American Journal of Orthopsychiatry, 24,* 266–277, 1954.

Long, S. Guidelines for treating young children. In K. MacFarlane & J. Waterman (Eds.), *Sexual abuse of young children.* New York: Guilford Press, 1986.

Lustig, N., Dresser, J. W., Spellman, S. W., & Murray, T. B. Incest: A family group survival pattern. *Archives of General Psychiatry, 14,* 31–40, 1966.

Machotka, P. F., Pittman, F. S., & Flomenhaft, K. Incest as a family affair. *Family Process, 6,* 98–116, 1967.

Maisch, H. *Incest.* New York: Stein & Day, 1972.

Malinowski, B. *Sex and repression in savage society.* London: Routledge & Kegan Paul, 1927.

Meiselman, K. *Incest: A psychological study of causes and effects with treatment recommendations.* San Francisco: Jossey-Bass, 1978.

Murdock, G. P. *Social structure.* New York: Macmillan, 1949.

Peters, J. J. Children who were victims of sexual assault and the psychology of the offenders. *American Journal of Psychotherapy, 30,* 398–417, 1976.

Raphling, D. L., Carpenter, B. L., & Davis, A. Incest: A genealogical study. *Archives of General Psychiatry, 16,* 505–511, 1967.

Rosenfeld, A. A., Nadelson, C. C., & Krieger, M. Fantasy and reality in patients' reports of incest. *Journal of Clinical Psychiatry, 40,* 159–164, 1979.

Seemanova, E. A study of children of incestuous matings. *Human Heredity, 21,* 108–128, 1971.

Selvini Palazzoli, M. At what point do systems consult an expert? Presentation to Second International Biennial Conference of the Mental Research Institute and the Emergency Treatment Center, Munich, West Germany, July 1984.

Sgroi, S. M. The sexual assault of children: Dynamics of the problem and issues in program development. In Community Council of Greater New York, *Sexual Abuse of Children.* New York: Community Council of Greater New York, 1979.

Symonds, M. The "second injury" to victims. *Evaluation and Change, Special Issue*, 36–38, 1980.

Weinberg, S. K. *Incest behavior*. New York: Citadel Press, 1955.

Weiner, I. B. Father-daughter incest: A clinical report. *Psychiatric Quarterly, 36,* 607–632, 1962.

Yates, A. Children eroticized by incest. *American Journal of Psychiatry, 139(4),* 482–485, 1982.

Yates, A. Psychological damage associated with extreme eroticism in young children. *Psychiatric Annals, 17(4),* 257–261, 1987a.

Yates, A. Should young children testify in cases of sexual abuse? *American Journal of Psychiatry, 144(4),* 476–480, 1987b.

6

The Boy Victim

The Freudian concept of a "latency stage" refers to the period of development, in both sexes, from the fifth year until puberty (Hinsie & Campbell, 1970, p. 427); for boys, the modal age at which puberty is reached is 13. This chapter addresses the subject of the molestation of boys who are in this process of preparing for their sexual role in life. These very formative years are especially crucial for little boys because (1) they remain relatively powerless in their relationships with adults and (2) they have not yet "discovered" girls; for those reasons, they are especially vulnerable to assault by pedophiles.

Boys in the latency stage are by no means inactive sexually, and if the term "latency" implies a dormant period, the term misleads. Especially from the age of nine or 10, most boys engage in a rich form of experimentation that is best characterized as "silent sex." Excited by fantasy but lost in perplexity, the boy muses for long hours on the subject, inventing vague theories of the differences between males and females. He conducts furtive researches into whatever encyclopedia, medical books, or magazines are available to him, in order to answer his trenchant questions about anatomy and destiny.

This prepubertal child, throughout these years of anxiety and confusion, is extremely needful of adult concern and guidance. Yet in most cases, the boy is afraid to confess his fantasies or to ask his questions of the father, and he is totally unable to find words to express these needs to his mother. (In fact, the core of the dilemma is that he is unable to figure out how girls or women feel about anything.) Because the subject of sex is such an important one to the boy, yet simultaneously is suppressed by the strongest taboo, the boy can only hide his feelings and retreat into his corner. There he is often discovered, in fact, daydreaming with his stamp collection or his computer, or engaged in some indecipherable dialogue with a trusting pet.

During these days of subterranean turmoil, the child's parents may be the dormant ones. They believe that they understand their boy, and yet because he has become uncharacteristically "quiet" (for which read "manageable"), they have a tendency to ignore him and turn their attention to other concerns. Often there is a younger sibling who is newly coping with separation anxiety as a result of starting school, or the parents may merely be feeling grateful for a time of holiday from the rigors of parenting. In any event, the father may well have forgotten his own phase of sexual repression, and the mother herself may have had no comparable experience that will give her a perspective. From the mother's point of view, the boy has grown moody and distant, no longer clinging so tightly to her as he did at six or seven. The boy, for his part, cannot permit himself the former closeness that he felt toward his mother, because he must discover and comprehend the "secret" of his relationship with her and—even more compelling—the relationship between her and his father. If he is unlucky enough to witness the "primal scene" at this age, the trauma is likely to have a profound effect upon him, not because of what he learns from the experience but because of the myriad questions that he will be forced to explore.

Whether or not a prepubescent boy encounters the primal scene, he can be thought of as a highly vulnerable child whose defenses are superficial and ill-formed. He is especially susceptible to adult influence from beyond the family, perhaps because the parents may have lost contact with his preoccupations and his fears. His mental space is a "blooming, buzzing confusion," and he finds himself prey to nearly any benign source of external control. It is in this state of mind that a victim is most often found by the molester.

PREVALENCE OF THE PROBLEM

In a much-quoted paper, Finkelhor (1980) estimated that approximately 9% of the male population of the country has been molested in childhood (p. 267). Earlier estimates were considerably lower.* And

---

* Estimates varying between 2.5% and 8.7% were reported by Finkelhor in his comprehensive review of prevalence surveys in the research literature (1984, p. 166). It is thought that to accept the higher estimate is the more prudent course, thus placing error on the side of caution.

while for many years it was believed that the prevalence of girls who were molested exceeded that of boys by between 10 and 12 to one, the currently accepted estimate (*San Franciso Chronicle*, 1985) is a two-to-one ratio (with the molestation of girls still predominating). If this figure is accurate, a highly pernicious social problem has at last been recognized after decades of neglect.

Another significant demographic characteristic that differentiates boy victims from girl victims is that a greater percentage of the molesters of boys are *nonfamily members* than are the molesters of girls. In one study (Finkelhor, 1979), this ratio was 83% to 56% (nonfamily molesters of boys to nonfamily molesters of girls). This follows from the fact that the most prevalent form of incest is father-daughter incest, and implies that molestation of boys is more often committed by men who are not their fathers. That the molester is a man in nearly every instance is confirmed by extensive research, the most recent being a survey by Reinhart (1987), who found that 96% of the perpetrators in his sample of 189 cases were male (p. 231).

EFFECTS ON THE CHILD

Being molested affects boys in a different way than it does girls. For example, it has been found that boys tend to be more secretive about this traumatic experience than are girls; they are thought to be fearful of revealing the molestation to family members, probably because of their perception of the need to play the "strong, silent" masculine role (Finkelhor, 1984; Fritz, Stoll, & Wagner, 1981). This phenomenon may also be due to the fact that boys are more strictly warned by the molester not to tell—with accompanying threats—than are girl victims. In general, a child's fear is likely to be positively correlated with the degree of threat implied by the feared object. In addition, boys may be reluctant to tell about the experience because of the taboo against homosexuality: that is, if the molester was male, the boy may feel the double jeopardy of censure because of (1) having been powerless and (2) confusion of sexual identity.

By contrast with girls, boys who are molested are believed to be less damaged by the experience. This research finding (Finkelhor, 1984; Fritz et al., 1981) may be the result of an artifactual error in the method most often used to collect these kinds of data (i.e., survey questionnaires of the recollections of men who had once been molested). Or, it may be a function of the problem referred to earlier, namely, that boys are more fearful of reporting molestation; if true, it would follow that men who once were molested might be anxious to minimize the effect that it may have had upon them. At least within American culture, men tend to practice a kind of emotional "damage control" in which, having confessed to a certain action, they will deny that the action meant something of importance to them.

In sum, boys who are molested differ from girls by being more repressive about the fact of having been molested and about its consequences. This tendency is *not* believed to be in the service of the ego. Hence, while girls may be far more severely traumatized by molestation, their natural candor about feelings, as well as their greater deference to parental authority, may increase the likelihood that they will find help sooner for their pain.

EFFECTS ON THE FAMILY

Little research exists on the subject of the impact upon a boy's family of the revelation that he has been the victim of molestation. For that reason, we shall rely upon the experience of clinical practice. Suffice it to say that the overt repercussions are devastating. The principal effect is one of massive confusion on the part of most parents who receive this news. For siblings as well, it is usually a matter of total incomprehension. This kind of assault can be so mind-boggling to the significant others of a victim that their first reaction can only be conceptualized as shock.

This is not to imply that the parents—and/or the sibling(s)—were no more than innocent bystanders to this event. The possible complicity of family members in the process that led to the assault will be discussed in detail in a section to follow. In the present context, it is worth noting that a component of the family members' reaction may be the need to deal with their own feelings of guilt.

In the aftermath of molestation, family dynamics are turned topsy-turvy. As when a serious accident occurs in the life of a family member, and each of the others must discover "how to feel" about it, so does this kind of assault bring conflict and inevitable change to the family process. Because of the societal taboo against "deviant" or "precocious" sexuality, the family must close ranks and cope with the neighbors who know what has happened, or with the community at large if the event has become a matter of public knowledge. The child who was molested needs to be protected from censure or ridicule by his schoolmates or playmates. It must be made clear to others that the child's sibling or siblings are not implicated in this scandal, and the parents may wish to absolve themselves of at least the deeper layers of blame.

Within the family itself, it is likely that a restructuring of roles will occur in which, at least for the time being, the role of the boy-victim is suspended. Since he is the "wounded" one, others must take over for him temporarily. The worst part is that no one knows how long this period will last. A significant element of the stress created by this kind of trauma is that those who care most about the victim first worry "will it ever end?" and later feel exasperated because "it takes so long." The boy himself is cast in the role of mysterious invalid in some families. In others, he is treated alternately as a pariah and as the newly repentant prodigal son. For example, the boy may be whisked away to a relative's home for a while, until the parents can collect their thoughts and dress their own wounds. During his stay, he takes on the aura of Odysseus on a quest abroad, for whom much is forgiven when he returns. These rituals have more symbolic than real value for the child. In whatever form it takes, this alienation from the boy's rightful place is one of the major obstacles to a reconciliation process that will be described in the treatment section later in the chapter.

LONG-TERM EFFECTS

The lengthy series of psychological losses that are typically suffered by the molested boy can be summarized as follows:

1. His trust in an (often) older person is betrayed.

2. He is plunged into a time warp in which the normal developmental sequences of sexuality are convoluted or vastly accelerated.

3. He is made to feel less masculine as a consequence of having been forced to do something against his will.

4. He is cast into a new and unsettling role within his own family.

5. He becomes vulnerable to possible ridicule, by peers and others, as one who must be "different" from them.

Clearly, none of these reversals is within the normal range of those calamities that are *expected* to occur during childhood or adolescence. Any one of them could contribute to neurotic adjustment. Taken together, these experiences are the active ingredients of trauma. More than the reality of the molestation itself, they coalesce to extend the traumatic ordeal far beyond the time when the physical acts have ceased. Hence, the nightmare may be less terrible than the awakening.

In helping the boy to recover, the clinician cannot lose sight of the fact that his emotional trauma has occurred during a period of rapid emotional growth. For that reason, treatment consists partly in helping him to catch up. This process resembles taking someone to a train and arriving too late at the station; it may be worth the effort to race ahead to the next station before the train gets there. Since, however, this effort could easily fail and make matters worse, it may be the wiser course to wait for a later train. Nevertheless, the child must reach the next developmental stage, and any intervention that is tried should take account of this factor of timing.

In conclusion, so much damage is done by molestation that a child or adolescent male victim can be considered psychologically and environmentally deprived. Effects on family equilibrium are profound. Reconstruction of this wounded ego and restoration of this weakened family stability may well be a protracted process, taking years in some cases.

SOURCE OF THE ASSAULT

This crime is rooted in a context of pathology that has two branches— one within the family of the child victim, the other within the distorted fantasy life of the molester. This section first examines factors in the boy's environment that can lead to his becoming a potential victim. Later, clues to the motivation of the potential molester will be traced.*

The Family Dynamics

Vulnerability to sexual abuse derives from more than a single source, and that is one reason why the ensuing trauma is so difficult to treat. Just as there is no typical family of origin, there can be no stereotypical approach to family therapy in these cases. There is a variety of pathological family alliances and defective coping styles that can increase

---

* A distinction should be drawn between two distinctly different types of molesters. Some pedophiles rape their victims; these psychopaths are similar to serial murderers, whose victims are for the most part chosen at random. In essence, these people hate children. The child who is assaulted is usually one who happens along at the wrong time and becomes a "target of opportunity." By contrast, the vast majority of pedophiles actually seek a relationship with the victim, to whom they are attracted physically or psychologically or both. The relationship, once established, is carefully cultivated by the molester. This distinction implies that, while some children are molested *against their will*, most victims are actively *courted* by the perpetrator of sexual abuse. This process sets the stage for molestation that occurs repeatedly over time (as opposed to a single event). This chapter discusses chiefly the more prevalent type of abuse concerning boys.

the probability that one of the children, in this case a young boy, will become the victim of a sexual assault. Some of these family environments are exemplified by the following types we have seen in our practice; by no means do they exhaust the possibilities:

- a situation in which the parents are on the verge of separation or divorce; this kind of contest may cast one or more of the children into the role of pawn;

- a nuclear family that contains a nonnuclear member such as an adopted son (or a son who does not technically "belong" because he was illegitimate); this kind of child is often the victim of neglect within the home; in addition, some family constellations require a scapegoat or "odd man out," for which the child of uncertain status may afford a convenient target; by contrast with the schizophrenogenic family, some families allow a member to be exposed to danger from people *outside* the family circle;

- a single-parent family in which, for example, a boy who remains with his mother is called upon to perform the role of "little man" (or substitute husband) for the mother;

- a family in which there is a boy who, because of unknown influences in early childhood, is effeminate; the resulting family conflict over this unsettling tendency can lead to the tactic of trying to ignore the problem, which itself may become a form of neglect.

Each of these family orientations or patterns of functioning will be described in detail below.

The child who is caught in a war between parents can suffer in many ways, and often the worst of it is not just "getting lost in the shuffle." Any clinician who does forensic work with custody cases will be aware of how cruel some parents can be when it comes to judging each other's parenting ability. This, of course, is a means to the end of obtaining principal custody or some other concession in the eventual divorce settlement.

The prepubertal boy who witnesses these squabbles is diminished by them, because he feels resentment toward the accusing parent and empathic guilt toward the accused. In the worst scenario, this child will feel responsible for the (alleged) failures of both parents. Although most children will not suffer permanent damage from their involvement in a divorce process, all will be touched by it and some will be unable to cope. The primitive and superficial defenses of some children will be strained to the limit when their families disintegrate. And if the boy should be asked which parent he wishes to stay with the majority of the time—as often occurs when the child is eight or nine or older—the stress created will be extreme, because he will find himself in a "no win" situation. Under these circumstances, when the center of a boy's life is in chaos, it is not surprising that he may be receptive to substitute parenting from a source beyond the home.

If a child has been designated as the family's scapegoat or the one who is "different" in some way, he may feel that an invisible wall separates him from the other family members, one that he cannot comprehend. This child may be the "middle child" who is squeezed out of the attention and affection of his parents because there are too many children and not enough love to go around. Or he may be the youngest child of parents who grew tired of parenting and had one more child than was wise for them. Further, in a blended family, he may be the child who "got lost." This boy may suffer a fate no more complicated than being ignored, but as his isolation from the core of the family increases, so does his alienation from the parents grow.

An example of the child who is an outcast in his own family can be found in the case of a boy who had been (from ages four to six) the victim of incest by his mother. When the parents divorced, the boy was placed in his father's custody because of the mother's lack of fitness to be a parent. In time, it became clear that the father, a man of borderline intelligence, could not properly care for the boy, so an aunt was persuaded to adopt him. This aunt proved the more acceptable parent for a short while, until she and the uncle had a child of their own. About then, the boy was just entering the difficult latency years, but these adoptive parents became more and more preoccupied with their new infant. Eventually, the boy was "farmed out" to the care of his adoptive father's brother, who molested him throughout one year. First the victim of his own mother and then of a relative, this child was twice betrayed by a defective family system.

The boy who must serve as his mother's "little man" is one whose childhood has been lost before he knew how to enjoy it. This fatherless boy needs his mother's love all the more, but she has her own needs, and her coping mechanisms may not be equal to the task of being both parents to her boy. In a case differing markedly from the one noted above, the boy was also caught in a labyrinth of allegiances. His natural father had abandoned the mother soon after he was born. After a while, a stepfather came along and gave him the fathering that he had never known; the boy's last name was changed to that of the stepfather whom he came to idolize. When the boy was about eight years old, the mother divorced this second husband and effectively prevented the boy from meeting with his stepfather during the next several years. When she at last realized that her son needed a male authority figure in his life, she enrolled him in the Big Brother program, whereupon he was molested repeatedly for several months by his Big Brother. Twice the mother had retreated from a disastrous marriage to a symbiotic relationship with her only son, whose loyalty to her came into sharp conflict with his need to learn masculine ways and to proceed in his development toward manhood.

An effeminate boy will find that the interval before puberty becomes increasingly painful. The parents will grow more and more anxious about their boy's "state," and their anxiety will accomplish nothing more than to confuse the boy still more about why there is so much tension in the household. The boy himself may have no standard by which to judge his own masculinity or the lack of it, and thus wonders what he has done to cause his parents to stare and frown at him. In one such case, a boy of 14 had successfully reached puberty and endured its conflicts by himself, but was afraid to confide this to his puritanical, divorced mother. Even though he had already had heterosexual experiences, the boy was still quite delicate, sensitive, and shy in manner. His mother, mistaking this for a homosexual trend, reacted by enrolling the boy in a youth organization, with the result that her worst fears were realized by the assault of a male counselor on her son.

A theme that pervades the preceding account of factors that contribute to a boy's lack of defense against molestation is the one of the absent father. The case vignettes that were cited give a trenchant description of the effect upon the child of rejection by his father in its many forms, the worst of which is abandonment. The source of the dilemma for the boy is the experience of losing a father at a most critical stage of learning the ways of men. In essence, many boy victims of molestation are, by one means or another, fatherless children. The father has contrived to be away from the home or has neglected his fatherly role at the very time when the son most needs his presence, his regard, and his encouragement. When this critical preadolescent time is not filled with masculine role modeling, the budding young man will experience a delay in his progress—as though spellbound—while his body continues to evolve according to its own schedule. The lost father becomes the idealized hero and, in fantasy, the boy's tormentor. The boy who is at risk to be molested is one who lacks male guidance about sexual values. Other teachers will be found outside the home, and they are as likely to exploit him as they are to be a positive influence.

The abdication by a father figure of the fatherly role in guiding a young boy into adolescence is the key to understanding a boy's susceptibility to molestation, as well as a starting place for psychotherapy with the child after his assault and ensuing trauma. This approach will be described at length in the concluding section of this chapter.

The Mind of the Molester

The person who assaults a little boy sexually is, by any reasonable standard of conduct, a psychopath who deserves no sympathy from right-thinking persons. But according to the police profile cited previously (Chapter 1, p. 4), a molester often masks his identity behind a cloak of respectability. To reiterate, this type is typically in his twenties or thirties, a college graduate, a married man who may have children of his own, and he has led others in his circle to believe that he is generally a "good citizen" and above suspicion. If the description fits, this type of criminal will be difficult to find and even harder to convict and punish. In order to prevent such a travesty, it is worth taking a look behind the mask.

A molester of boys chooses them as victims because they are "safe" objects over whom he can swiftly establish control. The boy, for his part, is typically starved for fathering, and the molester will at first take full advantage of this need. He will try to become the boy's mentor or confessor or "pal." In one case of a man who molested at least 30 boys between the ages of six and 15 in a residential neighborhood during a two-year period, his mode of operation was remarkably clever. He took a job in a convenience store which, because it was open until late hours, had become a hangout for local youth. He would secretly give them candy or soft drinks or comic books and sometimes beer, until they trusted him and thought of him as a "good guy." Later, he would use these favors as a means to coerce them into visiting his home. He would entice the new initiates to take pictures of other boys engaging with him in sex; finally, the picture taking would be used as a form of blackmail to force the new boy to have sex as well. This pattern of assault was only broken when one of the boys, who felt that the molester had neglected him, reported the events to his parents. We were involved in providing treatment for the trauma suffered by four of this man's many victims.*

---

* The perpetrator had been incarcerated twice previously for child molestation. After having served a total of six years in jail, he was released to probation with the requirement that he receive psychological counseling. When he had attended 45 group counseling sessions, a psychologist recommended that his probation be ended. It was later revealed

The preceding example shows how a shrewd pedophile can seek out and take advantage of the vulnerability of a needful child. He becomes the "good daddy" who never has a temper tantrum or never punishes arbitrarily, who accepts the boy for what he is and caters to his whims. Without necessarily being conscious of doing so, the molester can exploit a child's intense sexual curiosity and give him some answers (albeit wrong ones) to his questions about what adults feel and do.

The kind of man who fulfills his own needs through assaulting boys may well have been molested as a child. Whether he was or not, he has become fixated at an adolescent phase of development. This does not refer to how the person behaves, but rather to how he *feels*. This point was well taken by Geiser (1979), who wrote: "Molesters of young children are probably psychologically children themselves. They identify more easily with children and feel more comfortable in their presence" (p. 89). This grotesque Pan, whose psychosocial training came to a halt during the teenage years, is very likely one who lacked adequate fathering. His experience has led him to become, for his victims, the idealized, caring father; at the same time, he is perversely able to punish his own neglectful father by means of his misdeeds.

The molester is a man who, by default, tends to rely on women for support and nurturance. He has always found, in the adult women who guided him through the shoals of childhood, a source of solace. As a result, he has become dependent upon female authority figures, even though he resents this trait in himself. At an unconscious level, he feels a strong identification with women, but he would never be able to confront or admit this introjected *persona*.

The molester tends to deny his homosexuality. As Geiser (1979) put it, "It is not unusual for a child molester to express strong feelings against homosexuals" (p. 92). This self-deception is a key to understanding the fact that he is, in many cases, a married man who has fathered children. By not having overt adult-with-adult homosexual experiences, he manages (by a certain form of logic) to avoid the stigma of being the "gay" man who is living a lie by being married to a woman. He does not think of himself as bisexual because his homosexual relationships with boys do not "count." In this climate of self-deception and sham, it is not surprising that in many cases the marriage of a molester has been a superficial and unloving union prior to the husband's being found out. The secret of its lasting so long may be the dependency

---

that he had been molesting boys throughout the last several months of counseling sessions. When his probation ended, however, the true reign of terror began, and it was nearly two more years before he was caught. He was sentenced to 104 years in jail.

arrangement between these partners, in which the wife is content to play a motherly role.

In summary, the molester of young boys is an inadequate personality who clings to women and strives to prove his worthiness as a man. His victims are chosen because they are powerless to resist him, due to the same obsession with finding a father that the molester himself probably experienced as a boy. The molester is a homosexual with a difference, in that he cannot accept his homosexuality and expends much energy to divert suspicion from himself. Unlike the homosexual, he seeks not a mate but a slave. And because he is so psychopathic and so lacking in self-knowledge, he can harm others in many ways over long periods of time. That a molester of boys is extremely resistive to treatment and/or rehabilitation goes without saying, but the methods of overcoming that resistance are not the subject of this book.

There has not been much research on the subject, but some clinicians hold the opinion that the more severely disturbed male molester is ambivalent about whether or not his victim is a boy or a girl. That is, a person who has attacked a boy might just as well attack a girl if given the opportunity. One of these opinions was expressed sternly by Geiser (1979), as follows:

> Any group seriously interested in the sexual safety of children in the classroom would do well to concentrate on pedophiles—men sexually interested in young children, regardless of sex. (p. 93)

This point of view may be correct in concept but inaccurate in detail. There are certainly pedophiles who would have nothing to do with young boys. One such molester was encountered in prison, where he was beginning a 21-year term for having been convicted of kidnapping and raping a young girl; his long sentence was appropriate because he had twice before been convicted of the same crime.

The man boasted of his assault. He said that he had had many sexual encounters with women in the past (he had never married), but he found those women so difficult to satisfy. It was always such hard work, he claimed, to "make them come." By contrast, young girls were no trouble to please: "They'll let you do anything; they love it." This man freely admitted his crime and accepted the sentence he was given as deserved. Yet the sequence of events that began with his abduction of the young girl can be seen in another light. It led to a situation in which, for many years, the molester will be incarcerated, very likely, with another man as a cell-mate. He knew this in advance because he had previously spent time in prison. Through the victimization of a child, he had achieved the resolution of a homosexual fantasy that he could neither articulate nor understand. In short, there is an undercurrent of latent homosexuality in the sexual orientation of the pedophile who preys on young girls. His is the ultimately inadequate personality because he is both terrified by women and incapable of actualizing his attraction to men.

RECOMMENDED TREATMENT METHODS FOR BOY VICTIMS

A major consideration for psychotherapy with boy victims of molestation is the child's need for reconciliation with his father or, in the most difficult cases, the need for a father substitute. This consideration at once points to the appropriateness of a family therapy approach, because whatever healthy allegiance is to be restored between father and son will require changing alliances elsewhere in the family system—e.g., between the father and the boy's sibling(s) or between mother and son. This family approach will be addressed later in this section, following a discussion of the frequent case in which the father is effectively absent from the child's life, or in which reconciliation of the two would be ill-advised.

A key issue that should be mentioned here is the expectation that boys will imitate, as early as possible in their development, those qualities of manhood that are considered ideal in our culture. For example, men are expected to be sexual aggressors, and they are thought to be weak or foolish if they reveal fear or confusion about sexual functioning. By extension, boys are generally relied upon to find out for themselves what sex is all about, and to keep their doubts and dilemmas to themselves in most families. These factors compound the problem of the molested child, because his enticement into premature sexual activity may cast doubt on his fitness for the man's role. In effect, he has submitted to the blandishments of another person when he should have refused; he gave in to a physical impulse when he should have resisted steadfastly. It is clear that molestation does more harm than simply arresting a boy's sexual development. It calls into question his fortitude in defending the values he was taught at an early age—in effect, his moral fiber and masculine identity.

This kind of challenge to a boy's fitness for manhood would be even more poignant in the case of one who had been molested by a woman or girl. In such a case, the roles of aggressor and the one who submits have been reversed. For example, a boy of 10 was assaulted by a teenaged girl neighbor; although apparently only one incident of molestation took place, the boy's parents were alarmed at his inability to say no, and for a time could not restrain themselves from questioning the boy's resistance to temptation of various kinds.

When a person's trustworthiness is challenged, his own ability to trust can be shaken. For that reason, establishing trust will be crucial to the beginning of therapy with the traumatized boy. Considerable thought should be given to the subject of whether the therapist should be male or female. The sex of the clinician affords both advantages and disadvantages in this type of case. For example, latency-age and adolescent boys generally respond better to treatment by a man, while many little boys of six or younger are able to relate well to a female therapist. But if a male counselor reminds the victim of the molester in some way, such as in appearance or by some behavior, the necessary transference may not materialize.

With a female therapist, the boy will very likely have difficulty in telling the story of what has happened to him. It may be too much to expect that he would describe the details of a sexual assault to a woman whom he has not met before. In fact, as will be discussed below, the child of a single-parent mother may even be reluctant to tell *her* some details of the molestation. All things considered, the boy of nine or older should very likely be seen at least initially by a male therapist. The most significant advantage is the opportunity to use therapy as a means to disengage the tangled relationship between father and son, or to build a bridge to new sources of fathering for the son who has been abandoned. The transference itself, if successfully created, should serve to catch the attention of the father or closest father equivalent. It is important that this man pay attention, because his commitment to a new way of perceiving the boy will be vital to the closing stages of therapy.

Early Stages

In order to establish trust, patience is required. When a boy who has been molested is brought to the office of a clinician, it is highly likely that he will be fearful if he has no prior experience with counseling. If not properly prepared by his parent(s), he may be resentful as well. The main difficulty is that the child is less aware, on a conscious level, that he has a problem than are the grown-ups in his life. He knows that something "terrible" has happened to him and he may or may not feel awful about what happened, but he cannot be expected to intuit that he is "exhibiting symptoms" or "suffering from an emotional disorder." He is not aware that he is experiencing trauma because he is *in* the trauma.

What the boy wishes to do most of all, especially in the first weeks after his being molested has been revealed, is to forget about the matter entirely. He wants to play with his friends or go fishing with his father, or just watch television—whatever he perceives as the sign of living a normal life or whatever will reassure him that the nightmare has ended. Visiting a therapist's office is not on the child's agenda.

Recognizing and accepting these resistances as a natural phase in the recovery from trauma, a clinician will proceed with more than usual caution to establish transference with the boy. At the first session, when one or both parents will have accompanied the boy to the office, it is a good idea to greet them, introduce oneself, and ask the boy to come into the therapy room alone. The purpose is to avoid the child's sitting by himself in the waiting room for a long time while the adults discuss his "case" and his anxiety rises by the minute. (This procedure should be described to the parent[s] when the first appointment is arranged.) When the boy is seated in the office, it is best to begin immediately with a series of questions that he will have no difficulty in answering, such as his age, grade in school, name of school, favorite subject and least-favorite subject, and favorite sport. If the boy is extremely tense, these questions can be expanded indefinitely as a form of history taking that should eventually have a calming effect. Most children are put at their ease by this type of questioning, because it reminds them of ordinary school routine.

After a brief time of getting acquainted in this way, more than one course of action is available as a next step. For example, the therapist can begin the process of testing the boy at this first session, if psychological testing is part of one's approach to therapy. When the boy's fears have subsided somewhat, he can usually be persuaded to do several of the Draw-a-Person (Harris, 1963) drawings on the first day. As an alternative procedure, the therapist can tell him about some of the play therapy opportunities that are available in counseling, such as a game (checkers, chess, etc.) or building a model plane or car. The immediate aim is to give the child an idea of what possible benefits could be gained from his visits in future. A larger goal is to make clear from the beginning that the therapist is concerned about him as a person, instead of as a victim. Toward the end of this session, the boy can be excused to the waiting room, preferably supplied with a game or some other activity as a distraction, while the parent or parents trade places with him. Whether at this or in a later meeting with the boy's family members, it is important that the clinician learn as many details of the molestation as they can provide.

At a second session, the process of getting acquainted can be continued (as well as more projective testing if desired), but the main objective is to put the relationship between child and therapist on at least a preliminary contractual basis. Guidelines should be provided at this point so that the boy will know there is more involved in therapy than playing games or taking a test, and so that he will begin to form realistic expectations of what these sessions seek to accomplish. A suggested procedure for presenting these guidelines to a victim of either sex is provided in Chapter 3 (pp. 43–47). Their aim is to encourage the child to describe what happened to him in as complete detail as possible. This telling of the story will be vital to therapy, because it enables the clinician to understand how the boy *perceived* the assault. It also will clarify what the relationship between victim and molester was prior to the assault, as described by the boy himself. In effect, one needs to know what led up to the assault and what it meant to him from the one perspective that counts—the child's.

Whether it occurs during a second session or much later in treatment—as indicated by the clinician's intuition that the proper moment has arrived—this line of questioning is worth pursuing in some manner such as the following (these are suggested approaches that can be modified in any way and varied broadly in form or content):

1. I know that you have had an experience with an adult. Someone has done something to you that was wrong. It shouldn't have happened, but it's not the end of your life.

2. It's important that you tell me what happened when you are ready to tell me. I'm here to listen. I'm not here to ask a lot of questions or give you a lecture. If you don't want to talk about something, you don't have to.

3. If you want me to, what you tell me can be told to your [father, mother, significant adult]. I won't tell [him or her] anything that we say unless you agree that it's okay to tell [him or her].

It is understood that these remarks must be spoken gently and with restraint. In the case of an extremely fragile child, they must be lightened by even more subtle phrasing.

A recommended source of useful information about the boy's current personality dynamics is the standard battery of projective tests, such as the Rorschach and TAT (or CAT with very young boys). In the absence of other information, at least the extent of the trauma can be assessed. Further, if the boy has fallen behind in schoolwork as a symptom of post-traumatic stress, the degree to which his achievement ranks below that of his grade level can be measured (e.g., by the Wide Range Achievement Test). If the gap is significant, giving an IQ test may be worthwhile; the result could show that the boy is bright enough to perform at grade level, but has been unable to concentrate in school as a result of trauma.*

Collecting data about the actual events of the assault, from either the boy or his family members or both, as well as measuring the magnitude of the boy's post-traumatic pathology, constitute the primary tasks of the initial phase of therapy. One factor that may prolong this stage is the possibility that a child will "test" the clinician himself: that is, an oppositional phase may intervene when it becomes difficult to persuade the child to cooperate with any aspect of therapy. When this "storm" of displaced anger passes, and when it can be said that transference is firmly established between therapist and child and between therapist and family, the treatment process can begin in earnest.

Middle Stages

Treatment has the dual purposes of reconstructing the boy's ego and of restoring family unity, just as it does in the case of a girl who has been the victim of assault (see Chapter 3). Since the two desired outcomes are positively correlated, both will be pursued simultaneously in the well-planned treatment strategy. In an ideal scenario, the boy would be helped to move successfully through the several stages of the trauma response and recovery cycle, would then be restored to his level of functioning prior to the assault, and finally would be successfully reintegrated into his family system. This happens rarely, if at all, in real life. The child may punctuate the proceedings with periods of sullen opposition or episodes of acting out. One or more of the family members may give the impression of wanting therapy to fail, and there will be times when their lack of cooperation brings progress to a halt. Thus, the process is often one of false starts and frequent relapses.

The best treatment plan to begin with is one that is concentrated upon the victim, with the family members considered as collateral clients. In time and with progress toward recovery on the part of the boy, emphasis can be shifted to family concerns. Even so, family members can certainly be brought into therapy occasionally from the

---

* Because scores on IQ tests (e.g., WISC-R) are negatively affected by stress factors, it may be that the child's current score is an underestimation of true potential. Other sources of information, such as prior test results, should be reviewed in detail.

start, as long as the boy is made aware of the reason for their being present during that session.

Should transference be established, a male clinician will be in a good position to offer the child the father substitute that he may lack. This will be accomplished in several ways, not the least of which is by example and by presence. The boy needs to know that the therapist will "be there" for him when he feels shaky or wants to talk with someone. Even more important, the boy needs to know that the therapist accepts him without judgment. This is conveyed by *affirmation*. Through board games and other shared activities such as model building, a therapist can show his concern for the boy's ability to do well at whatever he attempts, as well as acceptance of his mistakes. Life is full of accidents, which tend to happen to people when they feel most lucky. And by extension, a person can suffer an accident as terrible— and as absurd—as having been molested. From such experiences one can learn and grow.

Because the boy endured what probably in his eyes, and those of his parents(s), was a failure experience, he is in need of reconstituting himself by means of a series of successes. The reason is that neither he nor his loved ones are likely to achieve the detachment that will enable them to look upon the molestation as one of life's cruel events. Nevertheless, the antidote for the self-doubt that is created by "failure" is a real or imagined demonstration of competence. Often this can occur in the subtlest of forms. For example, a child whose siblings have continually excelled at simple games can derive much self-esteem from defeating an opponent who is outside the family circle. Should the opponent be an adult, so much the better.

As the boy gains in confidence, his parent(s) can be expected to notice the change. The parent may then be aware that some progress is being made and may be better motivated to lend a hand in therapy. One way to give a parent a role in this recovery process is to invite him or her to join the boy and therapist during the 10 or 15 minutes before the end of a therapy session. The boy should be told about this plan in advance. It can be introduced by asking: "Do you mind if I ask your mother [father] to come in for a while today?" If the answer is "no," the clinician can ask, "Is there something that you would like me to ask your mother [father] when she [he] comes in?"

Later in the treatment process, it may be possible to ask (before the parent enters), "If I would ask her [him] what you've been doing wrong lately, what do you think she [he] would say?" Because this is phrased conditionally, it implies to the child that it may be a question that need not be asked, and in fact there is no reason that it should. The answer will inform the therapist of the child's present concerns vis-à-vis his parent, as well as the most recent themes of his discipline at home.

If the boy replies to the latter question by stating a complaint that the parent is likely to make, the clinician can ask him specifically for permission to mention it when the parent comes in. Usually, the child will agree, especially if he feels that the therapist will be his advocate in any discussion that follows. And in the event, the therapist will be introducing a subject that the child has been thinking about himself in a context in which he is protected from the parent's emotions by a third party. This technique is not really intended to mediate the many annoyances that aggravate the life of parent and child. Its aim is to create dialogue between people whose communication has become distorted by a traumatic event. The alienation that has intruded between son and parent can be lessened when they are called upon to speak their grievances in the presence of a caring outsider.

With the passage of time, one may wish to expand on this format for therapy sessions, gradually lengthening the portion of the hour that is given to the parent-child interaction. Later, the other parent (or surrogate) can be invited to take part, so that what began as a problem in and of the child may eventually be identified as a family issue. On occasion, it is appropriate to meet with the parent(s) separately in order to find out how he or she views the course of treatment so far. These meetings should be discussed first with the boy, so that he does not fear that his confidences will be betrayed.

In some cases, the boy's siblings should participate in therapy. These are the cases in which the boy is either quite "close" to a sibling, or those in which the relationship with a particular sibling has deteriorated since the assault occurred. Both situations call for an assessment of changes that traumatic events have forced upon the relationship, as well as a new accommodation between the two. The victim needs help in his relationship with his brother or sister in order to gain new sources of acceptance and support. In many cases, a sibling will be asked to express a degree of insight that is beyond his or her comprehension, or a degree of sympathy beyond his or her capacity to feel. A possible key to the sibling's empathic understanding is an awareness that he or she could just as easily have been victimized too.

Finally, the quest for the father must find resolution. If an existing father-son bond can be renewed or strengthened, so much the better for both. This will be achieved only when the father is fully in touch with his neglect of the boy and is prepared to rebuild the relationship. He must place no blame on his son for the assault and make an effort to see that the assailant is caught and punished. In short, the father should resume his fatherly role of protector and teacher by example. It may be that he will benefit from counseling designed to improve his fathering skills.

Certain fathers will not be equal to the challenge. These are the men who have long since distanced themselves from their child in one way or another. For some children, the stepfather or their mother's boyfriend is no consolation. Ironically, the problem begins and ends at the same place: the child seeks to fill a deficiency in his life by finding a father figure who, in turn, betrays him; and if the "natural" father figure rejects him once more, he will be vulnerable again. At different developmental stages, this vulnerability will invite differing forms of abuse, but abuse nonetheless.

A male therapist can only impersonate the "good daddy" for one or two hours a week, and for that reason it will be useful (if possible) to work with the father or surrogate intensively—both jointly with the boy and in separate sessions. Here, too, there is likely to be testing, by both man and child, to find out if the clinician is a "safe" person to permit closeness with the father-son system. In those too frequent cases when the father or surrogate denies the problem or avoids therapy, other methods are called for. The mother can be encouraged to find as many father substitutes as possible for her boy, from sources such as sports groups, scouting or other boys' clubs, special classes such as music or singing lessons, hobby groups such as model railroading or stamp collecting, church activities, and so forth. In effect, many part-time fathers may suffice for the boy whose male parent has been lost. These people should be screened very carefully by the mother before the child is enrolled in programs such as the ones mentioned, for obvious reasons.

Closing Stages

The trauma of molestation will never be fully erased from the memory of a victim. Although he may "adjust" to it, he cannot wipe it away. Hence, the boy and man to follow are forever altered by the incident. This fact by no means trivializes the contribution of treatment, but it can reframe our ambitions. As clinicians, we seek to help molested children to resume their lives as well as can be expected and to lead them to a safe place in which events like that are less likely to happen. These criteria of successful therapy may exhaust the possibilities. Above all, the therapist should recognize that these children may have to return to treatment more than once during later developmental stages.

From a realistic standpoint, we can conclude treatment when most of the following milestones have been reached:

1. The boy has experienced a working through of the trauma by such means as telling his therapist how he perceived the assault, venting his anger toward the assailant, and/or moving steadily through the steps of the recovery cycle.

2. There is evidence that the victim has arrived at or has regained an appropriate level of development for his chronological age; for example, the prepubertal boy should be able to compete with his peers in games or sports or schoolwork or in just plain horsing around. He should have at least one close male friend of his age, and he should be relatively well behaved in the company of adults. The boy who has reached puberty should exhibit each of the above characteristics, as well as demonstrate the first signs of male vanity (e.g., concern for hygiene and appearance) and be able to contemplate some form of relationship with a girl. If none of these indicators of adolescent *Sturm und Drang* is sighted, this boy is probably still in the process of recovery from trauma, in that period when he can best be described as treading water.

3. A better relationship has been achieved, or is in process, between the boy and at least one significant male authority figure, preferably his father; this is the touchstone of therapy, and the hardest part.

4. Boy and family are reconciled, with the child reinstalled as a fully fledged family member who has a secure status and an accepted role. If this had been lacking before the boy became a victim, it is doubly necessary now.

These considerations imply that the child needs to reintegrate his sense of identity and self-worth at the same time that he needs to find a protected niche within his environment. Therapy will not create these changes, but it can set them in motion and help them evolve.

REFERENCES

Finkelhor, D. *Sexually victimized children*. New York: Free Press, 1979.

Finkelhor, D. Risk factors in the sexual victimization of children. *Child Abuse and Neglect, 4*, 265–273, 1980.

Finkelhor, D. *Child sexual abuse: New theory and research*. New York: The Free Press, 1984.

Fritz, G. S., Stoll, K., & Wagner, N. N. A comparison of males and females who were sexually molested as children. *Journal of Sex and Marital Therapy, 7*(1), 54–59, 1981.

Geiser, R. L. *Hidden victims: The sexual abuse of children*. Boston: Beacon Press, 1979.

Harris, D. B. *Children's drawings as measures of intellectual maturity.* New York: Harcourt, Brace & World, 1963.

Hinsie, L. E., & Campbell, R. J. *Psychiatric dictionary* (4th ed.). New York: Oxford University Press, 1970.

Reinhart, M. A. Sexually abused boys. *Child Abuse and Neglect,* 11, 229–235, 1987.

San Francisco Chronicle. Many adults were abused as children, new poll finds. August 26, p. 51, 1985.

7

Adults Who Were Traumatized as Children

For as long as one can imagine, people have sexually abused children and adolescents—usually the more vulnerable ones, which compounds the tragedy. And when one attempts to infer the numbers of persons within the present adult population who were traumatized as children or adolescents, by using the estimated number of children believed to have been sexually abused each year as a baseline, the result is staggering. By the most conservative standard, this population is very large. At last, clinicians are beginning to discover widespread evidence of this well-hidden phenomenon and to examine its implications for psychotherapy with adult clients.

This chapter is intended to provide therapists with a clinical picture of the characteristics of adults who were abused as children or adolescents. The chapter is primarily focused on three categories of this often misunderstood population: (1) those who tried to tell someone, who responded in such a way that they made no further attempt to confide their secret; (2) those who told someone but did not receive the support or help they needed to resolve the trauma; and (3) those who told no one. Of course, there have been children and adolescents who were able to tell someone what happened to them and who did obtain the help and protection that they needed. And, once in a while, life spontaneously heals by providing corrective experiences. But in our experience, such cases are few and far between. The more likely instances are those in which trauma has lain festering beneath the surface like a "psychological time bomb" (Peters, 1973).

This chapter begins with a description of how some adults who were sexually assaulted as children find their way into treatment. The first section of the chapter places special emphasis upon helping a therapist to identify the previously "silent" victim of childhood sexual trauma. We suggest how a therapist might go about bringing this kind of trauma to light in a manner that the client can tolerate. We give reasons for the fact that some child and adolescent victims remain silent for years and frequently feel compelled to persevere in the victim's role throughout adolescence and adulthood—often in the form of self-destructive acting out. The chapter then describes some common mistakes that a clinician may make, which frequently serve to compound the original trauma and preserve the victim's silence. The chapter concludes with suggestions for the treatment of these clients who were sexually traumatized in childhood.

UNCOVERING THE SECRET

The present population of people who were sexually traumatized as children or adolescents is a tragic group. They were young in an era when their suffering was rarely, if ever, recognized. In many cases, the very real assaults that they suffered were dismissed as fantasies; or, they themselves were blamed for bringing on the assault by their "seductive" or bad behavior. Many have been cruelly mislabeled by society and, frankly, misdiagnosed by the professionals who were supposed to help them. Frequently, such misunderstandings only served to deepen their feelings of isolation and self-deprecation, and may have served to validate their self-destructive histories by confirming their feelings of worthlessness through the medium of a clinical label.

A therapist should be aware that many persons who were sexually assaulted as children or adolescents may not spontaneously tell the therapist about the event. Our clinical experience suggests that many victims can spend considerable time in a therapeutic relationship before they develop sufficient trust to broach the subject (see also Everstine & Everstine, 1983; Gil, 1971; Lister, 1982). Even when this topic is introduced, it may not be done directly. In some cases, the victim may not have defined what was done as a form of abuse. The person may defend himself or herself by rationalizing that such events were "just part of life." Or, the person may have accepted the rationalizations of the abuser as reality and thus have interpreted the event as what he or she deserves. Many adults who were traumatized in early life perceive the abuse as a "definition" of themselves, i.e., they construct a self-image that incorporates the abuse, instead of seeing it as something that happened to them. Past and present trauma are viewed as attributes of one's *persona*.

As with many young victims, these adult victims may initially tell the therapist more about the abuse by their behavior than by words. For example, people who have a long-standing history of self-destructive or suicidal behavior may well have been sexually abused as children; recent evidence of this phenomenon has been provided by Harrison, Lumry, and Claypatch (1984), Bagley and Ramsay (1985), Briere (1984), and Sedney and Brooks (1984). In addition, persons who choose abusive partners in their relationships or those who continually place themselves in situations in which they will be injured physically or emotionally should also be viewed with concern (Briere, 1984; Russell, 1987). Because many adults who were victimized as children have internalized the traumatic event as part of their personality structures—that of a person not worthy of care—they frequently develop a style of life which tends to perpetuate their being victimized (Miller et al., 1978). Although some are overtly suicidal, they are more likely to take extreme risks, abuse alcohol or drugs (Briere, 1984; Herman, 1981), or make life decisions that are self-defeating. Again, these people see themselves as unworthy, and so they lack the ability (or see no reason) to take care of themselves. Other, more desperate victims may consider committing suicide as the only way ultimately to get revenge on the adults who abused them (see Everstine & Everstine, 1983, Chapter 11).

Clients who have hysterical personality disorders or who depersonalize or "split off" should also be treated with particular concern. They may describe such symptoms as "going numb," "emotionally shutting down," or (literally) "going blank" in situations in which they experience intense anger, anxiety, confusion, or pain. One victim of childhood sexual assault accidentally inflicted second- and third-degree burns to her body during an intensely angry family situation. While she was cooking one day, her sister and mother began an extremely emotional argument. The sister rushed into the kitchen and angrily demanded that our client take her side in the battle, and while the sister was yelling at her, she touched the stove and burned herself severely. At the time, she was unaware of what was happening to her, and it was only later that she realized she had been injured.

We have observed that some persons (men as well as women) who are promiscuous or who appear to be unable to "attach" by establishing trusting love relationships may have been victimized as children. These people may easily involve themselves in sexual encounters with strangers, but have tremendous difficulty in forming and maintaining healthy partnerships. They may enter therapy with the complaint that they feel adrift and alienated from life. Many appear socially adept but in fact lead solitary lives, devoid of close ties or commitments. Because they so fear intimacy, they tend to equate closeness with being used or rejected, and thus retreat from relationships in general. For these reasons, clients who suffer from reactions of panic when they approach a possible love relationship should be observed carefully by the clinician, on the chance that a history of being abused as a child lies hidden.

Although childhood sexual trauma often plays a role in the history of a borderline personality disorder (see *DSM-III-R*, 1987, pp. 346–347), it is necessary to differentiate persons who have an unresolved childhood sexual trauma from the true borderline, masochistic, or manipulative client. Even though they may superficially share many characteristics, the emotional dynamics of the self-destructive or acting-out behavior of the borderline or masochistic person are quite different from those of a person who suffers from unresolved childhood sexual trauma. Many child victims of sexual trauma have been misdiagnosed as borderline, hysterical, manipulative or generally "bad" or "annoying" clients. Granted, working with this kind of person can be extremely trying, but in many such cases there is much more to the client's behavior than manipulation, pushing limits, or attention getting. The therapist should be wary lest his or her response to such behavior reflects anger and frustration at not being able to control the wayward client, instead of awareness of the message that the client is trying to convey by his or her behavior.

In order that there is no misunderstanding, we can affirm the need to set clear limits with clients who act out. But the clinician should also recognize that some clients (i.e., those who have suffered sexual trauma as children) may be trying to express the unspeakable by their behavior (Nelson, 1982). In most cases, thoughtful and cautious inquiry over a period of time is the best means of discerning which clients are suffering from the effects of sexual abuse (see also Gil, 1971; Katan, 1973; Lister, 1982; Peters, 1973). It is rarely a matter of asking a certain question, but rather of employing a period of sensitive and cautious inquiry, during which the client will be testing and scrutinizing a therapist's responses on every level in order to discern whether or not he or she is a safe person to receive the secret.

People who have been sexually assaulted as children may seek treatment because of some undefined anxiety when they contemplate parenthood, when they become parents, or when a child of theirs approaches the same age that they were when sexually abused.* More-

---

* The subject of parents who, having been sexually abused as children, later abuse

over, there are cases in which one of the parents who brings in a sexually assaulted child has himself or herself suffered an assault in childhood. This parent may have been abused at approximately the same age as his or her child. It is not uncommon for these parents to attempt to "work through" their own assault by means of the child's traumatic experience.

The Relationship Between Therapist and Client

The clinician's initial approach of cautious observation is a critical step because several forces are at work simultaneously in these cases. For example, the therapist may be seen, by the client, as shifting between two incompatible roles. First, a therapist can become confused with the "bad parent" who did not discover or did not respond appropriately to what was done to the client in childhood (the parent who could not or would not see that the child was being abused and was suffering, and who failed to protect the child; the parent who, the child believed, was indifferent to or condoned the abuse). In another guise, the therapist can become the fantasied "good parent," namely, a parent who would have been able to perceive what was being done to the child, who would have stopped the abuse and protected the child from further harm.

This initial observation phase may be further complicated by the client's defenses, in that the sexual assault may have been repressed and, consequently, may be inaccessible to the client at present. Hence, he or she may be asking the therapist to intuit what may not have been conscious when therapy began—in effect, to know what he or she does not know. Here is a paradox reminiscent of the dilemma faced by Prince Calaf in Puccini's "Turandot"—a mystery without clues.

The Client's Defenses

Apart from this obvious repression, a client may also have diminished the intensity of the event by some form of the dissociative process. As one woman so clearly summarized after describing years of brutal physical and sexual abuse by her father, "You know, being beaten up isn't that bad; after the first hit you don't feel it anymore." It is worth reflecting that these kinds of defenses may have been the person's protectors and friends—in many instances a victim's only solace. When

---

their own children was addressed in Chapter 5 in the section on the incestuous family system.

casting off these defenses and telling someone about the trauma, the person may feel that the only shield has been stripped away and that he or she is without anesthesia against the pain of the original assault. One client described a previous therapist, the leader of a woman's group who aggressively confronted the client's defenses before the group, in these words: "That therapist attacked me! She tried to take away my way of coping. I know I'm hard. I have a shell and there's some stuff I won't look at. But I protect myself the best way I know how. Who is she to attack me . . . trying to take away all I have that protects me from me? . . . Is she going to protect me? No!" Needless to say, the woman never returned to the group.

Because the defense mechanisms of these persons may be the only reason that they have not broken down before now, a clinician should proceed with restraint. By confronting these defenses head on, without laying considerable groundwork, the therapist will be considered to be yet another assailant by a victim. The client can choose between two alternatives: to flee from therapy or, if he or she is particularly dependent, to develop a pathological transference with the therapist. In such a relationship, the person may form an attachment with the clinician that is fundamentally masochistic and that, in the client's mind, may be reminiscent of his or her relationship with the abuser. When working with these persons, a therapist should be ever mindful that the power which is inherent in the therapeutic transference may be terrifying to adults who were sexually abused as children, because they do not possess the foundation of a healthy parent–child trust relationship. In fact, one of the primary clinical issues is this lack of trust and the person's accompanying inability to form intimate, nurturing relationships. The therapy experience must not mirror, in any way, the original abusive ordeal.

The fact that some people who were sexually abused as children can present themselves as hardened (superficially), successful, or wordly-wise adults can further confound the early stages of therapy. A clinician should perceive that this strong/tough demeanor is merely a veneer that masks the terrified child within. As noted earlier, psychological growth often stops when sexual abuse begins, and thus there may be two clients—the overly defended adult and the blocked child. This may place a therapist in the difficult position of having to phrase things in a way that communicates with both the child and adult aspects of the victim—a connotational balancing act that is not always easy to accomplish.

The Pact of Silence

One naturally must wonder about those who remained silent for so many years. Why have these people kept their secrets for so long? Why did they expend so much emotional energy in keeping the secret, perhaps driving away those who wished to help them by their acting out, or testing their loyalty by demands nearly impossible to meet? To understand the long silence of those who were sexually abused as children or adolescents, a clinician need only dissect the internal structure of the abusive relationship and look closely at the interaction that occurs between a victim and a molester. Once the elements of such a relationship are understood, the client's seemingly strange behavior begins to make sense. The reader might question our use of the term "relationship," considering the fact that some children and adolescents are sexually assaulted by total strangers. We take the view that even if the assailant and the victim were total strangers and have not met since the abuse ended, a relationship has been created, within the mind of the child or adolescent, that may have the malignant power to control elements of the victim's behavior for years to come. This kind of bond is complicated and strengthened when the victim *did* have a preexisting relationship with his or her assailant.

In most cases of child or adolescent sexual assault, two forms of threatening occur that can create silence. First, there is the threat that the young person must do what the abusive person wishes. This enforced submission may range from a subtle form of coercion that cajoles or lures, to an overt threat of physical violence. Once the person succumbs to this initial threat, he or she has acknowledged the power of the molester, and a form of relationship has begun in which the victim acquiesces implicitly. Acknowledgment of the molester's power is a critical first step, because it frames the relationship as one in which the victim does what the abuser says to do within the context of the relationship.

Compliance is further solidified by the second threat, the admonition of silence. Once a child or adolescent capitulates to this second demand, the abusive relationship takes on a life of its own in the internal dynamics of the victim. This bond becomes even more powerful if he or she is repeatedly assaulted by the same person, or if the adults who are close to the victim act in a way that confirms the molester's power over him or her (e.g., by ignoring the young person's attempts to reveal that something is wrong or by unwittingly reexposing the victim to the molester).

In some situations, the young person's fear of his or her parents' response to what has happened serves to augment the power of the pact of silence. Besides, in many cases such as this, the child or adolescent was assaulted while doing something that had been forbidden by the parents, and the molester had the added magical role of being an agent of punishment for the young person's forbidden act. In situations such as these, the young person enters into a kind of collusion with the assailant and makes a form of "promise." Lister (1982) described the process in this way: "One has 'promised,' been spared further pain and almost inevitably feels a sense of subsequent obligation, a wish for there to be no more pain" (p. 874).

What seals the contract between the young person and a molester is when the molestation ceases or the victim is let go. This may appear to be paradoxical, but the stopping of abuse strengthens the victim's promise because, in his or her mind, a molester who has the power to stop may have the power to begin again, and the next assault may be even worse than the one before. If the victim continues to submit to the abuser by keeping the secret, that person will choose not to attack him or her again.

Young victims of sexual assault, like older victims, ascribe superhuman powers to their assailants, although this misperception is amplified in children because the assailant may well hold considerable power over the child or adolescent under ordinary circumstances—i.e., as parent, relative, teacher, or other trusted caretaker (Everstine & Everstine, 1983). When one considers that most cases of molestation are ones in which persons known to the victim were the perpetrators (86% in the cases studied by Cupoli and Sewell, 1988; 99% reported by Kendall-Tackett and Simon, 1987; 96% reported by Reinhart, 1987), it becomes evident that for a child to tell his or her parents what has happened is a tremendous act of courage.

COMMON ERRORS MADE BY CLINICIANS

Even if a client has been in therapy before, one cannot assume that he or she has told a previous clinician about a past sexual trauma. It has been our observation that many persons whose trauma was undisclosed have had prior therapy experiences—some of them quite positive. In this treatment, for a number of reasons they were unable to tell the therapist about the abuse; in some cases, a therapist may have given the client messages that the subject made him or her uncomfortable or that he or she did not wish to deal with such issues. Lister (1982) has listed common errors that are made by therapists which may prevent a client from being able to reveal childhood sexual trauma: (1) a focus on intrapsychic processes at the expense of attention to external realities; (2) subtle insinuations that "if something happened, perhaps you set it up"; (3) frankly overlooking historical information that relates to violence, threats, or fear of violence; or (4) refusal to entertain the possibility that what one is being told may literally be true (p. 875).

It cannot be overemphasized that a clinician ought to be constantly aware of his or her own issues and how these could possibly hinder the treatment process. We have found that foremost among the errors that can be made is to imply that the victim "set up" what happened when he or she was young. This can be quite a complicated situation because many adults who were sexually traumatized as young persons may, in a sequel to the abuse, have selected abusive mates or, in other ways, "set themselves up" for current maltreatment. Tragically, these adults are, on the one hand, constantly searching for explanations and, on the other, re-creating the traumatic event in such a way that gives them further confirmation that they are loathsome people. Hence, a therapist's intervention should help diminish or break this cycle of self-defeat.

If a therapist focuses solely upon the current self-destructive behavior and does not grasp what the patient is attempting to communicate by means of such behavior; and if, in addition, he or she forgets that when the original trauma occurred the client was truly an innocent victim, the threats and guilt conveyed to the client during the abuse will only be echoed in therapy. Or, the clinician will be cast into the role of the victim's unseeing or uncaring parent. To avoid this, a therapist should interpret the meaning of the self-destructive behavior so that the client can understand it, and should also set appropriate limits. This balance between setting limits and interpreting is not always easy to attain. The best insurance that both messages will be properly conveyed is for a clinician to be certain that his or her own feelings about sex and violence, as well as how much people can control their own destinies, have been rigorously examined.

It is particularly difficult for mental health professionals, who consider themselves to have at least some control over the direction of their lives (providing they have a healthy attitude and make wise decisions), to accept the fact that this is not always a just world. Facing that harsh reality is frightening because it means facing one's own vulnerability. Nonetheless, if one is to think of unraveling the often complicated life histories of people who were sexually abused as children, one must at least be willing to consider that at one time in their lives these adults were innocent victims. Beneath it all, this truth cries out to be understood.

Victims Whose Children Are Victims

Even though it may take a pathological form, in some ways it is a positive sign for the psyche to force itself to communicate, by means of the person's behavior, that abuse was suffered. The most serious form that this can take is when a parent who was once a victim unconsciously places his or her child in a position to be victimized, so that the parent can work through what happened to himself or herself as a child. Parents who do this should be counseled with considerable care, because even though their action is extremely pathological, they are nonetheless attempting to heal their own childhood wounds. Bringing this to a parent's awareness needs to be done with much sensitivity, because the parent is usually unaware of what he or she may be doing vis-à-vis the child, and most such parents are deeply invested in being "a good parent." Hence, one should avoid implying that they may have been bad parents by exposing their children to harm. Instead, a therapist would be wise to focus upon their own infantile needs for understanding, nurturance, and protection, so that they can be directed toward a therapeutic resolution of the original trauma.

Hidden Messages

Some persons whose childhood sexual traumas are unresolved may communicate the trauma to a therapist by creating a new trauma during therapy. It is our experience that re-creations of this sort often occur after therapy has been ostensibly proceeding favorably for a period of time, and for this reason may take the clinician completely by surprise. This re-created trauma may assume one of many forms. For example, the person may be beaten up in a fight or mugged or become involved in a suspicious car accident or get in trouble with the police. The incident usually results from excessive risk taking which the therapist thought was well under control. If a therapist treats this event in the same manner as he or she would deal with acting-out, borderline, or masochistic behavior (i.e., by trying to make the person aware of how his or her actions may provoke the behavior of others), it may turn out to be a serious error, because it will miss the fundamental point of the behavior. Even though the victim has "set up" the event, it has occurred in the context of an attempt to tell the therapist about the original trauma. Hence, if one takes the traditionally accepted "firm hand" with acting-out clients as a means of forcing the person to take responsibility for his or her actions, one risks becoming like the adults who, in the victim's childhood, did not notice or respond properly to the abuse. In fact, if the clinician adopts a punitive position, he or she can seem worse than the imperceptive parents. Not only has the therapist been deaf to the victim's cry for understanding, but has punished him or her for trying to communicate what happened before.

In a situation like this, a therapist would be wise to investigate whether or not there was a message in the behavior of the client, and permit the client to respond to this kind of interpretation. He or she may initially deny the interpretation; for that reason the clinician should be patient and carefully observe details of the person's other verbal and nonverbal behavior, which may confirm or disconfirm the possibility of undisclosed childhood sexual trauma.

If the therapist believes that there was a trauma but the person persists in denying it, we do not recommend using confrontive techniques. The client is very likely rigidly defended, and such an approach would prove pointless. A better strategy is to focus on clinical issues, such as how to care for and protect oneself better, while avoiding the subjects of guilt and blame. In addition, a therapist should convey that he or she understands and respects the client's defenses and will not try to take them away. One can suggest that the person may have disturbing dreams or memories that could surface periodically, and that he or she need not try to fight such thoughts; instead, the client should tell the therapist what these thoughts are, no matter how vague or strange they appear.

TREATMENT ISSUES

Throughout the treatment process, one needs to balance careful, direct inquiry with a sensitive request for repressed material, while giving the client a sense of safety and control; the goal is that he or she does not feel compelled to leave therapy because it has become too dangerous. One must be cognizant of the fact that treating adults who have an unresolved childhood sexual trauma is not as simple as conveying that one recognizes the trauma, asking the correct questions, and—voilà!—resolving the problem. Instead, this therapy is in many cases a long, slow process of carefully bringing to light the original trauma, at a pace that the client can tolerate, while helping the person to understand why he or she behaved in certain ways after the trauma occurred. Finally, a clinician must provide an environment in which the client's true feelings about the trauma can be expressed. The therapist should let the victim know, above all, that he or she recognizes the full range of emotions that a child experiences during a traumatic experience of this magnitude.

Adults naturally look back upon childhood with adult perceptions and cognitive skills, forgetting how big and powerful adults appear to children: even their most subtle threats are terrifying to a child. Adults who were traumatized as children frequently make similar perceptual errors that serve to intensify their current feelings of inadequacy and depression. They often remember themselves as older and more competent than they actually were at the time when they were molested. Many lack an appropriate understanding of what a child of that age is capable of comprehending or doing. Hence, they feel intense guilt or shame about what they said or did during the traumatic event(s).

Case Example

An example of such distortion is the description of a childhood sexual trauma (first disclosed during therapy) by a 27-year-old woman. She was the daughter of a very young, single-parent mother who left her alone (at a very early age) for long periods of time while she did odd jobs. Once, when the client was about three years old, her mother sat her on the front doorstep with some toys, told her to stay there while she worked and that she would come home to make lunch. While the girl was sitting on the front step, a man came along who coaxed her to go with him to the basement of a nearby apartment house; there, he sodomized her. When her mother, accompanied by the police, finally found her huddling in the basement with her clothes torn off, the mother loudly exclaimed that she was a bad child for disobeying her and leaving with a stranger. After the girl was examined at a local hospital and questioned by the police, the police officer who found her (believing he was being helpful) also scolded her harshly for following the stranger.

When this woman told the story as an adult, she said that after the assault she never could sleep unless her bed was against a wall. She slept with her back to the wall so that she could see the man if he tried to sneak in and "get her" again during the night. She added that she had another fear that he was hiding under the bed and would try to stab her through the mattress.

The details of this assault were later verified during a private meeting with the child's mother. The mother said that she had been 19 at the time and struggling to survive during that period. She had thought it would be best if she and her daughter did not talk about the molestation so that they could forget it. She believed that the daughter had been so young that she really did not understand what had happened to her. Her reason for being "firm" with her daughter after the assault was so that the girl would be more careful in the future. Even though this mother used poor judgment in dealing with her daughter's trauma, she appeared to be a well-intended young woman who genuinely cared about the daughter but simply did not grasp the complexity of what had happened.

The victim had not spoken of the assault again until she was 12 or 13, when she began to brood on the event. Finally, she asked her mother why the man had attacked her when she was three. Intending to make the girl more cautious, her mother told her that it probably happened because she was a rebellious, overly mature child. Following this conversation, the teenager did not mention the event again, but shortly thereafter she began to abuse drugs and act out promiscuously. By the time she was 18, she had been the victim of another sexual assault, had suffered two drug overdoses, and was engaging periodically in prostitution.

Because the legacy of the first unresolved sexual trauma had not been recognized as the cause of her adolescent acting-out behavior, the victim had been misdiagnosed by several agencies (as well as therapists) as merely a rebellious adolescent who was promiscuous and abused drugs; in other words, she was a behavior problem. This further confirmed to her that she was a bad person who deserved punishment. She was first referred for therapy by the police after she was the victim of a brutal rape at the age of 27. During the rape she was badly beaten and several ribs were broken. She initially resisted the idea of seeing yet another therapist, but one of the detectives involved in the case was concerned about her and insisted that she see someone, so she "went along with it to shut him up."

When the young woman arrived for the first therapy session, she was still badly bruised. She tried to present herself as tough and worldly wise. When the therapist expressed concern about her injuries, she cynically replied that this was not the first time she had been beaten, and it was "no big deal" because she had learned how not to feel anymore. She gave her life history in a glib recital of facts and was very resistive to the merest inquiry into details or to any request for additional information.

The clinician believed that there was more to this young woman than appeared on the surface. She was very bright, sensitive, and quite insightful about other people, but not about herself. Her stepbrother and stepsister were fairly well adjusted, and the family, as she described it, was not consistent with the type of system that produces borderline or markedly self-destructive family members. But her own self-destructive behavior, fear of closeness, and ability to numb herself to pain caused the therapist to be suspicious that some undisclosed traumatic event might be the source of her problems.

In the early stages of therapy, this young woman was very defensive about discussing her early life. She would simply say that she and her mother had experienced difficult times before the mother married her stepfather, a fairly successful small businessman. She also said that she had no real memories of her life prior to beginning school at about six-and-a-half, which was approximately the time when her mother remarried.

As therapy progressed, she began to reveal glimpses of a tragic and neglectful early childhood. After each disclosure concerning her early life, she would become obstinate with the therapist and later indulge in risk-taking behavior such as driving while drunk or picking up strange men who would be abusive to her. She seemed to be trying to force the therapist to reject or dislike her. Each time this occurred, the clinician would point out the connection between what she would reveal in therapy and the behavior that followed, being careful to add that the woman was still, fundamentally, a good person. The therapist went on to say that, although she could not force the client to stop this self-destructive behavior, it would not suffice to drive her (the therapist) away. The therapist would then explain why she believed her to be a good person, worthy of better care than she gave herself.

Several stormy months passed before the story of the assault (at the age of three) came to light. When it finally surfaced, the woman experienced the memory as a terrified child: she tearfully admitted she was still afraid that the man who assaulted her could come back and kill her if he chose to, and that there was something evil within her which had attracted him to her in the first place. She had absolutely no conception of how inappropriate it was to leave a three-year-old child unattended on a doorstep for a long period of time.

After two stressful meetings, when logical arguments failed to convince the woman that she was not responsible for and did not cause the assault by some intrinsic fault, the clinician took a different approach. She asked a friend if her three-year-old daughter could join her and the client for a portion of the next therapy session. While playing and talking with this little girl, the therapist asked her some questions, including what she would do in certain situations that clearly illustrated what a three-year-old's actual capabilities are. After the child left the office to return to her mother, the client asked why the therapist had brought her there. The reply was that she would understand in a moment, but first she must answer a few questions herself.

The clinician asked the client how capable the little girl was, whether or not there was anything sexual about a child of that age, and if a child of that age should be left unattended for long periods of time. By her responses, it was clear that the woman understood that a little girl should not be left alone, was not sexual, and possessed very limited problem-solving skills. Then the therapist reminded the client that she had been the same age when she was left on the doorstep and later assaulted. The woman was truly shocked and amazed because, she said, she was sure that she herself had been bigger and older than this girl. It was clear that she had a totally distorted concept of herself at the time of the assault. Yet being able to see and talk to a child of the same age as herself when she was assaulted gave her a more realistic sense of what had occurred. It also proved to be a turning point from which she began to work on changing her concept of herself from that of an evil, unworthy person, whom she wished to punish and destroy, to a healthy one. She began to see the original assault as something that *happened to* a vulnerable child and not something that she brought on herself because of some internal flaw.

The necessity of helping a childhood victim to correct his or her self-deprecating persona cannot be overemphasized. The misguided loathing of these adults may take several forms, but each disguises the guilt and shame of an abused child. Some forms of hatred of the self are more obvious than others, such as the self-destructive behavior of the young woman just described. Other hidden victims exist as loners, aloof and isolated, unable to form close, lasting relationships. They may make themselves unattractive in some fashion—by their looks or by their actions—in order to drive people away from them.

Because their poor self-image cannot tolerate the love or care of others, these victims may assume the role of rescuer or caretaker in their relationships with others. In such relationships, they are always "doing for" or attempting to please the other person; yet they cannot tolerate the other's caring for them, because it is too threatening. In this type of reaction formation, the person cannot tolerate (on a conscious level) the relinquishing of control to another. As a result, they often feel used and unappreciated by people in general, but fail to see that they create the structure of such relationships. Many throw themselves into relationships with such cloying intensity that it drives the other person away, or they find themselves constantly being taken advantage of.

Care and caring are complex and emotionally loaded issues with these victims; often the only way they can tolerate being taken care of is to become ill or to injure themselves. Hence, many will display psychosomatic illnesses or seem accident-prone. There can be several reasons for such behavior. First, because these persons dislike themselves (especially their bodies, since it was supposedly the attraction of their bodies that led to the assault), taking care of themselves, and particularly their bodies, is something they cannot endure. They can rationalize that being cared for as a result of physical pain or illness is all right, because their bodies have now suffered or have been "punished." Second, a victim may have come to associate care with the assault itself, because the molester may only have been caring during or after the abuse. In this way they became conditioned to accept being cared for only through a painful experience or some form of abusive sexual encounter. Third, caring may have become linked with abuse of the secondary gains, such as gifts, privileges, or special attention, that were associated with the trauma.

The terrible sense of inadequacy and low self-esteem that is felt by adults who were sexually traumatized as children may be hidden behind hostile or overly aggressive behavior. Victims may be easily angered; childish rage may burst forth in temper tantrums due to real or imagined wrongs. These persons are often extremely opinionated, aligning themselves with the side of right or goodness. Because many of their perceptions of the world were arrested at an early age as a consequence of their traumatic experiences, they tend to see the world in black-and-white, concrete terms. People and events are only seen as good or bad. And despite the fact that some victims can superficially project a persona that is quite to the contrary, they see themselves as inadequate people. Either they believe they do not deserve anything good, or that if something good happens to them they will be punished. For the clinician, this is an extremely sensitive issue. One must work carefully but deliberately to help the client restructure his or her world view in a more flexible and less punitive way.

As Therapy Proceeds

As noted earlier, therapists are well advised to proceed slowly with adults who were sexually traumatized as children. Particularly during the initial stages of treatment, they will most likely need constant reassurance that it is safe to remember and to talk about what happened to them. They need to have the message, "If something bad happened to you it doesn't make you bad," framed in such a way that they will be able to hear it. One cannot overemphasize how important it is for them to be told this, time and time again, until they are able to incorporate the concept into their belief systems.

Clinicians should reflect that their own associations concerning change and the potential for personal growth may be very different from those of adults who were sexually abused as children. The difference is that the childhood experiences of the victim were frequently cloaked in shame, guilt, and fear. When one expresses a wish for change, it essentially implies a complaint about the status quo, and complaining may have been forbidden or punished with threats of worse abuse. One woman recounted that one time when her father began molesting her she began to cry. He put a pillow over her head, saying, "Shut up, or I'll really give you something to cry about"; needless to say, she never cried again. So even expressing a desire for things to be different may be more threatening for these persons than one might realize.

In order to grasp fully how this kind of client's defenses function, a therapist should investigate how the person *survived* the abuse, psychologically, as well as the logic underlying the survival techniques themselves. For example, did the child become "numb," pretend it did not happen, pretend that he or she was somewhere else or invisible, or "disconnect" from his or her body in some way? Or, was the defense one of trying to please *everyone?* Next, one can explore how the victim explained the abuse to himself or herself after it ceased. This will often yield considerable insight into how the person viewed himself or herself in relation to the molester. Such inquiry may also yield insight into how a client has incorporated perceptions of the abuser into his or her self-concept.

Once the degree to which a victim's defenses are functional has been determined, the clinician can utilize this information, along with an assessment of the degree to which the client's self-concept has been affected by the event, to begin helping the victim develop appropriate adult defenses. But one must be careful to base these clinical interventions upon the *client's* sense of who he or she is, recognizing the person's own views on how to protect himself or herself. One cannot emphasize too strongly the importance of forming a thorough understanding of how the client sees himself or herself in relation to what happened. This is vital because the childhood or adolescent experiences of the victim may be so far removed from those of the therapist that one literally cannot imagine how he or she felt at that time. The path to understanding may be obscured by defenses such as rationalization and dissociation, as well as by the unsatisfactory results of past therapy experiences. Once the therapist addresses this key issue, he or she can help the person to form a healthier, more positive sense of self.

When a clinician responds to an adult victim in a nonjudgmental manner, it will demonstrate concretely that things can change for the better. Of course, the process only begins there; it moves forward when the clinician works in increments that the person can tolerate. A therapist should alternate the focus of treatment back and forth between the client's inner world and self-perceptions, and the role that such issues play in defining how others, in turn, respond to the client.

At first, this process is very slow indeed, while the past is analyzed, interpreted, and put into perspective. Even so, the past need only be utilized in terms of how it influences present behavior. One can anticipate that a common defense of adults who were traumatized as children is to become involved in endless contemplation and discussion of their personal histories. This may be an attempt to relive a lost youth or to avoid dealing with the issue at hand, i.e., changing old behavior patterns. The therapist must weigh spending time on the victim's childhood issues against persuading him or her that it is time to move on to the present. Awful as these clients' past experiences may have been, in many ways these events in retrospect are less terrifying than a future filled with unknowns. Moreover, the person may not have an array of life experiences from which to draw in order to know how to respond when positive possibilities present themselves. There may be quite a struggle around this issue, but the clinician should take a firm position: namely, once a fundamental understanding of the victim's past traumas has been reached, the past is to be worked with only as it pertains to the person's present and future. While working to reorient a client toward present and future, the therapist should be prepared that there may be some anger on the client's part at not being able to "set things right" regarding the past.

Victims may need considerable assistance in accepting the fact that they may not have had particularly good or consistent parenting. This issue becomes especially complex when there has been a combination of alternating abuse and kindness, or abuse combined with other forms of secondary gain. Separating, in memory, the good aspects from the bad aspects of the molester can be quite a struggle. As a result of the black/white, good/bad way in which these victims see the world around them, it may require considerable discussion and working through before the person can come to terms with the duality of human nature. As with other victims of childhood abuse, adults who were victimized as children may face a dilemma in that, despite what was done to them, they still love or feel affection for the abuser. This is another situation in which a clinician should acknowledge his or her own feelings or biases. It is not always easy for a normal person, who would not consider sexually mistreating a child, to put feelings aside and see the abuser as someone who is both loved as well as hated. In such cases, one should strive to comprehend the relationship between the client and the abuser from the client's perspective, and then guide him or her to regard the abuser as realistically as possible.

At some point, a victim will very likely need to work through considerable rage toward the abuser. The client may feel tremendous relief at finally being able to express these repressed emotions; conversely, he or she may feel extremely frightened by them. In either case, a therapist should attempt to balance the need for ventilation with the necessity of control. The authors have noted that during this phase of treatment, many clients wish to confront the molester. Although some clinicians approve of and actually encourage such confrontations, we do not. It has been our experience, as well as that of Gil (1971), that such confrontations rarely proceed as victims might wish. Frequently, when planning such a confrontation, the victim forms a fantasy that the abuser will make some form of atonement for the abuse, when in fact just the opposite is more likely to happen. The abuser may have repressed or distorted the molestation in some self-protective manner that may enable him or her to dismiss the confrontation as a lie or as the absurd protest of a disturbed person.

We believe that such confrontations are best treated symbolically within the context of therapy; e.g., a victim can express these feelings toward an empty chair or through some other form of role play, instead of directly toward the molester. Of course, some clients will resist being dissuaded from this kind of confrontation. When that happens, one can only do one's best to see to it that he or she has realistic expectations of such an encounter, and is aware of risking the possibility of having no relationship with that person in future, as a direct consequence of the confrontation.

One way to help victims gain insight into how well they take care of themselves is to have them look at the process by which they make life decisions and to find out what sort of internal dialogue and decision-making process is taking place. How do they talk to themselves when they are deciding what to do? Are they self-deprecating or critical? Do they dare themselves to risk dangerous or potentially abusive situations because they "deserve" punishment? And do they rationalize that, this time, some fantasied "good person" will eventually rescue them? Transforming this internal dialogue from a negative one to a healthy, self-caring one is a major step that an adult must take toward resolving the trauma of childhood. Until this self-dialogue begins to change, most external interventions will fall upon deaf ears.

Latter Stages of Therapy

Relationships in general pose serious and complex problems to adults who were sexually abused as children because they lack some of the fundamental building blocks that are required to create healthy friendships and love partnerships. If the client is in a permanent or stable love relationship, the therapist may wish to meet with the other person. When taking up the many issues concerning relationships, a clinician should first explore with the client the question of disclosure of his or her past abuse to the friend or loved one—not because he or she has anything to be ashamed of, but because many people do not understand what sexually abused children suffer through, and the victim may not receive the support or empathy that he or she expects. The therapist should recall that even though there has been a considerable amount of public education and publicity concerning the subject of child sexual abuse, many hold unfortunately misguided opinions about the subject. So even though disclosure to others may raise intense feelings on the part of a client, it is better if the therapist brings up the unpleasant possibility of insensitive reactions in advance, lest the victim find himself or herself unprepared in a painful situation.

Another important issue pertaining to relationships is that adults who were sexually abused as children may, in one way or another, place their mates in the roles of the adults who abused them. They may choose abusive people as mates or, conversely, rush into a love relationship with the fantasy that, this time, the loved one will magically make their problems disappear. An adult who was abused as a child may feel let down or cheated when this latter type of relationship does not magically "heal." More frequently, the victim's intense dependency needs drive prospective lovers away, leaving the person feeling as though he or she was taken advantage of or feeling unlovable. Many victims attract people who find gratification in the role of rescuer or who are more at ease in a relationship with someone who is fragile or vulnerable. This kind of mate may become threatened if therapy begins to change the balance of forces within the partnership.

A clinician should be cautious that adults who have been molested as children may, consciously or unconsciously, turn relationships into abusive ones. They do not necessarily do this because they enjoy abuse: they are more likely to do it because they associate abuse with intimacy. This is above all the reason that many have such struggles with love and being loved. In some cases, when the relationship becomes intimate, a victim will do something to create distance or instability. Another reason for their causing instability or choosing abusive mates is that many have a fundamental self-concept of being people who will be punished if something good happens to them. In retaliation for daring to be happy, they do something to harm the relationship or accept mates who will continue to abuse them.

In many ways, it is hard to imagine that these clients cannot conceive of a relationship that, despite life's vagaries, is a fundamentally healthy one. To them the word "relationship" intrinsically carries with it a threat of emotional pain. Over the course of treatment, it will be one of the therapist's aims to transform this kind of definition into a healthier one.

Another way in which a victim's poor self-esteem interferes with being able to have fulfilling love relationships is that it blocks his or her capacity to identify and express needs appropriately. This incapacity may take several forms. A victim may magically expect others to know what his or her needs are—much as the idealized "good parent" would have been able to do. When the loved one fails to intuit these needs, the person feels betrayed or unwanted. Others who were sexually abused as children are largely unaware of their inner emotional needs; they feel unsatisfied and empty, but cannot clearly identify why this is so. They may go from one relationship to another, searching for the one in which they will find fulfillment.

To some child victims, the vulnerability that is part of loving is simply too much for them to tolerate. With these clients, a therapy group comprised of other adults who have had abusive childhood experiences may be an appropriate setting for them to learn to sustain emotional relationships with others. Through such a group, they may learn to experience adult relationships within a protected environment. Nevertheless, in the ideal case, clients who were abused as children should also be seen individually during the period when they are participating in a group.

The roles that these adults assume in relationships range from the dominant to the submissive. Some cannot tolerate being in a relationship unless they feel as though they have *total* control. Others are extremely submissive to their mates, fearing that if they do not constantly please them, they will cease to be loved. The ordinary ebb-and-flow, give-and-take of a relationship is a matter of continuing struggle for these persons, because affection and intimacy once had to be "paid for" and were associated with someone's arbitrary exercise of power over them.

A particular source of serious problems for persons who were the hidden victims of *incest* as children can be their adulthood relationships with their parents. Many incest victims continue to have relationships with either or both parents. Nevertheless, when the victim's current mate learns of this past sexual abuse, he or she may have considerable difficulty in understanding the victim's desire to maintain a relationship with "those monsters." The reactions of the mate of an incest victim can range from wanting to punish both parents to suspicion that the victim may not have been truly an innocent participant in the incestuous experience. Ideally, a therapist will work with the victim to help him or her deal with the reactions of the partner. But usually it will be advisable for the clinician to meet with the mate in order to clarify the complexities of these kinds of parent–child relationships, and to point out that the victim must be permitted to work through the trauma himself or herself. Naturally, a therapist may need to take more assertive steps if the incestuous parent has contact at present with the victim's own children or adolescents, to ensure that these grandchildren are not at risk of abuse. Apart from situations in which grandchildren may currently be at risk (and assuming the statute of limitations pertaining to the reporting and prosecuting of incest has expired*), a therapist should help the client's mate understand that the victim must be allowed to resolve the relationship with parents on his or her own terms.

In summary, a therapist who treats adults who were the victims of sexual trauma in childhood must be prepared to deal sensitively with a vast array of clinical issues. One can expect that these clients are likely to present themselves for therapy with complaints and symptoms that would not necessarily lead a therapist to guess that sexual trauma formed part of their experience as children. Moreover, once the truth of the earlier abuse has been revealed, they may at first display resistance to allowing this trauma to be the central focus of therapy. Even so, the clinician who perseveres and feels compassion for these victims will be much rewarded when they are eventually capable of achieving significant growth and change.

---

* A recent court case provides considerable comfort to those who might wish to sue for damages in cases of molestation that had long ago been "swept under the carpet." In Los Angeles, a 28-year-old woman has filed a civil suit against her father, claiming that she was repeatedly molested by him from the time she was seven years old until she was 19. The significance of the case is that current law (in California) prohibits the filing of such a suit after the victim's 19th birthday. Intended as a test of this statue of limitations, the case may well be taken all the way to the California Supreme Court. Its progress will be carefully watched by persons who have never been compensated for their trauma, as well as by those who care for them (*San Jose Mercury News*, 1986, p. 8B).

REFERENCES

American Psychiatric Association. *Diagnostic and statistical manual of mental disorders, Third Edition, Revised.* Washington, D.C.: American Psychiatric Association, 1987.

Bagley, C., & Ramsay, R. Disrupted childhood and vulnerability to sexual assault: Long-term sequels with implications for counseling. Unpublished paper presented at the Conference on Counseling the Sexual Abuse Survivor, Winnipeg, Canada, 1985.

Briere, J. The effects of childhood sexual abuse on later psychological functioning: Defining a "post-sexual-abuse syndrome." Paper presented at the Third National Conference on Sexual Victimization of Children, Washington, D.C., 1984. (Cited by Browne, A., & Finkelhor, D., in *Psychological Bulletin, 99*(1), 66–67, 1986.)

Cupoli, J. M., & Sewell, P. M. One thousand fifty-nine children with a chief complaint of sexual abuse. *Child Abuse and Neglect, 12,* 151–162, 1988.

Everstine, D., & Everstine, L. *People in crisis.* New York: Brunner/Mazel, 1983.

Gil, D. G. Violence against children. *Journal of Marriage and the Family, 33,* 637–648, 1971.

Harrison, P. A., Lumry, A. E., & Claypatch, C. Female sexual abuse victims: Perspectives on family dysfunction, substance use, and psychiatric disorders. Paper presented at the Second National Conference for Family Violence Researchers, Durham, NH, August 1984.

Herman, J. L. *Father-daughter incest.* Cambridge, MA: Harvard University Press, 1981.

Katan, A. Children who were raped. *Psychoanalytic Study of the Child, 28,* 208–224, 1973.

Kendall-Tackett, K. A., & Simon, A. F. Perpetrators and their acts: Data from 365 adults molested as children. *Child Abuse and Neglect, 11,* 237–245, 1987.

Lister, D. Forced silence: A neglected dimension of trauma. *American Journal of Psychiatry, 139*(7), 872–875, 1982.

Miller, J., Moeller, D., Kaufman, A., Divasto, P., Fitzsimmons, P., Pather, D., & Christy, J. Recidivism among sexual assault victims. *American Journal of Psychiatry, 135,* 1103–1104, 1978.

Nelson, S. *Incest: Fact and myth.* Edinburgh: Stramullion, 1982.

Peters, J. J. Child rape: Defusing a psychological time bomb. *Hospital Physician, 9,* 46–49, 1973.

Reinhart, M. A. Sexually abused boys. *Child Abuse and Neglect, 11,* 229–235, 1987.

Russell, D. E. H. *The secret trauma: Incest in the lives of girls and women.* New York: Basic Books, 1987.

San Jose Mercury News. Woman challenges age limit in incest law by suing at 28. November 12, p. 8B, 1986.

Sedney, M. A., & Brooks, B. Factors associated with a history of childhood sexual experience in a nonclinical female population. *Journal of the American Academy of Child Psychiatry, 23,* 215–218, 1984.

Westermeyer, J. Incest in psychiatric practice: A description of patients and incestuous relationships. *The Journal of Clinical Psychiatry,* 643–648, August, 1978.

8

Legal and Ethical Considerations

with Richard Gregg, Esq.

The law concerning sexual abuse of children and adolescents unfolds on a daily basis, as do other legal conventions in our society. Legislation is being passed in every state, and everywhere court decisions on individual cases are establishing precedent in a continuous process of correction and renewal. For the responsible clinician, being current with these laws that regulate his or her profession is a perpetual task. In this chapter, broad trends will be charted and pervasive themes described, but the reader should remain current with the letter of the law by means of self-education such as reading relevant journals, joining study groups on legal issues, or subscribing to a newsletter that abstracts recent court decisions. Here, the law will not be catalogued; instead, its intent will be summarized and suggestions will be made for the clinician's prudent conduct.*

Richard Gregg, Esq., coauthor of this Chapter, is a member of the Boccardo Law Firm, San Jose, California.

* We are licensed in, and practice in, California, and for that reason have firsthand knowledge only of legal procedures and rules pertaining to that state. We have read extensively in literature that pertains to both nationwide requirements and those that differ in spirit from state to state. In this chapter an attempt is made to describe and interpret general principles of conduct that are appropriate in any setting. Some discrepancies between what is set forth here and the most recent laws that apply in certain regions are inevitable, and we recommend caution on the part of the reader.

The law properly recognizes a child's vulnerability and lack of re-sources for self-defense. In that regard, the law is compassionate. Even so, children have few rights in our culture, being considered subservient to adults until the 18th birthday in most states. This means that children are regarded—in the eyes of the law—as agents or extensions of their parents. With parental authority comes responsibility: the parent(s) in charge can be held liable for any *civil* wrong that a child may commit, notwithstanding the fact that the child can be convicted of a *criminal* act and punished for it if a court so decides. Ultimate power rests in parental hands, and the state insists upon parental accountability. In that aspect, the face of the law is patriarchal.

Even though it is fair to characterize our legal system as adult-oriented, an important principle benefits children in myriad ways. This is the recognition that a child has all of life ahead and that his or her development as a person will be a key element in social progress. This unfulfilled quality of childhood and the vitality of children's potential are a founding rock for much of our legal view of the child.

When it comes to child abuse, the ethical principle referred to above provides a framework for the construction of many of our laws in the following way. The purpose of the major legislation of recent years, as well as the preeminent case law decisions, has been to prevent children who have been abused from being abused again. Certainly there has been a strengthening of laws that define the scope of abuse, and the penalties for this crime have been increased manyfold; but the legal advances of the 1970s and 1980s are primarily those promoting early detection and swift prosecution of abuse. The theory behind this movement is that a protective net should shield the child from any threat or attempted form of abuse. Further, the existence of this net should deter those who would commit abuse from making the threat or attempt in the first place.

The attribute of this deterrent scheme that most directly involves the work of the psychotherapist is the legal requirement to report child abuse, as defined and described in the section to follow. A related issue, namely that of clinical record keeping, will be discussed in a subsequent section.

CHILD ABUSE REPORTING

Although the term *child abuse* is often used to refer specifically to the physical beating of children, it is best employed as a generic term that refers to both physical harm and many other forms of maltreatment, including the psychological. In this book we are concerned mainly with sexual abuse, and in that regard primarily the mental damage caused by those physical acts. Hence, this discussion of reporting requirements will concentrate on the laws relating to a therapist in his or her role as a guardian of the *emotional* life of children.*

If a clinician has a "reasonable suspicion" that a child has been sexually abused, he or she has a legal duty to report this suspicion.** In fact, not to do so would be a crime committed by the therapist. Current law on this point has been summarized in a number of writings (e.g., Heymann, 1986; Weisberg & Wald, 1986). A fuller account can be found in the authors' earlier text, *People in Crisis* (Everstine & Everstine, 1983). Major provisions of the law, as outlined in this present chapter, will be drawn from the statutes currently in force in California.

In California, the legal definition of *sexual abuse* includes incest, molestation, and exploitation for pornography or prostitution. When therapy leads to a suspicion that a crime such as this has occurred, the reporting process begins. In what form must this report be made? The report must be made by telephone *and* in writing within 36 hours of the incident in which evidence first appeared, to: (1) the local police or sheriff's office; (2) the juvenile probation department; or (3) the county welfare department.

For psychotherapy, this justly strict reporting requirement means that when child sexual abuse is suspected the "client-therapist confidentiality privilege" is immediately null and void. This privilege, which normally pertains to the content of conversations between a therapist and a client, tapes of therapy sessions, and/or therapist notes or test results, becomes invalid when information concerning child sexual abuse is being exchanged in some way. When abuse is a factor in a therapy case, any information pertaining to the case can be handed over to an agency of law enforcement or to the judicial system. In addition, information can be provided to other professionals who may have some legitimate interest in the case.

What is the penalty for failure to report? The person who does *not* report will be charged with a misdemeanor. If convicted, the person will be required to pay a fine, faces possible loss of licensure or

---

* In effect, we extract the specific reporting requirements concerning child sexual victimization from the legal context that pertains to child abuse in general. Our basic source is Conidaris, M. G., Ely, D. F., & Erikson, J. T., *California laws for psychotherapists.* Gardena, CA: Harcourt Brace Jovanovich, 1988.

** This "reasonable suspicion" can be based upon either observation or knowledge. The latter stipulation suggests that a practitioner who forms the suspicion might never have seen the child in question. This provision of the law has not yet (as far as we know) been tested in an actual case. In a sense, the clinician is being credited with both keen intuition and sound judgment.

certification, and may be sent to jail for as long as six months. And it may be that the clinician will be sued for a civil liability (i.e., malpractice) for not reporting well-founded suspicions. In effect, a therapist would be accused of not adequately performing his or her duty of care toward the abused child. Every clinician should be informed of this prospect, and a most valuable document is the seminal paper by Kohlman (1974), in which a lawyer advises other lawyers how to prepare a malpractice case on these grounds. What happens if a therapist *does* report a suspicion of abuse? Unless the report was falsely made, "civil and criminal immunity is accorded those who report" (Kohlman, 1974, p. 248). That means a person cannot be sued for reporting (in good faith), nor be charged with a misdemeanor for doing so (Everstine & Everstine, 1983, p. 244).

RECORD KEEPING

From the earliest days of his or her practical training, a clinician is taught the art of taking "case notes." These jottings are intended to serve varied purposes, for example:

1. as an *aide-memoire* that can be referred to from time to time when plans are made for the next step in therapy;

2. as a record of visits, interventions attempted, and results achieved, for billing, insurance claims, or other paperwork requirements;

3. as a means of proof in case of the need to prepare a defense in a lawsuit or other legal proceeding.

Hence, for practical reasons and as a form of self-protection, note taking is considered worthwhile. The zealousness with which this is done will vary among therapists as a function of their training and/or their tendency to compulsivity.

Problems associated with record keeping often arise from the clinician's lack of knowledge of the legal system and the workings of courts. From the point of view of those who administer justice, any information that may assist in making a just decision is within the scope of their "right to know." In effect, any knowledge possessed by a person who is in some way connected with a court case "belongs" to the court. Moreover, the court can seek out case-specific information from the person who is connected with a case, without being aware in advance of the nature of that information. Thus, it can appropriate *any and all* information that may or may not be relevant and discard that which it believes to be irrelevant.

In order to lay hands upon the information to which it feels entitled, a court can grant an attorney subpoena powers to demand that it be supplied by a clinician. A subpoena is simply a court-sanctioned demand that a person become a witness in a proceeding before the court. And since being a witness means being one who supplies information to the court, this demand may be the kind that involves turning over documents *(subpoena duces tecum)* in lieu of testifying on a witness stand. Failing to comply with a subpoena could be construed, by the judge, as "contempt of court," and the person who refuses could be punished.*

Clearly, clinical records are potentially incendiary objects. Because they are so readily accessible to the justice system, they become in effect latent public documents. For that reason, it is necessary to reassess their utility as adjuncts to therapy. Some attorneys who work closely with clinicians in the field of civil litigation on behalf of child sexual abuse victims advise that case notes not be written at all. By contrast, we advocate that a middle course be taken.

In the best interests of the victim, keeping some data on file is recommended. The chief justification for that would be to ensure a smooth transition in treatment if a change in therapists is required. No other compelling reason exists, with the possible exception of information that is recorded for research purposes.**

But what should be contained in this record? Essentially, one may write what can be ascertained from some other public source of information. In addition, the clinician may document certain actions that were taken in pursuit of his or her legal duties of care toward the client and the community: specifically, such actions as making a *Tarasoff* (1976) warning, making a report of child abuse or neglect, and/or establishing a no-suicide contract with the client. This documentation,

---

* In an infamous case, a California psychiatrist went to jail for several days because he refused to comply with a subpoena to produce clinical records (*In re* Lifschutz, 2 Cal. 3d 415, 431–32, 467 P. 2d 557, 567–68, 85 Cal. Prtr. 829, 839–40 [1970]).

** Some observers feel, with good reason, that doing therapy and doing research simultaneously is unethical. This view is based upon the belief that the aims of treatment (to heal) and a research study (to discover a scientific truth) are incompatible. Whatever position one takes in this controversy, it is generally accepted that there are rules of privacy and confidentiality pertaining to research subjects in much the same way that therapy has rules to protect clients. For example, a principle of the recruitment of subjects for research is that the participant freely gives his or her informed consent to participate. When research data are being collected during a course of treatment, it is the clinician's duty to obtain this consent before keeping that kind of record. And a therapist must be aware that even the research record itself can be made public in a court of law.

if accurately recorded, is not likely to harm the client and may certainly serve as a form of self-protection for the therapist. What should *not* be a part of this record? The rule is to omit whatever one would not want to hear if it were read aloud in a court of law. In general, the concept is not to write what could only be learned about the client from a therapy chart.

In summary, information storage in psychotherapy should be approached as discreetly as one would handle a loaded weapon. There is no harm in taking a child's personal or family history, because details such as date of birth, grade in school, and names and ages of siblings are already matters of public record or common knowledge. The criterion for *excluding* information from one's notes is that it would be harmful to the child (and/or the parents) for those comments to be made public. Hence, chartings such as "feels betrayed by her mother" or "needs to defy parental authority" or "dresses seductively" are inappropriate. In many instances, notations of the kind cited have no more validity than as a representation of the clinician's internal monologue about the case; from another point of view, they seldom rise above the level of gossip.

The primary consideration in respect to keeping records of therapy with a child victim is whether or not his or her right to privacy is properly respected. In order to make a fair judgment on this point, it is ethical to look beyond the current needs of therapy to the child's right to transcend the past and build a future.

CHILDREN AND THE LEGAL PROCESS

The clinician's duty of care to a client does not end with the duty to report suspected abuse or with prudence in record keeping. For a young victim of sexual assault, the legal process that follows may be a source of prolonged or even worsened traumatization. The therapist's responsibility extends to helping a child or adolescent through the criminal proceedings that will follow when a suspect has been arrested and is accused of the assault, the civil trial that may take place no matter what the result of these criminal proceedings, and/or any issues that may arise concerning the child's custody.* Our view is that assistance to the child during these events is simply another phase of treatment, and one that will play a vital part in recovery.

---

* The custody issues that are commonplace when parents divorce are often complicated by accusations of abuse or neglect. In the context of this chapter, we are more concerned with the challenges to custody that arise when one parent is convicted of incest, or when a mother is declared unfit to care for her children, as well as related causes of custody review and reassignment.

The child in a courtroom is in many respects a displaced person. The most famous illustration of the plight of a child in an adult's world is *Alice in Wonderland,* in which the plucky Alice is perplexed and terrified by "courts" of various kinds. Part of her bedevilment is a result of the tendency of adults to subject children to their more advanced language skills, leaving the child awash in a verbal swamp of paradox and double entendre. Should a child founder, he or she can be asked, condescendingly, "You don't understand, do you?"

There is nothing even vaguely comforting to a child about the traditional atmosphere of the court of law. The youngster who is at ease in the family room and schoolroom, in the neighborhood and on the playground, finds no source of warmth or nurturance in the courtroom, and a judge in his or her black robe could appear as the embodiment of a child's bad dream. The worst part about a court is its lack of wonder and its stony heart.

It is ironic that the child victim of molestation, in whose interest the court is presumably acting, is the one participant who may feel most out of place, most intimidated by the court process. In recent years, first steps have been taken toward acknowledging the child's alienation and alleviating it, as will be outlined in the sections to follow.

COURT PROCEDURES

It cannot be overlooked that those who work in the justice system and those who work in the mental health system think differently about many things (for myriad illustrations of this point, see Everstine & Everstine, 1986). To begin with, attorneys who practice criminal law wish to convict and punish criminals, while attorneys who do civil law seek to settle disputes fairly. By contrast, psychotherapists strive to heal emotional wounds. There are times when these unlike approaches work at cross-purposes, but they need not if each side is aware of the other's aims throughout their interaction.

As a result of television and cinema portrayals of lawyers, judges, and trials, the popular image of the workings of a court is very different from reality. The clinician should be aware of these misconceptions, since adults will experience constant frustrations and these will be communicated to the child. Many dilemmas can be avoided if the processes of the criminal and civil systems are understood.

THE CRIMINAL PROCESS

As a means of protecting the child victim, clinicians and other members of the helping professions have accomplished much in recent years toward "childproofing" courtroom procedures. These reforms are described in a publication that catalogs developments on a nationwide basis. Entitled, "When the Victim Is a Child," it was sponsored by the National Institute of Justice (Whitcomb, Shapiro, & Stellwagen, 1985).* The significance of this new foundation for the child abuse trial was noted by James K. Stewart, the Institute Director, who wrote in the Foreword:

> More than 90 percent of all child abuse cases do not go forward to prosecution. In many of these cases, the decision not to proceed is based on concerns about the child's possible performance on the witness stand or the impact of the court process on the child victim's recovery. The unfortunate result is that many suspects are released without the imposition of justice. They not only escape any penalty but have the opportunity for further abuse of their initial victim or other children.
>
> Both community members and criminal justice professionals are increasingly concerned about our apparent ineffectiveness in dealing adequately with the crime of child sexual abuse. (Stewart, 1985, p. i)

The remedy for this ineffectiveness lies, according to Stewart, in making it more likely that the child victim will be a credible witness. By implication, a greater percentage of cases will be prosecuted if the child's story of what happened can be believed by a judge or a jury. Apparently, it is assumed that by relieving the stress upon a child of giving testimony, he or she will more likely be perceived as telling the truth. Although this assumption reveals a great deal about the way some adults feel toward the veracity of children, it could be that the justice system has succeeded in doing the right thing for the wrong reasons. In any event, these changes will be welcomed by anyone who advocates children's rights.

New departures in *criminal* court procedures can be categorized as follows:

1. measures to protect the child when he or she is giving an initial statement to police (or other authority) about an assault;

2. measures to exempt the child from testifying in a courtroom, by means of:

---

* This report is concerned only with criminal court procedures and does not address civil court procedures. Even so, the prevailing rules in one sphere of the judicial system are often applied in the other. The reader can consider many of the rules outlined in this chapter as applying to both legal enterprises.

a) videotaped testimony,
b) testimony given in an adjacent room and televised live in the courtroom;

3. other measures designed to make the courtroom a more pleasant place for those children who must appear there.

Some of these innovations are described in more detail later in this chapter.*

First Statements

Upon discovering that their child has been the victim of a sexual assault, many parents respond with shock, dismay, and confusion. Most adults have little training or preparation in how to handle such an event. Hence, a therapist can offer immeasurable support and help to the family if he or she is knowledgeable concerning the workings of the criminal justice system and what can reasonably be expected from this system.

When a case of child molestation comes to light, once the initial report has been made the child will be interviewed by either a child protective services worker or a police officer. Who conducts the initial interview may be determined by factors such as the nature and severity of the assault. For example, when there has been a serious assault or there is concern for the immediate safety of the child, the initial interview is usually done by a police officer. This may differ in various locations, depending upon how the intake system for child sexual abuse cases is structured.

A police officer typically begins the process by speaking to the adults who are close to the child who has allegedly been sexually abused. The officer will then speak to the child and, if he or she believes that there has been abuse, attempt to gather all of the evidence necessary to show that a particular law—as defined by that state's penal code— has been violated. However, if the officer has difficulty in developing necessary evidence or feels that the case has other complicating problems that will make the availability of evidence questionable (e.g., the reluctance of witnesses to testify or the child's difficulty in communicating

---

* Throughout this review, the number of states that have implemented a specific reform will be indicated for each procedure. Considering the small number of states that have adopted these relatively new court rules, the reader may feel that they are merely exceptions that prove the existing rules. Even so, there are observable trends toward adoption of the reforms by more and more states each year. The current state of affairs has been abstracted from Whitcomb, et al., 1985.

information about the molestation, very little investigative effort will be given to the case. Essentially though, all that the police officer requires in order to proceed to investigate a complaint is that the complaint be received and the officer, in his judgment, believes that it has some merit.

When a child is initially questioned by an officer of the law or child protective worker (etc.) about an assault, a videotape can be made of the interview. Even though this kind of statement is considered "hearsay" testimony (because it is not produced under oath), three states permit such a tape to be introduced as evidence in an eventual trial. For this to occur, the questioning must have been conducted by a nonattorney, and both questioner and child must be available for cross-examination if the defense requests it. The latter provision naturally makes it possible that the benefits of videotaping a first statement will be negated at a later time. Still, this does amount to a major concession—to the special status of children—on the part of court traditionalists.

Even though one would prefer that the child would only have to tell his or her story once, that is not the way things usually work; indeed, a child may have to repeat the story many times to many different adults throughout the process. Consequently, the clinician should try to lay a supportive foundation for this as part of the initial stages of therapy. From the onset of the process, a therapist should take an active role to ensure that the child is sufficiently protected from further trauma.

Identifying a Suspect

After the child's story has been taken he or she may be asked to identify a suspect if the perpetrator is unknown to the child. The entire experience of identifying and accusing someone of a crime is an anxiety-laden one, even for an adult victim, and vastly more disturbing for a child. This identification procedure can be fraught with especially acute fears for a child, because he or she will now have defied the threats of the assailant. Moreover, the child must struggle with the fearful idea of causing someone to be sent to jail. Being put in jail is a horrifying thought for children, and being responsible for it being done to an adult can be a source of complex and conflicting emotions—most of them negative. The role of a therapist is to help the child understand that full responsibility for the abuse lies solely with the adult, and that it is adults who must account for their actions and accept punishment, or receive treatment, if they sexually assault children.

One task of the clinician is to find out what the likely outcome of the legal proceedings will be, and with that knowledge prepare the child to accept this outcome without additional feelings of guilt or blame. A victim may be comforted by the notion that the perpetrator is a sick person, and because of the child's actions he or she will receive help and hopefully never molest anyone again. Certainly not all children are filled with fear when it comes to testifying against a molester; in fact, some are eager to speak out, but this occurs in only a minority of cases.

The Role of the District Attorney

A district attorney will receive the report of sexual abuse that was prepared by the police, review it, and decide whether or not to file a criminal action.* The district attorney must evaluate if there is a substantial amount of evidence to show, beyond reasonable doubt, that a person abused the child at a specified time, at a specified place, and in a specified way. District attorneys are especially concerned about sexual molestation cases, because a child will have to be asked specific questions about an embarrassing subject and must answer the questions in a convincing manner. District attorneys frequently find it difficult enough for an adult witness to answer questions in a public setting without becoming nervous and confused; these problems are magnified when a child is the witness.

District attorneys are, typically, elected officials, and a key issue that can be raised to criticize an incumbent during an election is that his or her conviction ratio is low, or that he or she has attempted to prosecute cases with insufficient evidence—thus wasting taxpayers' money. Hence, a D.A. may decide not to file a criminal complaint if it appears reasonably clear that a defendant will be able to raise some doubt that the alleged molestation occurred. If a complaint is filed, the matter will proceed toward a trial.**

---

* If the district attorney subsequently believes that the case might eventually be lost, he or she may offer to plea bargain with the defendant. If a plea bargain is not arranged, the case will have to be tried.

** In order to avoid the problem of attempting to resolve disputes whose roots are in the distant past, each state has laws requiring that a complaint be filed with the court before a certain time has passed from when the injury occurred. Each state has established its own time criteria; these laws are called "statutes of limitation" or "limitation of actions." For example, in California, a criminal action for child molestation must be filed within six years of the date of the molestation (*Penal Code*, Sections 799 through 803). A district attorney in California would be powerless to prosecute a person who was

The Rationale for a Criminal Proceeding

A child victim and his or her supporting adults may view a criminal trial as the vehicle by which a molesting defendant will be punished for what he or she did to the victim. In this view, the trial will show either that the defendant is guilty and did these terrible things to the child or that he or she is innocent and did not do these things to the child. However, this is not how the legal process works. In fact, the jury in a criminal case does not determine whether an accused is guilty or innocent but rather that the accused is guilty or not guilty. A finding of guilty means that a jury concludes that the district attorney has proven, beyond a reasonable doubt, that an accused person has violated a specific law as defined in the state's penal code. A finding by the jury of not guilty means that the district attorney has not proven, beyond a reasonable doubt, that the accused person violated a specific law. The defendant in a criminal case does not prove his or her innocence; instead, the D.A. must prove him or her guilty. Hence, a jury finding of not guilty does not indicate that the jury could not believe that the defendant did the crime, but only indicates that a violation could not be proven to the standards required by law.

Another issue that commonly arises in a criminal trial is the perception, by the victim of sexual abuse, that he or she is not protected and is being made to feel like a liar or a bad person, while the defendant appears to be protected and may not even have to testify. To understand better how these feelings come about, it should be noted that a district attorney is not the child's attorney as such, but rather the government's attorney who represents the people of the state in general. In effect, it is not the child's case but the government's case against a defendant for the violation of a state law. The child is a witness to help prove the government's case. As such, the child is subject to examination as a witness. Because the credibility of a witness is relevant, his or her capacity to testify accurately must be examined. A history of truthfulness or prior inconsistent statements, and/or any bias against the accused are subjects on which a witness may be questioned. Since these are legitimate topics, a district attorney must permit this type of questioning to proceed—however embarrassing it may be to the child. The more the D.A. attempts to keep a child from being questioned on these matters, the more the defendant's attorney can argue to the jury that

---

accused of molesting a child if it occurred more than six years previously. These laws were designed to protect someone from being tried so long after an incident occurred that he or she would not be able to find the witnesses necessary in defense of the case.

the child is not being completely truthful and that there is something to hide.

The Preliminary Hearing

Soon after a suspected abuser has been identified, arrested, and charged at an arraignment hearing, he or she will appear before a judge and enter a plea in response to the charges. At this time, a date will be set for the preliminary hearing of the evidence. A defendant is entitled to have this take place within the next 10 days but may waive that right. The child's next involvement in this process will come when the preliminary hearing is held. One can expect that the interim period will be a difficult one for a child victim, clouded with apprehension about what might happen. Throughout, the clinician should work toward allaying the child's fears and preparing him or her for giving testimony in court.

In places where court rules have been modified for the benefit of children, it may be a good idea to take the child to the courtroom for practice in sitting on the witness stand. Whether or not that is possible, the therapist can have "pretend" question-and-answer sessions with the child prior to the preliminary hearing. During this time of preparation, it is important to be extremely careful not to tell the child what to say or to influence him or her in some way; the aim is to enable the child to tell the actual story in a clear manner and in full detail. For example, the child should learn to pause before answering a question in order to give the district attorney enough time to object to a question. The answer given should be a direct response to the question, simply stated. The child may ask for clarification if he or she does not understand what is being said.

The subject of who can be present in the courtroom to provide support for the child should be decided upon well in advance of the court date, and the decision should be left to the victim. Some family members or other relatives may believe that they should be there for support and protection, but the child may feel awkward or embarrassed about telling the story in detail with these persons listening. In such a circumstance, it is the therapist's role to extricate the child from a difficult situation and see to it that the family members wait outside the courtroom if the child wishes.

Prior to the preliminary hearing, there may be many delays and postponements. These can be emotional ordeals for the child and his or her family. A clinician can reassure the family that these delays probably mean nothing to this particular case; the majority are due to scheduling difficulties in the court calendar. Nevertheless, most victims tend to personalize developments such as these and fear the worst. In some jurisdictions, district attorneys take advantage of this inactive period to meet with the child and prepare him or her for court, but unfortunately this practice is rare. In many cases, the child and parent(s) may not meet the district attorney until the day before or even on the morning of the hearing. That is all the more reason for a therapist to help the family in coping with the often mysterious legal system.

The parent(s) and their child should be aware that the preliminary hearing is not the trial itself: instead, it represents a meeting to find out if the evidence is sufficient to require that a trial take place. Before this hearing concludes, the judge will decide whether or not the case will proceed to an actual trial. If so, another waiting period will ensue. In the interim, the district attorney and the defense attorney may conduct plea bargaining. In this procedure, a defendant may plead guilty to one or more of the lesser charges, in order that the more serious charges will be dropped and a trial avoided. Most capable district attorneys will discuss this sort of negotiation with the parent(s), as well as the child if he or she is old enough to participate in such a discussion. (It is our opinion that adolescent victims *should* be included in this negotiation process.)

The Actual Trial

Most trials on sexual assault charges last from three days to two weeks. The length of any trial depends upon factors such as the difficulty involved in jury selection, the number of witnesses to be heard, and the complexity of the evidence. Usually, a victim will be kept on the stand for one or two hours. Even under the best of circumstances, this situation is uncomfortable for an adult, but in a case of molestation the child or adolescent must endure questioning about the details of a painful and intimate experience before a roomful of strangers. The defense attorney may intentionally attempt to bully, trick, or confuse the child; in addition, the defendant may also try some kind of nonverbal behavior to influence the child's testimony. An enlightened judge will put a stop to such inappropriate maneuvers by the defense, but some are not so perceptive.

Environmental Measures

Many jurisdictions have made extensive changes in court environments for the purpose of conducting preliminary hearings or trials in which a child is to be the key witness. For example, seating arrangements are often modified so that the judge sits at the same level as the child, and the judge may wear ordinary clothing instead of a robe. Testimony can be elicited in a conversational way, even with the aid of dolls that the child can use to describe what has happened; or, the child may be asked to make a drawing that tells about his or her experience. This introduction of the techniques of play therapy and psychological testing to the normally sterile court atmosphere is a most encouraging development in the current reform movement.

Although some states permit a judge to close a courtroom to visitors when a child abuse case is being heard, this option is seldom chosen (Whitcomb, 1985, p. 3). Moreover, recent U.S. Supreme Court decisions have generally upheld the constitutional emphasis on open trials. The main difficulty is that when a court is kept open to the public, the press and other media often rush in. Fortunately, there is a growing awareness that publicity can harm a child victim, and efforts have been made to enforce responsible reporting. In 1984, an Attorney General's Task Force on Family Violence made this recommendation:

> Court proceedings involving a child victim or witness must not become a media event. When a youngster is a juvenile offender, his name is withheld and the court proceedings are closed to the public. At a minimum, the same considerations should be given to the child victim. (p. 40)

A recommendation such as this is not likely to be written into law, chiefly because of First Amendment mandates in favor of the "public's right to know." Often, the media account of a child's ordeal in court includes the names of his or her parents without mentioning the child's name, thus bending the rule until it is broken. A change in this state of affairs will only follow from self-regulation by journalist groups.

A total of 14 states now permit videotapes of children's testimony, under oath, to be made prior to a trial—from which the child will be excused. One of these states has a rule that the child can be called into the trial at some point if required to "serve the interests of justice." And although in general this development implies a new sensitivity toward the needs of children, it must be pointed out that 12 of the 14 states in question *require the defendant* (accused molester) to be present during the videotaping; seven of those states allow a defendant (himself or herself) to cross-examine the child during this proceeding. The law giveth and the law taketh away.

When the court session is underway, a child can testify from an adjacent room (by closed-circuit television) in four states. Prosecution and defense attorneys will be in this room, of course, but as a companion to the child a victim assistance worker or one of the child's close relatives can be present; in turn, the persons who operate the camera and microphone must be out of the child's sight. Whitcomb, Shapiro, and Stellwagen (1985) fear that even this innovation will be struck down on constitutional grounds because of the Sixth Amendment provision that an accused person must be permitted to "confront" witnesses who testify against him or her (pp. 50–54).* This principle is drawn from common law, and like the common cold is no more desirable for being common. The technology of our time will modify this archaic convention in due course.

In retrospect, one can only be grateful for the self-imposed changes that have been implemented by people in the justice system—from police to prosecutors to judges. (Legislators have done their part, but they are often thwarted by political realities and, after all, children do not vote.) By means of a glacial process of procedural revision, the courts have been made more accommodating to children. But reform is cosmetic unless the children themselves are capable of taking advantage of these improvements. For that to happen, a child must be *ready* from an emotional standpoint. And the child in question is not an ordinary child, but one who is suffering from trauma. He or she is being asked to enter the dark forest of crime and punishment, while at the same time trying to recover from an emotional earthquake. For this almost impossible task to be accomplished, sympathy and support of the child must be increased to a maximum.

The End of the Trial

When the questioning of a child has finally been completed, the child and his or her loving adults frequently want to hear words of praise from the district attorney that the child's performance as a witness was good and that the attorney is pleased. However, this seldom occurs in

---

* A fundamental right guaranteed by the Sixth Amendment is that the accused be permitted to see and be seen by witnesses who are against him or her. This right has its foundation in the logic that the conscience of a false witness will manifest itself through physical actions when the false witness must tell a lie in the presence of the person who knows it is a lie ("I want to see him look me in the eye and say that"). This logic is popularly believed to apply also to children. A child may lie about what someone else did, but the child will tell the truth if confronted by the person he or she is lying about. Consequently, the testimony of a child victim that is elicited when the defendant is not present may fail if challenged on constitutional grounds.

a way that is satisfying to the child victim, for even though the child's contribution to the trial has been completed, the district attorney's has not. The D.A. may be concerned about what the next witness will say, or may be evaluating nonverbal reactions from the jury to the testimony. Often, he or she is so wrapped up in other details of the trial that any supportive attention that could be given to the child is subordinated to the purpose of getting a conviction against the accused molester. Then, too, parents or others who wanted the child to testify with computer accuracy will often point out any mistakes that the child made or something that he or she forgot that was important. These comments, combined with a lack of positive reinforcement from the attorney, may leave a child feeling dissatisfied with the experience of testifying. The clinician's support at this moment will be especially valued.

In the best of all possible worlds, things work out for the best. A court system is a highly imperfect world where things do not always turn out as one would wish. Sometimes the person who sexually abuses a child is not convicted. This possibility must be confronted realistically—first by the clinician and (with his or her help) by the family members and, eventually, by the child. If the accused is convicted, the event can represent an important symbolic victory for the child that may help to resolve questions of self-blame, giving the child a clear message that there are forces in society that will act to protect children. A positive court verdict can also help to heal the pervasive sense of powerlessness and devaluation that a child victim frequently feels.

THE CIVIL PROCESS

Even if there is no favorable outcome in the criminal case against an accused child abuser, the parent(s) may seek compensation in a civil lawsuit. The suit is filed in the name of the child victim, with an attorney representing the child on behalf of the parent(s). The molester may or may not have resources to pay for damages if the child's suit is won, but often this person (especially if the person is a homeowner) has insurance that will pay for the damages that he or she has caused.

Any decision to sue should not be made lightly. One needs to consider that many aspects of the child's life which are not admissible in criminal proceedings are, in fact, admissible in civil proceedings. Court protection is available to prevent the dissemination of personal information before the trial, but once the trial begins, a family's private life could become quite public.

Before retaining counsel, the parent(s) should be advised to interview several attorneys who specialize in the field of personal injury litigation, and to evaluate carefully their expertise in the process of deciding whether or not to proceed with a civil case. For one thing, the parent(s) will need a qualified personal injury lawyer's assessment of what the recoverable damages would be in the case, before deciding.

Although some attorneys have had experience in personal injury litigation, a thorough inquiry should be made to determine whether or not the prospective attorney's expertise has been recognized by either the National Board of Trial Advocates, the American Board of Trial Advocates, the State Trial Lawyers' Association, or by one of the certified specialist programs of the State Bar Association. Reputable attorneys are not offended by such inquiries concerning their backgrounds and their actual trial experience (including jury verdicts obtained and so on) with respect to personal injury work. During this critical decision-making phase, a therapist can act as a sounding board to help the parent(s) weigh the wisdom of civil litigation.*

The Rationale for a Civil Proceeding

The criminal process focuses on punishing the perpetrator for violating a law, but the civil process focuses on attempting to compensate (monetarily) a wrongfully injured victim. The focus of a criminal process is on the accused. The focus of a civil process is on the victim. Although a criminal case requires that proof of molestation be shown beyond a reasonable doubt, in a civil case it is normally only necessary to show by a *majority of the evidence* that the molestation occurred, in order to establish the liability of the molester.

The child victim's attorney will read the police report, including any statements by witnesses and any court records if there has been a criminal trial. Once the attorney feels satisfied that there is a reasonably good chance to be successful in proving that the molestation occurred

---

* The civil law also has its statutes of limitation. For example, in California an *adult* must file an action for personal injury suffered as a result of a sexual assault (e.g., rape) within one year after the assault occurred, or the court will refuse to take jurisdiction of the matter. However, in many states, the same statute does not apply to a child during his or her minority. This is done to protect a child who may have been injured, in case there is no adult who is willing to bring suit on the child's behalf during the child's minority. Hence, many states will allow a child to sue as long as it is done within a period of time after becoming an adult. For example, in California a child has one year after he or she becomes an adult within which to file a lawsuit for personal injuries received while a minor. And if the child was molested by a parent, stepparent, or other adult who was *living in the house* where the child lived at the time of molestation, the law permits filing the lawsuit within three years of the child's becoming an adult.

by a majority of the evidence, it will be necessary for him or her to obtain information regarding the extent of the emotional damage done to the child by the assault. This is best obtained by means of a consultation with the child's therapist. This discussion can be very important, because an attorney must look to the therapist for information that will permit him or her to know whether or not to proceed with the litigation; and, if a decision is made to proceed, what special steps must be taken to protect the victim from harm that could be caused by the litigation process itself.

In the case of a child who has suffered minimal harm from the molestation, the monetary compensation that a child can receive will also very likely be small; thus, the potential upset that could be caused by a litigation process will not justify the compensation anticipated. Similarly, the child may also have been the victim of other emotionally damaging experiences that could overshadow the damage done by the sexual assault. These other incidents may serve to lessen the relative impact of the molestation on the child's life in the eyes of the jury, thus making any potential compensation to the child not worth the stress of the litigation process.

Another factor that must be considered is the availability of funds (to the defendant) by which the eventual judgment would be paid. If the defendant has no assets by which a judgment can be paid, the child and the child's family will be left with a feeling that the molester has gotten away with impunity for his acts. For this reason, it may be necessary to conduct a preliminary investigation into the assets of the defendant, as well as to find out if his or her homeowner's insurance provides coverage that would compensate a victim for the perpetrator's actions.

If the foregoing considerations are resolved favorably, a complaint will be filed and a *discovery* process begins. This process permits the attorneys from both sides to gather information that will allow them to evaluate their potential to win or lose the lawsuit, in addition to information that will help them estimate the probable monetary value that a jury may assign.

The Role of the Therapist

A psychotherapist can have one of two roles in a civil proceeding, namely that of treating clinician or that of an independent, expert witness who is called upon to determine the degree of trauma suffered by a victim of abuse. It is best if these roles are performed by different therapists, but in many situations a therapist will be asked to perform both roles. In the expert witness role, he or she will evaluate the child's pretrauma condition, emotional trauma suffered, and how the trauma has affected the child's personal life and development.

When a therapist is called upon to testify as an expert witness, he or she should be prepared to present an opinion concerning the case in terms that a lay person (i.e., a member of the jury) can understand. The clinician as expert witness should be aware that it is useful to provide a certain amount of educational foundation that will help jury members in formulating their decision. For many, the clinician represents a profession that the average person may not fully accept or understand; or, the jury member may hold some stereotyped conception of psychotherapy that must be dispelled. It is vital to make clear the basic principles and supporting facts upon which one is formulating an opinion, so that the testimony of the expert witness will not be dismissed as esoteric "mumbo jumbo" or "purchased" evidence.

The Examination

The parent who seeks compensation for a child's injury will need to prove the nature and extent of the damages that the child has suffered. This usually entails the victim's being examined, by attorneys and experts on both sides, on the subject of the alleged traumatization. For example, someone who claims psychological damage will most likely be examined by at least one psychologist or psychiatrist employed by each of the opposing sides. The child's therapist should help him or her to prepare emotionally for these examinations. The child victim once again needs reassurance that he or she is not being judged. Further, if the child feels that an examination is upsetting or inappropriate in any way, he or she can report it to the attorney. In a case in which the child is extremely fragile, a therapist can request that: (1) the examination be postponed or limited in its length; (2) he or she (the therapist) be present during the examination; or (3) the entire examination be audiotaped or videotaped. The purpose is to make sure that nothing is done that would add to the trauma or be intrusive in any way.

Depositions

One of the methods used by attorneys to gather information is called a deposition. A deposition is the interrogation of a witness by an attorney. It normally takes place in an office, not in a courtroom. The witness is placed under oath and is asked questions by the attorney.

Depositions are normally taken of the child, the parents of the child or the adults with whom the child lives, and the child's therapist. The child's attorney will be present at each deposition taken and will have prepared the child by explaining what will happen and by asking the child questions similar to ones that the defendant's attorney will ask.

Before the child's deposition occurs, a clinician should be prepared to advise the child's attorney if the victim is emotionally strong enough to have his or her deposition taken. If the therapist feels that the deposition, as scheduled, will interfere with the therapy process or that the child has not yet reached a level of emotional adjustment to be questioned by a stranger regarding the incident, the lawyer can postpone the deposition to a later time. If the therapist feels that a child has insufficient emotional support from parents or other adults, the therapist should be present at the child's deposition. There should be an agreement between clinician and attorney that the therapist will immediately notify the lawyer during the deposition of any concern for the child's well-being or for the need to break for a few minutes, or if the defense attorney appears to be intimidating the child. The deposition may be stopped at any point, and the child's attorney can seek special orders from the court providing controls—for the protection of the child—when the deposition is resumed.

The therapist will also be deposed. Topics of questioning will include the academic training of the therapist, experience that the therapist has had in treating the emotional trauma of sexually abused children, and what therapy has been given the child up to that point. The attorney will also want to know the clinician's diagnosis and prognosis concerning the child, as well as the facts upon which these are based.

Following a deposition, the attorney will closely scrutinize a copy of the deposition transcript in order to check it and correct any errors that it may contain. After all the evidence of both sides has been compiled, the court will schedule a settlement conference, at which the two sides will attempt to come to a negotiated settlement without having to go to trial. If that is not possible, the case will proceed to the courtroom stage of the civil process.

The Actual Trial

One major source of difficulty in respect to a civil trial is that it may take place long after the criminal process has concluded. In many cases, the delay can be a matter of years. The sole advantage of this may be to permit both family and victim to recover from their earlier ordeal.

When the trial does occur, it almost invariably awakens traumatic memories and reopens old wounds. For these reasons, a clinician should be available to prepare the child or adolescent and the family for the procedure, and support them through its hazardous course. If the person who committed the abuse has been convicted of the crime, the child victim may not be required to testify in the civil trial, but if that has not happened, he or she will very likely be called to the stand.

Often a child or family member feels that *he or she* is on trial, and the therapist can help to deal with this experience. Also, the therapist can give those who will be participating in the trial a perspective on the rigorous and often confusing kinds of questioning that they can expect in the courtroom. A clinician must refrain from coaching the child or family member in what to say, but rather should strive to get the person ready—emotionally—for testifying truthfully.

In those cases in which many years have elapsed between the traumatic event and a civil trial, the testimony of the therapist can make clear to a jury that the victim who is telling his or her story now is different from, and much more mature than, the child or adolescent who was abused. Further, the clinician can explain to the jury what the assault meant to the victim when it occurred. In addition, a therapist's testimony may serve to clarify the fact that a child may not even now understand, or have the cognitive resources to explain, how he or she was affected by the assault.

As an example of the foregoing, there was the case in which a nine-year-old girl was raped. She was able to say that it had hurt and that she was afraid. She was also able to say that she had had bad dreams and that she did not want to be away from her parents. But, being only nine, she was not able to explain the connection between the rape and her current phobias, her bedwetting, and her temper tantrums; she could not connect the trauma with her serious behavioral problems both at home and at school. And she could not see the relationship between being raped and the fact that she had regressed to the approximate level of a six-year-old for as long as nine months. It was the therapist's role to describe these phenomena, which the child's cognitive development could neither comprehend nor convey.

The End of the Civil Process

When a case has been successfully resolved and has won for the child a sum of money, the clinician will be asked to advise the attorney on structuring the disposition of money. Typically, any monies received by a child as a result of litigation will be placed into a blocked trust account, so that none can be removed without court approval prior to the child's becoming an adult. When the child becomes an adult, he or she will receive the entire amount, to do with as he or she sees fit. In some cases, a child may be ill prepared to deal with the eventuality of receiving a sum of money with responsibility. It may be prudent in those cases to place a portion of the money in some kind of structured fund, by which the child will receive portions of it serially, such as at 18, 21, 25, and 30 years of age; or, it could be released in five equal yearly installments beginning at age 18, in order to provide income during the college years.

In conclusion, when a family is awarded a judgment or is able to negotiate a favorable settlement—just as those cases in which a criminal assailant is successfully prosecuted—the outcome serves to convey a message that society recognizes the child's loss. One learns that there are forces that attempt to right wrongs and compensate those who have suffered them.

REFERENCES

Attorney General's Task Force on Family Violence. *Final Report*, September, 1984.

Everstine, D. S., & Everstine, L. *People in crisis*. New York: Brunner/Mazel, 1983.

Everstine, L., & Everstine, D. S. (Eds.). *Psychotherapy and the law*. Orlando, FL: Grune & Stratton, 1986.

Heymann, G. M. Mandated child abuse reporting and the confidentiality privilege. In L. Everstine & D. S. Everstine (Eds.), *Psychotherapy and the law*. Orlando, FL: Grune & Stratton, 1986, pp. 145–155.

Kohlman, R. J. Malpractice liability for failing to report child abuse. *The Western Journal of Medicine*, 121(3), 244–248, 1974.

Stewart, J. K. Foreword. In D. Whitcomb, E. R. Shapiro, & L. D. Stellwagen, *When the victim is a child: Issues for judges and prosecutors*. Washington, D.C.: U.S. Government Printing Office, 1985, 0–488–113.

Tarasoff v. Regents of the University of California, 17C 3d 425, 551 P2d 334 (Cal 1976).

Weisberg, R., & Wald, M. Confidentiality laws and state efforts to protect abused or neglected children: The need for statutory reform. In L. Everstine & D. S. Everstine (Eds.), *Psychotherapy and the law*. Orlando, FL: Grune & Stratton, 1986, pp. 157–203.

Whitcomb, D. Prosecution of child sexual abuse: Innovations in practice. *Research in brief, 1*. Washington, D.C.: National Institute of Justice, November, 1985.

Whitcomb, D., Shapiro, E. R., & Stellwagen, L. D. *When the victim is a child: Issues for judges and prosecutors*. Washington, D.C.: U.S. Government Printing Office, 1985, 0–488–113.

Name Index

Subject Index

Symptoms:
  key, 17–18
  somatic, 18, 50

*Tarasoff v. Regents of the University of
  California,* 178
Target of opportunity, 134
Team, therapy, with incestuous families,
  114, 125
Television, closed-circuit, in court, 189
Territorial boundaries, loss of, 68
Testing:
  psychological:
    of boy victim, 144–145
    of child victim, 25, 30, 62, 188
    of incest victim, 105–108, 109
  of therapist:
    by adult client, 154
    by boy victim, 145, 148
    by child victim, 25–26
    by incest victim, 113, 121
Thematic Apperception Test (TAT), 25,
  62, 105, 144
Therapist; *see also* Clinician(s)
  aggressive acting out toward, 25
  and child's mother, 38–39
  hinting of child to, 26
  introduction of:
    to child victim, 45
    to boy victim, 143
  role of, civil proceeding, 192–193
  sexual acting out toward, 26
  testing of, *see* Testing of therapist
Therapy:
  degree of trauma and, 16
  doing of, and doing research, 178
Therapy relationship:
  with adult client, 155
  with child victim, 44–45
Therapy team, with incestuous families,
  114, 125
Threats, made by molesters, 21, 157
Touching, by therapist
  of child victim, 46–47
  of incest victim, 120–121
Toys, 46, 47–49
  aggressive acting out toward, 25, 54
  to encourage discussion and fantasy, 48
  regressive, 47
  taking apart of, 53
Transitional phase, in incest, 94
Trauma, sexual; *see also* Rape trauma
  assessment of, 12–30
  child before, 28

child's perception of, 52
definition of, ix
re-creation of, by adult client, 160–161
unresolved, revival of, 79–80
Trauma response and recovery cycle, 145,
  149; *see also* Rape trauma syndrome
Traumatic sequelae of childhood sexual
  abuse, 16
Traumatization as children, adults who
  experienced, *see* Adults
Treatment:
  of adolescent victim, 66–86
  of adult client, 161–172
  of boy victim, 141–149
  of child victim, 33–65
  of incest victim, 115–126
Trial:
  in civil proceeding, 194–195
  in criminal proceeding, 187
  end of, 189–190
Trust, in others:
  limited, as symptom, 17
  rape and, 68
Trusted offender, molestation by, versus
  stranger, degree of trauma and, 15

Understanding:
  of child, by therapist, 25–27
  of family, by therapist, 27–28
  of trauma, by child, 8
United Way, xi
Unresolved cases, 29–30
Unresolved trauma, revival of, 79–80

Victim(s):
  adolescent, *see* Adolescent victim
  boy, *see* Boy victim
  child, *see* Child victim(s)
  other, whom child knows, 55
  psychological condition of, and degree
    of trauma, 15
Victim-Witness Assistance programs, xi
Videotaping:
  of child's testimony, 188
  of examination in civil proceeding, 193
  of incest evaluation session, 110
  of initial interview with officer of law
    or protective worker, 183
Violence, in TAT, 62

"When the Victim Is a Child," 181
Wholeness, sense of loss of, 68
Wide Range Achievement Test, 145
WISC-R, 62, 145